WRITING TO
INFORM AND ENGAGE

WRITING TO INFORM AND ENGAGE

THE ESSENTIAL GUIDE to BEGINNING NEWS AND MAGAZINE WRITING

Conrad C. Fink
University of Georgia

Westview
PRESS

A Member of the Perseus Books Group

Westview Press books are available at special discounts for bulk purchases in the United States by corporations, institutions, and other organizations. For more information, please contact the Special Markets Department at the Perseus Books Group, 11 Cambridge Center, Cambridge MA 02142, or call (617) 252-5298 or (800) 255-1514 or jmccrary@perseusbooks.com.

Published in 2003 in the United States of America by Westview Press, 5500 Central Avenue, Boulder, Colorado 80301–2877.

Find us on the World Wide Web at www.westviewpress.com

A Cataloging-in-Publication data record for this book is available from the Library of Congress.
ISBN 0-8133-4074-8 (HC)   ISBN 0-8133-4075-6 (pbk)
The paper used in this publication meets the requirements of the American National Standard for Permanence of Paper for Printed Library Materials Z39.48–1984.

10   9   8   7   6   5   4   3   2   1

Contents

Preface

Good writing communicates facts, imagery, emotion — your thinking — to readers clearly and efficiently. Good writing stimulates and engages readers.

It's easy to define good writing. But, oh, so difficult to deliver it!

It's difficult to arrange words in crisp, effective sentences. It's difficult to marshal them smoothly in punchy paragraphs, to write with the flow and vivid descriptive of memorable storytelling.

First lesson, then, in this book: If a better writer you want to be, prepare for much hard work. Toughen up for many hours at the keyboard and, yes, for aggravation and even occasional deep disappointment, for the skill you seek is elusive.

But stick to it and you'll find the effort worthwhile.

What joy you'll know when you finally reach for just the right word — and grasp it; when that word falls in place just as you desire; when your thoughts take shape with clarity and precision that drive them home, into the minds of others.

I hope "Writing to Inform and Engage" will ease your journey toward becoming a better writer. If all goes well, if we — you and I — *really* click, the book will help you reach your destination.

But understand this: You cannot merely read a book to learn to write. A book — this book or any other — can only assist you. To learn to write, you must write. So get to a keyboard and write. Then rewrite. Then rewrite your rewrite.

This book will lead you through that learning process within the context of the journalism of our day. We'll look at reporting and explaining compellingly important political, economic and social issues amid societal changes and new technology that are forcing all media to reposition themselves for competitive and marketing unknowns still beyond the horizon.

Questions raised by these changes are fundamental: Will newspapers and magazines flourish or die? Will radio, television and Internet services remain distinctly separate? Or will all media, print and electronic, merge one day in dramatic convergence? Will science yield a new and better but still unknown way to communicate from one mind to another?

Don't let the futuristic hubbub distract you.

First, the traditional media — newspapers, magazines, radio, television—are doing well with readers, viewers, listeners and advertisers. All likely will be around for a very long time.

Second, whatever the future, whatever its shape, the basics of good writing and the fundamentals of strong reporting that are essential to good journalism will be unchanged. Learn those basics and you'll be ready for the medium of your choice.

Not that all media writing is the same. It isn't.

Each medium, whether print or electronic, presents news and information in ways that best use the medium's strengths and overcome its weaknesses. Understanding that — understanding how your medium identifies and reaches its audience — is crucial to your success as a writer.

It's on achieving that understanding that we begin "Writing to Inform and Engage."

ORGANIZATION OF THIS BOOK

PART ONE: GETTING READY

Before you touch a keyboard understand that good writing can flow only from strong preparation. Learn first how your medium defines news, then research and report thoroughly—all within the context of your audience's needs and desires.

CHAPTER ONE: KNOW YOUR AUDIENCE

Only by understanding who your medium's readers are and learning their demographic and psychographic characteristics can you tune your writing properly to facilitate understanding. Meet your readers in *their* marketplace of ideas on matters of *their* interest and with concepts and language *they* will comprehend easily.

CHAPTER TWO: KNOW YOUR SUBJECT

Readers today are better educated and more sophisticated than ever. They'll spot immediately any weaknesses in your reporting. Be comforted: You have more expertise than you think. Your challenge is to focus on what you know and find authoritative sources for reporting on what you don't.

PART TWO: SHARPENING YOUR TOOLS

Without strong language skills you lack the essential tools of your trade. You are a soldier without a gun, a baseball player without a bat.

CHAPTER THREE: ACHIEVING PRECISION AND CLARITY

A quick refresher on grammar — parts of speech, nouns/pronouns, verbs and adverbs, adjectives. Write to make your subject come alive.

CHAPTER FOUR: BECOMING A STYLIST

Fashion a crisp writing style unique to your personality. Wage war against language bloat, abstractions, redundancies and cliches. Use simple language to translate the complex into understandable ideas.

PART THREE: CAPTURING—AND HOLDING—THEIR ATTENTION

It's a busy world out there. Attract preoccupied readers with an intro that catches their attention. But you cannot stop there; you must lead them gently through your entire story, or they're off to the comics or stock market tables.

CHAPTER FIVE: HEY, READER! LOOK AT THIS!

Use a variety of hard-news leads and intros to tell your story. Capture its essence in a lead but don't hype it or stretch beyond its intrinsic news value. Many story structures are available. Use them.

CHAPTER SIX: LEAD READERS GENTLY BY THE HAND

You've attracted readers with your intro. Now what? Now you help them along by constructing a *bridge of confidence* from intro to conclusion. That requires keeping the cast of characters straight and handling carefully all switches in locale and time elements. Knit a whole fabric. Don't throw jumbled ideas and facts at readers. And handle numbers carefully!

PART IV: GETTING STARTED IN SPECIALTY WRITING

Using hard-news and soft featurish approaches you can start—now—to get published.

CHAPTER SEVEN: SPORTS, SCIENCE, BUSINESS

In these and other specialties lie enormous opportunities for writing news and feature stories for publication. Media, on campus and off, thirst for coverage of these news complexities, where many beginning writers fear — needlessly — to go.

PART V: FEATURES, PROFILES AND "SOFT" PIECES

Being first with hard news is important in journalism. But nothing is faster than the Internet and other electronic services. So newspapers and magazines must emphasize writing that focuses on the human element, that provides background and, on occasion, entertainment.

CHAPTER EIGHT: HANDLING LONGER NARRATIVES

You cannot function effectively in journalism today without knowing how to write profiles and features. Learn to handle longer narratives without getting tangled in blind-alley writing or excess verbiage.

PART VI: WRITING THAT EXPLAINS AND ADVOCATES

Some hard-news stories are so complex that readers need analysis and interpretation, so in Chapter Nine we move into writing that goes beyond recital of the Five Ws and into explanatory writing. Then, starting in Chapter Ten, a huge step—this time, into writing that advocates.

CHAPTER NINE: EXPLANATORY WRITING IN NEWS

Learn to come in behind a spot-news development with explanatory writing that lays out true meaning for readers. Learn to alert readers of forthcoming events that affect their lives. Use the newsfeature and news analysis to truly unfold complex stories.

CHAPTER TEN: WRITING EDITORIALS

Strongly reported news stories persuade readers to understand facts as you intend. Beyond balanced and dispassionate newswriting, however, lies advocacy writing—writing that takes a stand and expresses the institutional position of a newspaper or magazine.

CHAPTER ELEVEN: WRITING PERSONAL COMMENTARY

Of a more personal nature is advocacy writing in a signed column or review. Humor, the arts, the dim closets of childhood memory—all are subjects for writing commentary.

PART VII: ETHICS, THE LAW AND YOU

There is more — much more — to effective journalism than solid reporting, strong opinions and facile writing. You must be on the moral high ground and within the law.

CHAPTER TWELVE: CODES OF ETHICS, RULE OF LAW

History demands your adherence to the highest principles of good journalism; your duty to readers requires fairness and balance. Learn existing codes of ethics adopted by journalism organizations, then develop your own personal code of what is right and wrong in journalism. And *always* remain sensitive to the laws of defamation, privacy and false light.

Conrad Fink
Athens, Georgia

Acknowledgments

My thanks to Jill Rothenberg, Westview Press senior editor, who saw merit in my proposal for this book, and to Judith Serrin, an expert copy editor who handled my manuscript gently but discerningly, and to Barbara Greer of Westview, who supervised production of this book.

A salute to the many fine professionals whose strong writing is illustrated in the pages that follow. Your bylines are marks of excellence.

Thanks to Michael Giarrusso, Associated Press news editor in Atlanta, whose thoughtful essay on computer-assisted reporting is in Chapter Two.

Sophie Barnes, my typist on many writing projects, deserves special thanks for once again whipping my manuscript into presentable form.

C. F.

PART ONE
GETTING READY

Getting Ready

Newspapers, long tied to paper and ink, enter cyberspace to operate Internet services.

Magazines take to the electronic road and offer Web sites.

Internet news services publish print magazines, and television airs news shows titled "First Edition" and "Front Page."

What's going on?

A revolution, that's what—a revolution within the media, print and electronic, the new and old, in the way they do journalism.

Technology, ideas and operating methods traditionally associated with one medium are being borrowed liberally by others. Driving this *convergence* is a determination among journalists to use all technologies, new and old, and every workable idea, whether original or borrowed, that will help them communicate better with the American public.

Journalists trained in print seek the immediacy of electronic transmission; Internet and broadcast journalists forge alliances with newspapers and magazines to lean on their brand identities and popularity with readers.

Understandably, you may be a bit confused by all this as you launch into study of newswriting and try to figure out what "journalism" likely will be in years ahead.

Keep this in mind: Though *technologies* are used interchangeably by all media, each individual medium in fact is carving out its distinct identity and unique role that will maximize its strengths and disguise its weaknesses.

Thus, you will need to write differently for each.

If you want to write for Internet services, learn to write quickly, in minimalist language. Internet news is fast and lean.

If newspapers will be your game, focus on in-depth reporting and analytical writing. Going deep into important issues every day is something newspapers emphasize—and television and other media don't.

For a magazine career, take a longer view and sharpen your skills in less-timely narrative writing and in reporting techniques used in specialized journalism.

That is, to write effectively you must begin by understanding your medium and its audience. To that we turn in Chapter One.

1

Know Your Audience

FOR MANY AMERICANS it was just another weekday morning. Not so for New York Stock Exchange investors.

Minutes after trading opened, the Dow Jones Industrial Average, a leading indicator of trading, soared 107.28, a very substantial gain in such a short time.

Why was trading hot and heavy? Why did hundreds of millions of dollars trade hands while most of us lingered over morning coffee or toddled off to begin our day?

Because there was news.

But, it was news not seen or heard by all Americans. Rather, it was news reported by journalists who specialize in business and finance, news then sped to investors via electronic services that most Americans don't monitor carefully.

Here is how one service, CNNfn, flashed news via the Internet at 9:56 a.m., Eastern Time:

2Q productivity jumps
    9:56 a.m. ET

    U.S. workers were even more productive in the second quarter while wage costs for companies declined more rapidly than previously thought, the government reported Wednesday — more evidence that the world's largest economy is chugging along without much inflation. (full story)[1]

CNNfn's full story, available with click of a mouse:

2Q PRODUCTIVITY JUMPS

Worker productivity in U.S. advanced revised 5.7%; wage costs drop 0.4% September 6, 2000; 9:56 a.m. ET

New York (CNNfn)—U.S. workers were even more productive in the second quarter while wage costs for companies declined more rapidly than previously thought, the government reported Wednesday— more evidence that the world's largest economy is chugging along without much inflation.

The Labor Department said that *worker productivity* jumped 5.7 percent in the second quarter—above the 5.5 percent increase anticipated by analysts polled by *Briefing.com* and the 5.3 percent rise initially reported. Labor costs—a measure of what companies spend on worker output—fell at a revised 0.4 percent annual rate, a bigger drop than the 0.1 percent drop initially reported and Wall Street forecasts for a 0.2 percent decline.

The numbers provided more evidence for analysts and investors that massive strides in technology have boosted productivity, a measure of worker output per hour, and kept costs down for companies—a combo that is expected to convince the Federal Reserve to hold interest rates steady when the central bank's policy makers meet on Oct. 3 . . . .[2]

Note these characteristics of the CNNfn dispatches:

- Writing is direct, almost blunt in its minimalist language. The flash headline ("2Q productivity jumps") is designed to get word out quickly, taking advantage of the Internet's principal competitive strength over other media—speed.
- The CNNfn writer clearly is an expert writing for experts. Readers are expected to know the meaning of the flash news. Explanation is left until the third paragraph ("graf," in news parlance): Interest rates likely will hold steady, which is good news for the stock market.
- There is no featurish "color" in the writing. When big money is changing hands, investor-readers don't care if the sun is shining over the New York Stock Exchange or whether traders are shouting, "Hurrah!"
- Insider shorthand is used by this expert writer for expert readers: "2Q," for example, means "second quarter," the period April, May, June.

Now, here's a news story written for the front page of another medium, a newspaper:

Note characteristics of that newspaper writing:

After a Fourth of July spike, gasoline prices in the Philadelphia region have dropped back nearly to where they were at the start of summer. But prices at the pump are still high compared with a year ago, a new report by the American Automobile Association said.

During the Memorial Day weekend, the price of a gallon of regular unleaded gas ranged from $1.45 to $1.50 in Pennsylvania, New Jersey and Delaware, according to the AAA.

Prices crested at $1.58 to $1.64 eight weeks ago.

This week, gas in Pennsylvania is averaging $1.50 a gallon, 27 cents higher than for the same week a year ago . . .

Analysts said prices should start falling a bit after Labor Day, which ends the peak summer season . . .

Wendy Tanaka
Philadelphia Inquirer[3]*

- It's aimed broadly at *consumers*, not stock market investors or a narrow audience of experts. Newspaper writing is aimed at gathering the largest possible number of readers.
- The writing is highly detailed on what a consumer-reader (not investor) wants to know: How does the gas price *I* am paying compare with prices paid by others? And, importantly, the writing has an analytical dimension—what's ahead ("prices should start falling . . . ").
- The lead is tightly attributed to an authoritative source (American Automobile Association) and dollar figures are put in perspective with comparatives (as in the fourth graf's "averaging $1.50 a gallon, *27 cents higher than for the same week a year ago"*).

So, Internet services deliver news to their expert readers *right now*. Newspapers hit front porches with broadened coverage for general audiences *tomorrow morning*.

---

* For reasons of space and easy reading, I have eliminated an initial "The" from some newspaper titles.

Can magazine writers, who don't reach readers until *next week* or *next month*, possibly compete? Yes, and here is an example of how they do that:

The key question for magazine publishers following the decision by Philip Morris to suspend cigarette advertising in 42 magazines is whether the rest of Big Tobacco will follow its lead. The decision will cost the industry more than $130 million in lost advertising revenue.

"If you look at the tobacco industry as a whole, one company pulling out is not going to drive magazines to bankruptcy," says Robert Garfinkle, director of print media in the New York office of McCann-Erickson. "But if others follow suit, it will have significant ramifications."

Dave Morris, publisher of *Entertainment Weekly*, one of the hardest-hit titles, doesn't think they will. "I've talked to the other tobacco companies and they say they don't plan to do the same."

R. J. Reynolds, the second largest tobacco company in the United States, after Philip Morris, is sticking with its existing policy of advertising only in magazines with at least 66 percent adult readership . . . .

The surprise announcement by Philip Morris on June 5 was the result of pressure from the National Association of Attorneys General to stamp out tobacco ads in magazines with more than 15 percent youth readership (ages 12–17) or more than two million readers under 18 . . . .

Bob Moseley
Folio[4]

Folio, a trade publication covering the magazine industry, published the story above on July 1 — almost a *full month* after the news story, the Philip Morris announcement, broke on June 5. Internet services and newspapers covered the June 5 development at the time, so weeks later the magazine writer takes this approach:

- Focus the lead on a *look-ahead element*, the "key question" publishers face in weeks ahead, and not backward to the *spot-news development*, the June 5 "surprise announcement," which is subordinated to the fifth graf.
- *Interpret* the meaning of the Philip Morris announcement—$130 million ad revenue is lost.
- *Round up* authoritative comment (from Roberta Garfinkle and Dave Morris) to help readers *analyze* what's likely to happen.

- *Background* the Philip Morris announcement by explaining what caused it — pressure from the National Association of Attorneys General.

You noted, of course, that though highly effective for their own audiences, the three writing styles above are *not* interchangeable.

The fast, lean Internet writing is designed to flash bare-bones developments to experts who know how to interpret it themselves and trade appropriately on the stock market. This writing style is not appropriate for the front page of a general-circulation newspaper.

The newspaper is much too slow in reaching its audience for investors who move on news *right now* and its writing is too consumer-oriented for the CNNfn audience of experts.

The magazine story is crafted beautifully to overcome the even slower delivery of magazines. Indeed, *Folio's* writer *turns the slowness into an advantage* by taking time to create a reflective, well-rounded account with analysis and interpretation almost impossible to write for instantaneous delivery via the Internet and difficult even to create for tomorrow morning's newspaper.

Clearly, despite the so-called convergence of media *technology*, you must learn different writing styles for different media. That, in turn, requires you to understand how each medium selects and courts its audience and, thus, how each defines news.

THE MEDIA: THEIR ROLE AND AUDIENCES

American media divide into two broad categories:

- *Advertiser-driven* media offer news, information and entertainment attractive to audiences that, in turn, are attractive to advertisers. Traditional print media — newspapers and magazines — must define news, then report and write it to pull in readers who can be "sold" to advertisers that provide most of their financial support.
- *Subscriber-driven* media derive relatively little revenue from advertisers and, instead, deliver news and information to users who pay a fee. These media mostly offer hard news that subscribers

use to make stock market investments or other business decisions. Subscriber-driven media include private financial news services such as Dow Jones, Reuters and Bloomberg.[5]

THE NEWSPAPER

As you ponder a writing career, note that this battle-scarred veteran of media wars still is the dominant force in local news and advertising across the nation.

About 1,500 dailies sell around 55 million copies each day and nearly 60 million on Sundays. Each copy sold reaches two or more readers on average, so paid-circulation dailies reach more than 100 million readers daily.[6]

In developing your reporting technique and writing style, you must recognize that research shows Americans who read newspapers generally are upscale demographically.

That is, *you must be in tune with the news needs and desires of readers with higher than average education and income.*[7]

Paid and free-circulation weeklies (about 8,000, at last count) distribute more than 74 million copies, and provide careers for writers who want to live in and be part of small-town America.[8]

In defining what is news, editors first consider the *geographic market* their newspaper serves.

For national newspapers — *USA Today*, the *New York Times*, *Wall Street Journal* — the market, of course, is nationwide.

However, for virtually every other newspaper the relevant market is the city of publication and a tight geographic area around it. For example, the 36,000-circulation *Athens (Ga.) Banner-Herald* defines its geographic market as the city of Athens and five surrounding counties.

Geographic-market outlines are drawn in response to advertisers, who willingly pay to reach nearby readers (nearby, and thus potential customers) but aren't willing to pay to reach distant readers who shop elsewhere.

So, the Athens newspaper strives mightily to increase circulation in its five-county market (defined as the "retail trading zone") but makes no effort in south Georgia, 350 miles away.

First lesson, then, in developing your news sense: News that breaks within your geographic market takes high priority, but so does a news event that develops even far off *if* it is of compelling importance to readers in your market.

Second, you also must define news in a vertical sense—as in a deep, narrow *interest area*. Specialized newspapers do this when they virtually dismiss the geographic factor — where a story breaks—and concentrate instead on interests crucial to their readers.

The *Wall Street Journal*, for example, assigns high priority to any story anywhere, regardless of origin, if it concerns reader interest in business, finance and economics. Newspapers specializing in sports, farming or other "niche" subjects do the same.

Obviously, you 1) improve your chances of being published and 2) better serve your readers if you bring in stories that combine geographic and interest factors. Note the local reader constituencies served in the following story from the *Boston Globe*:

Federal investigators will soon cite a contractor building part of the $600 million Silver Lake transitway with 15 serious safety violations, sources said yesterday, raising the specter that the project could face far stricter regulations and grow far more expensive.

Although officials . . . said they had not been officially notified . . . such findings, if upheld on appeal, could rock the project's bottom line.

One source said the results could mean "millions and millions" in ad-ditional costs on new equipment, new crews, new procedures, and new ventilation systems required for all tunnel work. The transitway, currently considered a "cut-and-cover" highway project, is being constructed under far less stringent guidelines. Even so, it has already grown from initial cost estimates of $413 million . . .

Raphael Lewis
and Thomas C. Palmer Jr.
Boston Globe[9]

The *Globe* story above broke locally with enormous impact on many areas of reader interest — local business, worker safety, law and order, taxation, commuting.

Such "general news" — news from here and there and about a lot of things — surfaces in our research as what readers want most from newspapers. Editors generally interpret that to mean readers each morning want a wide view of what happened overnight in many news sectors.[10]

Nevertheless, responding to increasing reader demand for specialized coverage — and to competition, particularly from magazines — newspapers practice "internal zoning." Newspapers break their offerings into separate sections dealing in depth with sports, business, health, recreation, travel, the arts.

That is, even if you work for a general-circulation newspaper, you will need precision skills for in-depth specialized reporting plus the ability to write in expert detail for readers with specialized background and interests.

Other characteristics of newspapers affect how you define and write news for them.

THE PUBLISHING CYCLE

Most newspapers publish only in the morning or afternoon in a 24-hour cycle. Inevitably, other media — television, radio, the Internet — often reach the public first with major breaking stories.

Indeed, not since radio grew strong in the 1930s have newspapers been the public's first source of breaking news. And since those days, as television and cyberspace services developed, newspapers have moved toward analyzing and interpreting the deeper meaning of spot-news breaks.

For example, an Internet story sounds immediate alarm that the price of a stock is plunging on Wall Street; the later newspaper story is what was behind the plunge and, importantly, what's likely to happen tomorrow.

Or, take the death of a state governor in a plane crash. The crash — wreckage, body bags, horrified onlookers — is a picture story for television, right now or, at latest, on the 6 p.m. news.

For the next day's *Boston Globe*, the crash itself is almost incidental to how the unfortunate death leads to a wider story. Note below how the wider implications (emphasis added) distinguish newspaper writing from breathless television reporting:

St. Louis—In the flash of a fireball, an airplane crash killed Missouri's governor, *cast a pall over this year's final presidential debate and freshened doubts about Democratic* *hopes of reclaiming the US Senate.*

Governor Mel Carnahan, 66, his son Roger, and a political aide, Chris Sifford, died Monday night when their six-seat Cessna plunged amid a thunderstorm into hilly, wooded terrain about 25 miles south of St. Louis . . . .

The impact was felt all the way in Washington, where Carnahan was viewed as one of the Democrat's strongest hopes for gaining a US Senate seat in next month's elections.

The two-term governor, who under a term-limits law could not seek reelection, was running even with Senator John Ashcroft, the Republi-

can incumbent . . . .

The GOP controls the Senate 54–46, with 34 seats up for election. Thirteen seats are considered up for grabs, with Republicans controlling eight and Democrats five. Democratic prospects for gaining a majority were seen as a longshot, but *Carnahan's death was a blow to the party psyche.*

Glen Johnson
Boston Globe[11]

Lesson: Your newspaper writing must give readers something competing media don't (and, because of their own limitations, can't). Interpret, analyze and, whenever possible, *move the story ahead*, beyond the spot-news event, to its deeper meaning.

THE NEWSPAPER'S TECHNICAL LIMITATION

Even without competition (a rare condition), you must write to overcome the severe disadvantage you suffer due to the newspaper's cumbersome, time-consuming production and distribution process.

Putting ink on dead trees, then shipping pieces to various sectors of a market near and far takes many hours.

Important to a writer? You bet.

For example, most morning newspapers have a newsroom deadline of well before midnight — as early as 11 p.m. or so, to provide time to edit and lay out the paper, print it and truck it to subscriber doorsteps by 6 a.m., optimum time for catching readers before they depart for their work day.

Just think: You must write a story this afternoon or by early evening tonight that will "stand" — be journalistically valid — at 6 a.m. tomorrow!

Meanwhile, radio, television and an increasing number of 24-hour Internet services are all over important stories, updating and carrying them forward minute by minute between 11 p.m. and 6 a.m.

If you're writing for an afternoon paper, deadline pressure is merciless. Newsroom deadlines are about 10 a.m., and sometimes much earlier, to give production and circulation staffers a chance of getting to subscriber doorsteps by 4 p.m. — before the evening meal and television.

Lesson: No writer can succeed without understanding how to "write around" the mechanical complexities of newspapers.

THE FRESH NEWS WINDOW

News of spontaneous origin — air crash, fire, stickup — breaks at any hour, of course, day or night.

But *programmed news events* — Senate hearings, press conferences, board of education meetings — mostly produce news late in the day or early evening. And, that of course is "a.m.'s time" — the morning newspaper cycle.

News that breaks today between roughly 10 a.m., when afternoon papers "close," and 11 p.m., the deadline for morning papers, can appear in print only tomorrow morning.

Thus, the "fresh news window" in the United States opens most frequently for morning papers. Rarely do afternoon papers get a "today" angle on *local* news stories. (However, foreign news, from other time zones, sometimes gives afternoon editors a "today" angle. For example, a story out of Britain, which is six hours ahead of the U.S. East Coast time zone, could arrive in predawn in New York and Boston and put a "today" time element on afternoon front pages.)

Consequently, many afternoon papers adopt a "soft," featurish approach to news, emphasizing timeless stories, analysis and interpretation, and, particularly, columnists.

Newswriters for afternoon papers try for "second-day" angles because morning papers get first crack at much of the breaking news. For example, the "first-day" story on a bridge collapse is that the thing fell down. The next morning, readers learn it's down. For afternoon papers, the "second-day" angle has to be *why* — perhaps that investigators found old, brittle rivets and bolts gave way.

THE MAGAZINE

Do you have a hobby or special interest you would like to write about?

You're in luck. Almost certainly, a magazine is published somewhere in the United States that caters to readers interested in your hobby—and needs writers who can cover it.

An estimated *18,000* magazines focus on topics as varied as health and nutrition, travel, finance, home furnishings, sports—you name it. They are issued weekly, monthly, quarterly.[12]

What? The magazine, even slower to reach readers than newspapers, is flourishing in this era of instantaneous cyberspace communication?

Yes, but to succeed as a magazine writer your understanding of your audience, your news sense and your writing precision must be particularly acute.

Here's why:

In the 1950s, television burst forth as a commercially viable medium and began scooping up mass audiences of viewers. Advertisers found it cheaper to use television to reach millions who buy razor blades and laundry soap than to court them through national magazines. *Look, Life, Saturday Evening Post* and similar general-interest national magazines starved for ad dollars and withered.

In a brilliant strategic move, however, the magazine industry shifted to highly specialized "niche" publishing that features in-depth focused reporting and expert writing on narrowly defined topics.

Thus were born, for example, magazines covering not water sports broadly but, rather, narrow segments such as scuba diving or surfing.

Large-circulation magazines that published features on, say, farm life in rural America were supplanted by specialized magazines covering the economics of farming — and not just farming in general. Rather, they are "zoned" to present information on seeds, fertilizers and equipment — and advertising — peculiar to defined geographic areas, the upper Midwest, for example, or the Southeast.

For readers, specialized magazines present in-depth information they cannot get elsewhere in such handy, low-cost form.

For advertisers, specialized magazines present well-defined target audiences, which lowers the cost of reaching potential customers. A scuba-diving equipment company, for example, reaches relatively few potential customers by advertising in a general-circulation newspaper. But nearly every reader of a scuba-diving magazine likely is a potential customer. Some magazines offer advertisers incredibly affluent audiences.

Forbes, a business news magazine, boasts its average subscriber has household net worth — assets less liabilities—of $956,000.[13]

For writers, specialized magazines offer challenging careers: You command higher pay *if* you have strong understanding of the magazine's subject matter and know authoritative sources in the industry it covers, then are able to digest highly technical information and write it with authority for readers who themselves probably are experts.

If you want a career as a *generalist* writing hard news for magazines—*Time, Newsweek* for example—develop skills in four areas:

First, aside from occasional exclusives, newsmagazines break relatively few spot-news stories. Radio, television, newspapers—virtually all other media—get to the public faster than do weekly magazines. So, learn to sum up, quickly and in minimal language, a news development from the *past week*, then quickly pitch your writing ahead to what's likely to develop *next week*.

For example, violence in Israel is covered at the moment it happens by other news media, well before a newsweekly writer even turns to the keyboard. So, for the magazine writer, last week's violence is merely a "peg" for an interpretive and analytical look-ahead to the outlook for the Middle East peace process next week.

Second, learn to spot and write helpful how-to-do-it stories readers may not find elsewhere. *U.S. News & World Report*, a weekly, does this with explanations of how to finance college tuition, how to find the best home mortgage, how to live a better, more fulfilling life.

Third, develop expertise in one or more of those back-of-the-book specialties — art, cinema, books, religion, medicine — that weeklies, *Time* and *Newsweek*, particularly, offer with penetrating insights and clever writing.

Fourth, develop an eye for anecdotal probings of life, those stories that make you laugh or maybe cry a little. Newsmagazines relish off-beat human interest stories that can be developed exclusively to give readers one more reason to buy a copy each week.

INTERNET SERVICES

For print journalists, it was a dream: If only we could get to readers immediately and have infinite newshole (space for news) for explaining long, complicated stories.

The dream comes true with Internet services. Communication is instantaneous and cyberspace had infinite newshole.

Still, questions arise:

- Are Internet services evolving into e-mail and e-commerce functions—competitors principally for the U.S. Postal Service and shopping catalogs?
- Or, will the reading public shift from printed page to screen, not only for chatting with friends and computer-assisted research but also for their daily news?

Certainly, technology permits the shift. In some cities, 60 per cent or more of households have Internet access — deeper household "penetration" than most big-city newspapers can boast. Well over 100 million Americans are online, and Web sites record many millions of hits by users seeking sports scores, weather, stock prices, movie reviews, news headlines and other types of basic information long a strength of newspapers and magazines.[14]

Yet, newspapers at 50 cents or so a copy stay popular with millions of readers. New magazines are launched successfully every year. And, to an extent yet unmatched by the new media, the "old" print media attract affluent information seekers who generally are the movers and shakers — the decisionmakers — of our society.

That is, even after years of Internet expansion, it's impossible to predict the future of electronic services in the types of news and information that are the strengths of newspapers and magazines.

And that, in turn, makes it difficult to counsel you, a beginning writer, on what the Internet future will require.

Nevertheless, some things are clear:

For example, in working for an Internet service you must remember the medium's basic strength—speed. Internet users want fast access to your site *and* fast absorption—quick comprehension — once they get to your writing.

As a Web site designer, then, you must facilitate quick understanding through your display of various elements such as graphics, headlines and tabular material, as well as words.

As a writer, you must create copy that is read easily and quickly, whose meaning is open and readily apparent.

WRITE TIGHT.

Offer headlines, abstracts and summaries that are easily scanned. Tables and lists differentiated by "bullets" or dashes enable users to get quickly to operative information.

DON'T FORCE REPEATED SCROLLING.

Shape your writing whenever possible to fit a screen. Break longer stories into separate click-on sections. Newspapers lose many readers with "jumps" — continuations of long stories to subsequent pages; you'll lose site visitors if you force interminable scrolling.

WRITE SHORT.

The Internet is not best used for delivering poetry or displaying your skill at fashioning long, meandering, if colorful and descriptive sentences constructed of complex and convoluted language that forces users to read once, then backtrack for a second (or third) reading before comprehension finally dawns. Get it? Use short words. Short sentences. Short paragraphs.

DON'T JUNK UP YOUR WRITING.

Links embedded in every graf (or sentence!) distract users. Collect them at the bottom of your story or in sidebars.

REMEMBER THE BASICS.

Good grammar, active verbs, strong sentences — the fundamentals of *any* good writing — are the basics of good Internet writing. That is, the writing lessons in this book are lessons for Internet writers, too.

Your News Judgment Is Crucial

With a world of information truly at their fingertips online, how do non-journalist users cope on the Internet?

With difficulty, it seems.

The Pew Research Center for the People and the Press finds 30 percent of a sample of online information-seekers feel overloaded by the amount of information available.

Your crucial role as a journalist is to exercise professional news judgment in sifting through the unending flow of information and finding bits and pieces crucial to your readers.

Internet users can bypass traditional media and their sifting and editing process. They can interrogate directly the libraries of the world and a multitude of news sources.

But can they take to that the winnowing and sifting skills of a professional journalist? With difficulty, clearly.

The Pew research finds the number of surfers who feel overloaded is increasing — 30 percent in 2001, up from 23 percent five years earlier.

Nevertheless, use of the Internet for spot news is increasing, particularly by investors who increasingly are turning to the Web for stock quotes and trading information. Of active traders, 45 percent say the Internet is their main source for stock market updates.

After giving some ground in the 1970s and 1980s, newspapers are holding steady in the competition against Internet sources, the research finds. Broadcast television is hardest hit by the competition in the fight for younger viewers. Researchers find only 17 percent of those under age 30 say they regularly watch network news, compared with 50 percent of those aged 65 or older.*

---

*The poll, of 3,142 persons, was conducted from April 20 through May 13, 2001. The poll has an error margin of plus or minus 2.5 percent.

CONVERGENCE: THE FUTURE OR FOLLY?

So, will the dominant communications medium of the future be a hybrid of all media we've discussed so far?

Must you, the journalist of tomorrow, prepare to write for convergence of print, broadcast and Internet media into some new, yet-unshaped form of communication?

Or, is it folly to think the habits of confirmed readers will mutate with those of television viewers and Internet users to create an information-seeker demanding we use an all-media combination of reporting and writing skills?

Certainly, many large media companies, already diversified in ownership of print, broadcast and Internet properties, are changing their *corporate structures* and implementing *new technology* as if such convergence is coming.

Executives with titles such as "vice president for new media" are being placed in subsidiary organizations charged with developing new subscriber and advertiser support.

Alan Horton, senior vice president of newspapers for E. W. Scripps Co., a major and longtime publisher of newspapers, says, "We are in the 'information business,' not the 'newspaper business.' And we need to serve readers and advertisers in the ways that would most benefit them. That means we provide the information — commercial and editorial — in whatever form they wish to receive it.

"New media is just one of the natural extensions of the traditional boundaries of journalism."[15]

Though careful to say newspapers won't disappear, Horton speaks of "renaissance journalists" who "will be newsgatherers, not newspaper or broadcast reporters or Web reporters."

Now, cost-conscious managers might expect a reporter to work in any or all media — or in a future hybrid. But "renaissance journalist" also could mean "jack-of-all-trades," a journalist somewhat capable in all media but outstanding in none.

More likely, perhaps, is print and electronic media remaining separate and distinct *but* using each other's strengths to full advantage.

Is synergism — complementary use of various technologies—but not merger ahead? Example:

Showing a limitation of newspaper publishing, the *Atlanta Constitution*, a morning paper, went to press with most of its editions before the final game of the 2000 World Series was over (won by the New York Yankees).

On its front page, the *Constitution* published this:

LATE GAME
Thursday night's Yankees-Mets game was not completed in time for this edition. Complete coverage can be found:

In the Sports Final Edition of the Constitution, on sale around the metro area.
In the *Atlanta Journal*.
On the Internet at accessatlanta.com/sports/[16]

The Journal was the Constitution's afternoon sister paper (and now is merged with it).

Next to the "boxed" information above, the *Constitution* published a pre-game feature on the Yankees versus the Mets by one of its leading baseball writers.

His byline:
By Jack Wilkinson
jwilkinson@ajc.com

There, I believe, is convergence: For 50 cents, dear reader, get Wilkinson and much more in our pages. For further detail—and a chat with Jack himself — come into ajc.com.

Thus a newspaper remains a newspaper, a Web site a Web site, and the twain meet only in mutually advantageous technological synergism.

And for both — and for any other medium — you'll need basic reporting and writing skills. To them we turn in Chapter Two.

SUMMARY

- Technological convergence is enabling newspapers and magazines to use the Internet's speed to publish print products.
- But each medium likely will retain a distinct identity and unique role in serving the public, meaning newswriters must learn to write differently for each.
- For a career in Internet journalism, learn to write quickly, in minimalist language.
- For newspapers, focus on in-depth reporting and analytical writing that take your readers deep into compellingly important issues of our time.

- For a magazine career, take a longer view and sharpen your skills in less-timely narrative writing and, particularly, specialized journalism.
- Whatever your career destination, you first must understand your medium, its audience and, thus, how it defines news.
- American media divide broadly into two categories: advertiser-driven, which gain most of their revenue from advertisers, and subscriber-driven, which, instead, deliver news to users for a fee.
- Newspapers are advertiser-driven, so they report news that attracts readers who are upscale in education and income and who can be "sold" to advertisers.
- Newspapers define their "market" in geographic terms—a city and five surrounding counties, for example—and news that breaks in that area takes high priority.
- About 1,500 dailies sell around 55 million copies each day and nearly 60 million on Sundays, and because they average more than two readers for each copy sold, reach more than 100 million Americans daily.
- More than 8,000 weekly newspapers distribute over 74 million copies each week, serving mostly small towns with community journalism.
- Newspapers "zone" content into separate sections for sports, business and so forth, and you must write news expertly in such narrow interest areas for readers.
- Newspaper journalists must "write around" technical limitations of newspapers, particularly their relative slowness in reaching readers.
- An estimated 18,000 magazines focus mostly on narrowly specialized journalism, requiring writers to be experts in their subjects and to write with precision for expert readers.
- Many magazines boast upscale reader demographics (*Forbes* claims its subscribers' average household net worth is $956,000), and your writing must be tuned appropriately.
- In many cities, Internet services reach or "penetrate" more households than do newspapers, and well over 100 million Americans are on line.
- However, the future still is unclear for Internet journalism in areas of news and information long staples of newspaper and magazine journalism.

RECOMMENDED READING

The best way to learn how professionals define news is to make disciplined study of their daily efforts.

Go to an Internet site, CNNfn, for example, and examine the types of news being transmitted and how it is written.

Watch leading newspapers the next morning — a nearby metro, perhaps, or the *New York Times* national edition — for how they cover the same story.

Then, check next week's *Time*, *Newsweek* or other magazines for their versions.

I discuss media market strategies in "Strategic Newspaper Management" (Boston: Allyn and Bacon, 1996), "Introduction to Magazine Writing" (New York: Macmillan, 1993), "Inside the Media" (New York: Longman, 1990) and "Introduction to Professional Newswriting" (New York: Longman, 1998).

EXERCISES

1. This exercise will a) start you toward shaping your personal view of the communications future, and b) give your instructor a sample of your writing. In about 350 words, describe how you and friends your age obtain news and information operative to your lives. Which media do you use regularly? Which when big news breaks? Knowing what you do about the reading habits of persons your age, where will your generation seek news in a decade or so? Write carefully, in minimalist language. Try for a snappy lead.

2. Your instructor will provide you with a copy of a news story transmitted by an Internet service or direct you to an appropriate Web site. Examine the writing of the selected dispatch. Comment on the writer's style, use of language and apparent intent. In your opinion, what is the writer trying to communicate? Who is the selected target audience? Write in newspaper style, in 250–300 words.

3. Examine the front page of a newspaper designated by your instructor. In about 300 words, describe the types of stories pre-

sented, their subject matter and the style in which they are written. Are they hard-news offerings, features or interpretive and analytical? Can you surmise the type of audience the newspaper's editors sought?

4. Your instructor will designate a *Time* or *Newsweek* story on a news event from last week—that is, one already reported with the immediacy of the Internet and in fuller details by daily newspapers. In about 300 words, discuss how the magazine writer overcomes the time-lag disadvantage inherent in weekly magazine publishing. Does the writer pitch ahead the story, as discussed in Chapter One? Does the story bring new understanding to someone already aware of earlier news coverage? Or, does the writer merely rehash facts already known?

5. In Chapter One you had a quick look at news strategies followed by print and Internet media. In about 300 words, describe how you view the relative strengths and weaknesses of each. What roles do you see them performing in the future? Will Internet services be aimed principally at quick transmission of bare-bone facts, leaving deeper reporting to newspapers and magazines? Or, will your generation take easily to lengthy, in-depth stories via the Internet?

NOTES

1. CNNfn, "the financial network," followed this story throughout the trading day, of course. The Dow Jones Industrial Average rose as high as 142, then trading subsided and the average ended up 50.

2. Note the full account followed immediately after the abbreviated version and was transmitted at 9:56 a.m.

3. "As Summer Wanes, Price at The Pump Remains Hot," Aug. 30, 2000, p. A–1.

4. "Smoke in Publishers' Eyes," July 1, 2000, p. 11.

5. I discuss media management structures and marketing strategies in "Strategic Newspaper Management" (Boston: Allyn & Bacon, 1996) and "Inside the Media" (New York: Longman, 1990).

6. "Facts About Newspapers: 2000," published by the National Newspaper Association, pp. 15–16.

7. Ibid., p. 7.

8. Ibid., p. 31.

9. "U.S. Said to Eye Silver Line Project Safety Violations," Oct. 18, 2000, p. B-1.

10. "Facts About Newspapers: 2000," p. 8, reporting a Scarborough Research finding that 90 percent of adults look at "main (local) news," compared with, for example, 68 per cent for entertainment, the second-most popular category.

11. "Mo. Governor Dies in Crash; Impact Seen on Senate Balance," Oct. 18, 2000, p. A–18.

12. The Magazine Publishers Association, New York City, counted 18,047 consumer and business magazines as of 1997, quoting data from National Directory of Magazines, Standard Rate and Data Service and Audit Bureau of Circulations.

13. Peter Brimelow, "Who's Got The Bucks," Forbes, July 5, 1999, p. 88.

14. Jeff Bennett, a Knight Ridder dispatch for Sunday papers, Oct. 29, 2000, reporting on "Surveying the Digital Future," a study by the University of California at Los Angeles Center for Communication Policy.

15. Mark Alan Braam, "The Renaissance Journalist," Scripps Howard News, Fall 2000, p. 7.

16. Jack Wilkinson, "Quick Hook a Stunner for Neagle," *Atlanta Constitution*, Oct. 27, 2000, p. C–1.

2

Know Your Subject

THE VARYING WRITING styles you studied in Chapter One — fast and lean for the Internet, detailed and analytical for newspapers — must be based on one commonality: strong reporting.

How you write in journalism can vary. But, regardless of your medium, *what* you write always must flow from accurate, factual, balanced and fair reporting.

With strong reporting skills you can fashion a rewarding — perhaps great — career in any medium, even if your writing is not outstanding.

Many journalism greats who preceded you, men and women whose work changed our nation, weren't outstanding writers. But, oh, what reporters they were — bulldog reporters committed to the people's right and need to know, reporters determined to dig out facts to serve that right and need.

To report effectively you must know your subject thoroughly. On some stories you'll have time — days, weeks even — for reflective, methodical, time-consuming reporting. Mostly, however, you'll need to background yourself quickly and assemble facts *right now*, to meet a deadline *right now*.

In Chapter Two, we'll look at that challenge in two parts:

First, we'll discuss the elements of a strongly reported story and how to structure your writing around them.

Second, we'll look at beginner techniques for reporting and interviewing — helpful hints on where to take your hunt for news and how to operate when you get there.

HOW TO REPORT STORY ELEMENTS

Is news what *readers* say is news? Or what *editors* say?

It's a combination, really. We report what research shows readers *want*, then add what we journalists think they also *need* to know.

That combination, the *news mix*, contains elements you must consider for any news story. Varying nomenclature is used to describe them, and editors sometimes place different emphasis on each, but the elements are recognized throughout journalism as *impact, proximity, timeliness, conflict, prominence, novelty*.

Let's look at each:

IMPACT

In reporting an event, look first at how many people it affects and how deeply.

All media give top priority to news crucial to large numbers of people — war and peace, disease and death, hope and despair, dollars and taxes.

Reporting precisely how an event has impact on people, then describing that in clear, accessible, readable writing marks the professional journalist. Take a look:

As the MTA strike paralyzed Los Angeles County mass transit for the second day Sunday, about 450,000 commuters — many of them minorities and low-wage earners with few options — prepared to bear the full impact today of the labor dispute on their jobs and families.

With contract negotiations suspended, those dependent on public transportation planned to carpool, take cabs, walk or use neighborhood entrepreneurs who charge less than taxis for a cramped ride in their personal cars or trucks.

Others who cannot afford private transit said they have canceled shopping trips, errands, even doctor's appointments for their children. Many employees, desperate to keep their jobs, said they will call in sick or simply get up a few hours earlier this week and walk to work—some for distances of 10 miles or more.

"What else can I do?" asked (Fred Smith), 40, who said he has no other option but to set out before dawn from his home in Pico Union to get to his restaurant job in Santa Monica on time . . .

Dan Weikel
and Jeffrey L. Rabin
Los Angeles Times[1]

Note the story above focuses immediately and intently on impact: 450,000 commuters and their families will suffer — and so, obviously, will all of Los Angeles.

Such widespread impact—and writing that illustrates it—won for this story front-page display (which all true reporters covet) in the Los Angeles Times.

Note also how the writers describe impact in real-life terms any reader can understand: commuters must carpool or walk and cancel everyday activities. Reporting that personalized detail is much more effective than simply writing that commuters will be "inconvenienced."

In reporting impact, translate the meaning with language and scenarios that express your story in human terms: Poor Fred Smith, forced to set out before dawn to get to his restaurant job!

Can you spot three words in the lead below that underline impact?

Breaking from the norms of City Council decorum, two Los Angeles lawmakers on Tuesday blasted each other for allegedly wasting taxpayer funds.

Tina Daunt
Los Angeles Times[2]

Yes, of course, "wasting taxpayer funds" defines the impact of the story above. You'll remember from Chapter One that many newspaper readers have upscale incomes and thus are taxpayers, so this story has great appeal to Los Angeles Times readers.

Incidentally, the writer later reported in the story above that one lawmaker was accused of "spending $45,223 in taxpayer funds on a new Lincoln Navigator 2000."

Can't you hear readers exclaiming, "What? I pay taxes so those guys can buy expensive cars?"

That's how you *translate* impact!

PROXIMITY

It's not true, as journalists joked in times bygone, that any story breaking on Main Street — even a kitten stranded in a tree — is bigger news than any story, even a revolution, on the other side of the world.

It *is* true, however, that the closer to home a story breaks, the more carefully you must analyze its news merits.

Look at it this way:

A single-engine plane plunges into a swamp 500 miles from your town and the sole occupant, little known to all but his family, is killed. News? Not for you.

How about this: A plane crashes in your town, in the backyard of the town's leading banker, and the pilot is killed. News? *Big* news.

The difference? The second crash occurred *here*, not way over *there*. It affected *us*, not the anonymous far-off *them*.

Here's how *proximity* often is the total focus in small-town reporting:

A Blackshear man has been arrested for forgery after cashing over $200 in stolen checks at two local convenience stores.

The Blackshear (Ga.) Times[3]

Note above that the man's name, his age, his occupation, his momma's name—all are secondary to the fact that he's a local man, from Blackshear.

What? One of *our own* is forging checks? At *local* convenience stores?

However, proximity in reporting is not only a question of geography. Spot another type of proximity in this:

As many as 10 teenagers in the Antelope Valley are under investigation over counterfeit money allegedly made with their home computers and used to buy food in their middle school cafeteria, authorities said.

The bills, mostly of low denominations, appeared real enough to fool lunch room employees at the Joe Walker Middle School in Quartz Hill. They were discovered only when a cashier was counting the money late last week . . .

Josh Meyer
and Richard Fausset
Los Angeles Times[4]

Yes, proximity — *closeness* — for readers in the story above is that we all are in school, have been or have children there now. So children counterfeiting money and spending it in school cafeterias strikes very close to home.

If you define "proximity" liberally, a story on the other side of the world indeed can have major interest locally. Let's say you live in a U.S. coastal town endangered by beach erosion. An Australian city learns how to build underwater barriers that halt erosion. Does that news from afar meet the proximity standard? You bet.

CONFLICT

Conflict — between people, armies, nations, ideas — frames much news, and reporting it fully but carefully, colorfully but calmly is central to your responsibility as a reporter.

Below is an example of conflict reporting that's frequently in the news. As you read, look for 1) the superficial and obvious news element and 2) the deeper story behind the conflict.

Harare, Zimbabwe — Riots sparked by rising food prices spread Tuesday as crowds stoned cars, trashed suburban shops and marched through the streets. Police fired tear gas in response and soldiers patrolled the poorest neighborhoods.

With Zimbabwe's economy in tatters, the government last week announced increases of up to 30 percent on bread, sugar and soft drink prices. Bus and taxi-van fares rose Monday. The new higher prices followed a series of increases in the cost of gasoline, milk and corn meal — a staple food . . . .

The Associated Press[5]

Yes, riots are the superficial news in the story above. The deeper, much more important meaning is that Zimbabwe's economy is in tatters.

Lesson: Conflict frequently is news simply because it escalates into violence. Sometimes, blood, agony and tears alone are news. More often, though, *what's behind the conflict is the real news.*

Note below how a *Boston Globe* reporter gets quickly to the deeper meaning of conflict.

A sudden groundswell of opposition to the city's master plan for building on the South Boston Waterfront is gaining strength, threatening to delay construction of the first major projects there.

Activists in neighborhoods far removed from the 1,000-acre industrial plain — where officials want to construct a mini-city of hotels, condos, and office towers — are holding living room meetings, organizing petition drives, and planning public rallies to find a way to kill the plan.

"People are furious," said (Jane Smith) of the Alliance of Boston Neighborhoods, which has been receiving calls from residents of Ja-maica Plain, West Roxbury, and the Back Bay. "People are suddenly realizing what's being planned over there and they're not happy."

The uprising has alarmed city officials, who believed until recently that the plan was due for approval by Robert Durand, state secretary of environmental affairs . . . .

Steven Wilmsen
Boston Globe[6]

Note in the story above five factors your reporting must cover in writing about conflict:

- Characterize the conflict. (In this case, it's a non-violent "groundswell of opposition.")
- Isolate the deeper meaning. (Opposition to the master plan.)
- Report how conflict is manifested. ("Living room meetings . . . petition drives")
- Quote participants. (And note how much more effective the writer is in quoting Jane Smith—"People are furious"—rather than merely reporting that "people are angry.")
- Show the effect of the conflict. (City officials are alarmed.)

One danger in reporting conflict is sketching even non-violent confrontation with inappropriately warlike terms. Note below how teachers are characterized as "battling" in what really is a nonviolent dispute over pay:

While their colleagues in neighboring cities celebrate double-digit pay raises, teachers in two Silicon Valley school districts are battling to get what they say is their fair share of a cash windfall from the state.

State mediators will be brought in to settle disputes in the San Ma-teo-Foster City and Mountain View school districts, where negotiations between teachers' unions and district administrators have deadlocked . . . .

Julie N. Lynem
San Francisco Chronicle[7]

Note below how a writer carefully characterizes conflict in non-warlike terms but still captures for his readers its "sharp" edges (emphasis added):

The criticism was *calm and respectful*, but it was *sharp nonetheless* and hit at the heart of Columbus State University.

About 50 members of the CSU community met Tuesday with two top administrators to air complaints about a newly required freshman technology course besieged by problems . . . .

Mark Rice

Columbus (Ga.) Ledger Enquirer[8]

Two points need emphasis:

- In reporting conflict, don't automatically ride to the sound of the cannon believing noise and smoke always are news; find the deeper meaning — the reason for the conflict—and you'll find the real news for your readers.
- Watch your language. Writing that politicians are "attacking" each other and school teachers "battling" may pump your story beyond its intrinsic newsworthiness and mislead your readers.

TIMELINESS

News by definition is new, current, timely.

Reporting how Earth was formed billions of years ago is interesting, and there's a certain fascination in reporting that billions of years from now Earth may freeze up (or, alternately, burn up) in climate changes.

But that type of reporting isn't why people turn with urgency to *news*papers, *news*magazines, *new*casts or Internet *news* sites.

To be a professional reporter you must stay on the cutting edge of daily events. Watch who and what emerge into public view today, right now. Look for hidden meanings, and try to understand what likely will be the next act in the human comedy. It takes total immersion in current events and more reading and viewing of news than is healthy.

Timeliness — the *time element* in news — will be discussed repeatedly in this book. For now, recognize that one of your responsibilities in the competitive game of reporting is to be first to *tell folks what happened*. Here, in its most basic but perhaps most important form, is that type of reporting:

A city police officer was reported shot in the forearm last night while he and his partner were working in the Fairhill section of North Philadelphia.	Tom Infield, Dale Mezzacappa and Marc Schogol *Philadelphia Inquirer*[9]

Yes, readers want your reporting on the compelling economic, political and social issues of the day. Yes, they want your in-depth analysis on what all that means.

First, however, they want your report on more fundamental questions — such as, "What was all that fuss over in Fairhill last night?"

Warnings:

- Competing to be first can lead to sloppy, inaccurate reporting. Be first, *if you can*; be accurate *always*. Don't let the drive for timeliness override your need to be careful, thoughtful, *accurate*.
- Old news is new news if your readers don't know it yet. Don't get so hung up on timeliness that you automatically discard news unless it broke within the past 24 hours. We inevitably are late in breaking some stories. Your challenge is to come from behind and report and write those stories in ways that illustrate their topicality and meaning for readers *today and tomorrow*, even if they developed days, weeks or months ago.

PROMINENCE

Prominence — and, thus, newsworthiness — attaches to persons or things that thrust themselves *or are thrust even unwillingly* into public consciousness.

So, your priorities for reporting crucial elements of a news story must include this question: Is this person or thing of compelling interest to my readers?

Those who seek the limelight often find it follows them everywhere:

Vandenberg Air Force Base — Authorities arrested peace activists, including actor Martin Sheen, during a protest Saturday to return the study of outer space solely to scientific research instead of military purposes . . . .

The Associated Press[10]

Being singled out for mention by name happens, as well, to people who don't seek prominence:

Bureij Refugee Camp, Gaza Strip — He died huddled in his father's arms, caught in a hail of bullets — captured in the viewfinder of a television camera in a shocking scene viewed all over the world.

Twelve-year-old Mohammed Jamal Aldura — shot as his desperate father tried to shield him after they blundered into the middle of a fierce Israeli-Palestinian clash outside a small Jewish settlement — was mourned yesterday in the teeming refugee camp where he spent his short life . . . .

Laura King
The Associated Press[11]

Did you note the prominence factor was reported differently in the two examples above?

Martin Sheen got lead-graf mention because his name and face are known to millions. Leading with "a prominent actor" being arrested and subordinating his name to the second graf would not focus properly on the prominence factor so important in newswriting.

In the second story, *who* the boy is by name is not as important as *what* he is — an unfortunate victim of the capriciousness of war, whose death was watched on television worldwide.

Here is another example of the *what* of prominence being more important than the *who*:

Huntsville, Texas — A Mexican-born killer was executed by injection Thursday amid protests from countries that say he was denied his right under an international treaty to contact the Mexican consulate after his arrest. About five hours before Miguel Flores was strapped to a gurney for the execution, the U.S. Supreme Court, in a 5–4 vote, denied his request for a reprieve . . . .

The Associated Press[12]

Poor Miguel! Prominent — and thus news — only because international foes of capital punishment came to his aid, to no avail.

Merely being near a major news event can attach prominence to a person's life — and death. Note:

Jean Hill, an eyewitness to the assassination of President John F. Kennedy who became known as "The Lady in Red" in the Abraham Zapruder film of the killing, has died.

Hill, 69, a retired schoolteacher, died of complications from a blood disease Tuesday at Parkland Hospital in Dallas, where Kennedy died.

The grainy, amateur film shot by Zapruder . . . shows Hill clad in a red raincoat as she stood . . . on Elm street on Nov. 22, 1963. The Lincoln Continental carrying Kennedy, first lady Jaqueline Kennedy, Texas Gov. John B. Connally and his wife, Nellie, passed about 15 feet away . . . .

Los Angeles Times[13]

Warning: Legitimate pursuit of news to serve the people's right to know on subjects of true newsworthiness can degenerate, unless you're careful, into mindless personality voyeurism. Don't chase well-known personalities in their private as well as public moments to serve nothing more exalted than the base instincts of people who like to peer into other people's closets.

Prominence attaches, of course, not only to people. Ideas, issues, things — all can fit your news definition of prominence, and you must adjust your reporting priorities accordingly. For example:

- Graffiti on a subway wall in New York City isn't news; graffiti defacing the Lincoln Memorial in Washington is.
- Demonstrations against water pollution are relatively minor news; demonstrations against the ideal of racial, gender and ethnic equality among Americans are big news.
- Taxes, health care, education, crime are news. Why? Because they are nationally prominent issues that affect every American.

THE TRAGIC, NOVEL AND UNUSUAL

A story can be news even if it fails every reporting standard we've discussed—prominence, timeliness, conflict, proximity and impact.

How can that be?

Well, some stories are news simply because they are so unusual, such radical departures from the expected, that they fascinate many readers (whose interests, of course, are central to our definition of news).

For example, a priest — a man of God, an advocate of peace and love — gets violent. And that's news:

Rockford, Ill. — A Roman Catholic priest smashed a car into an abortion clinic yesterday, then chopped at the building with an ax until the owner shot at him, police said.

The clinic was not open, and nobody was hurt in the attack, which occurred two days after the Food and Drug Administration approved the abortion pill RU–486.

The Rev. (Fred Smith), 32, drove through a door at the Abortion Access Northern Illinois Women's Center around 8:15 a.m. He was swinging the ax when the owner fired twice with a 12-gauge shotgun. He did not hit (the priest), authorities said . . . .

Nicole Ziegler Dizon
The Associated Press[14]

The Illinois story above (with several hundred words more) was published a half continent away by the *Boston Globe*, not, of course, because it broke close to Boston or had direct impact on Bostonians or because the priest was prominent (he wasn't).

Rather, the news value is in the odd contradiction of a man of God angrily wielding an ax — and, of course, in the deeper controversy over abortion and RU–486.

Note above how carefully the writer focuses on the contradiction — *priest* gets *violent*. The writer would have failed if the lead referred only to "a man" getting violent, with the fact that he was a priest held until later.

Lesson: If a story interests you because it is odd, that's likely what will interest your reader. So focus your writing on the oddity.

Some stories are news simply because they are tragic, even if they have no deeper meaning (than, perhaps, that life is fickle). Here is one:

A 6-year-old girl was in critical condition and her father in fair condition after both were hit Sunday by a falling tree branch as they walked in a Westwood park, a Los Angeles Fire Department spokesman said.

The incident occurred as the fa-

ther, his daughter and 5-year-old son were walking in Holmby Park near the 600 block of South Club View Drive about 1 p.m., said Fire Department spokesman Brian Humphrey.

"There was no one climbing in

the tree, according to witnesses, or any other cause for it to suddenly give way," said Humphrey. "It is just a tragic, tragic case" . . . .

Los Angeles Times[15]

Note above how the reporting underscores the story's central meaning — that life is fickle. Always support your lead's thrust.

Do you see news value in the following story?

A woman who claims she was permanently scarred after a hot pickle from a (fast food) hamburger fell on her chin is suing the restaurant for $110,000. (Jane Smith) claims in a lawsuit filed in Knox County Circuit Court in Knoxville, Tenn., that the burn also caused her physical and mental pain. Her husband (Fred), is seeking $15,000 for being "deprived of the services and consortium of his wife." In 1994, a New Mexico woman was awarded $2.7 million after suing (a restaurant) for burns she suffered from coffee she spilled in her lap. A judge later lowered the award to about $500,000, and the parties reportedly settled for a lesser amount.

The Associated Press[16]

The story above meets not one of the reporting standards we've discussed — prominence, impact and so forth. But it is news. Why? Because it's so *odd*!

NOW BEGINS THE HUNT!

With core elements of news now identified, where — and how — do you hunt them down and report the story behind them?

Understand, first, that entire books — nay, *libraries* — are written about the art of reporting, and, second, even after years of experience, the really good reporters still are adding tricks to their trade.

Nevertheless, three factors central to your success can be identified immediately: people skills, interviewing and note-taking, and computer-assisted reporting.

PEOPLE SKILLS

Think about it: People are news, and most news is about people.

But, much news of and about people lies hidden, its meaning cloaked in questions of nuance and subtlety. Seldom will computer data banks or courthouses full of documents — the paper trail — volunteer the answers unbidden.

You need *people sources*, people who know where news is in the vast databank of cyberspace, where — on which page — it is in those tons of courthouse documents. You need people with *authoritative credentials* to translate those nuances and subtleties into meaning for your readers.

That requires locating sources who are *positioned to know*.

We're talking here about people skills far beyond simply "liking" or "getting along" with people. Your goal must be to develop professional relationships that enable you to extract from people the facts and figures you need.

First, study the geographic area, subject or "beat" you're covering. Where is news likely to break? Who likely will know about it? If, for example, city government is your beat, learn its table of organization. Trace how power — political, economic, personal — flows.

You need sources on the riverbanks overlooking that news flow, sources positioned officially or unofficially to alert you when something significant floats by.

Think about it: Somewhere on your campus, someone knows whether a tuition increase is being considered, which football players were benched for flunking drug tests, which club is being investigated for binge drinking.

It's that *someone* you must find and at whom you must direct your winsome personality and smile.

Some hints:

- *Never* try to develop sources by telephone. Nobody spills news to strangers on the telephone.
- Personal visits are necessary — and, as in love, you must start slowly and gently. "Hi, I'm John Smith of The Recorder, and I'm new on this beat . . . just thought I'd drop in and say hello . . . what's your name? . . . what do you do around here?" And, don't ask for a kiss — a scoop — on this first meeting.
- Make your rounds regularly. Get to know potential sources and let them understand you. Coffee or an occasional lunch together can cement your relationship. Yes, it's time-consuming hard work. Re-

porters, with reason, call this "legwork," and you'll spend much of your time at it.

- Keep a source notebook with names, telephone numbers (*home* numbers, too) and news specialties. Over years, this notebook will become perhaps your most valuable possession. And, track sources when they — or you — move to other jobs. Today's city hall clerk may be tomorrow's mayor; today's mayor may be tomorrow's governor.

- Don't let your relationship become personal rather than professional. Avoid entanglements that compromise your independence and integrity as a reporter.

INTERVIEWING AND NOTE-TAKING

Interviewing is a hugely important tool for reporters, yet (if you're a typical beginner), you probably don't know how to do it and, truth be told, are a bit timid about trying.

Right?

Well, be of good cheer. Your interviewing techniques will improve rapidly with experience. But that experience begins only when you force yourself to begin. So start now.

PREPARATION

Your success (or failure) will depend largely on how well you've prepared for an interview.

Go in fully briefed on the subject *and* the interviewee, and you'll improve greatly your chance of coming out with a good story. Prepare poorly and you'll 1) look stupid and/or 2) be led by the nose wherever and whenever the interviewee desires.

You can control an interview — take it where you want it to go — only if you develop a strategy in advance. You must know enough to ask intelligent, pointed questions.

It's obvious: You wouldn't interview a football coach without knowing his won-lost record and what a "down-and-out" pass play is, or an

English professor without determining whether Shakespeare or Hemingway is the professor's life work.

So, don't interview bankers, scientists or government officials without knowing what their game is.

And, an old trick: Have a list of prepared questions in your notebook. Especially in your beginner years, you can refer to them if you feel the interview prematurely running out of gas — and you draw a mental blank on what to ask next.

YOUR ENTRANCE

Ever watch two prize fighters enter Round One? They circle, jabbing a bit, looking each other over — setting the tone, really, for what follows.

Opening moments of an interview are like that.

If you jump in swinging — in a sense, demanding, "You've got news; give it to me" — you'll not score a knockout. Open gently, on a friendly note, with reporter's notebook and pen still in your pocket.

The interviewee will signal impatience (perhaps a frowning look at a clock) if you're stretching the preliminaries too long, or, hopefully, acceptance, by returning the chatter and ordering coffee.

If you see a frown, quickly get to business with an *open-ended question*, such as "What are the team's chances this year?" That lets the interviewee take the conversation anywhere. The tactic serves several purposes.

First, it shows this isn't going to be a one-sided inquisition but, rather, a two-way conversation. (Sometimes you can see a source visibly relax when that become apparent.)

Second, it gives you a chance to say something like, "That's interesting. Let me take a note to be sure I quote you accurately."

Than enables you to get the tools of your trade — pen and notebook — into action in a non-threatening way. And, importantly, it makes clear this is an interview on the record — meaning the source will be quoted by name.

If your source strays (and most will), redirect the interview by gently interrupting (yes, despite what your mother said, you'll have to interrupt on occasion) with a *closed-ended question*. That's one requiring a direct answer: "Who will start at quarterback?" and it gets the interview back under your control.

NOTE-TAKING

Some reporters use tape recorders so they can concentrate on the conversation.

If you intend to record an interview *always* state that in advance. Secretly taping a conversation is highly unethical.

I advise strongly that you develop note-taking skills. You'll need them sometime, somewhere, even in this wired world. And if you're writing on deadline your notebook will give you quicker access to facts and figures than listening to an hour-long playback on tape.

Warning: Your instinct will be to tuck your face into your notebook and scribble furiously, trying to catch a verbatim account. Don't.

Learn to *listen* to the interviewee and take *selective notes* on just those points you know might fit into your story. Maintain eye contact, asking, probing, thinking ahead to the next question, and always keeping priorities in your mind — "Ah, that's my lead! Yes, I've got to return to that point for details."

Some reporters use shorthand. (Some can catch conversations without looking at their notebooks.) But most rely on personalized systems of abbreviations, symbols, circles, arrows — all designed to catch essentials and highlight them for fast reference later, when writing.

NOW, ABOUT ARM-WRESTLING!

Ah, if only they would just *give* us the news!

Unfortunately, some interviewees 1) don't understand the news business and thus don't know what you want, or 2) if they know, they try to hide it.

Either way, you eventually must end the pleasant little chat and get what you came for — news.

Sometimes you accomplish this by circling a question, coming at it from different directions, with different questions. Ask it several ways, and maybe you'll trigger a response.

If that doesn't unlock the news, you may be forced to wrestle for what you want. That can require blunt questioning: "Why do you decline to answer that question?" Or, "I believe the public has a right to know this. Don't you?" (And the toughest of all: "I don't want to write that you refuse to answer my question.")

However, two can play the tough-guy act.

Sources experienced in the ways of reporters may try to intimidate you ("That's a dumb question!") or fend you off ("Well, what do *you* think?")

Completely *un*intimidated, you must push back into the fray: "Oh, I'm just a reporter; *you* are mayor. What's *your* view?"

Two points:

- We get to ask the questions as we wish; they get to answer them as they desire. That's how it works.
- And, don't try tough-guy stuff until late in the interview, after you've gotten everything else you need and have nothing to lose if the interview is terminated suddenly!

YOUR EXIT

Well, the interview concludes and you have the story you sought.

Or have you?

Did you think of every possible angle, ask every pertinent question? Maybe not. So, *always* conclude by asking, "Is there anything else I should know? Anything more you want to tell me? Is there anyone else I should see?"

Many important stories develop through such open-ended invitations to the interviewee to volunteer news.

Be prepared also for something else as you exit: The source, suddenly aware of having been too revealing, might say something like, "This interview is off the record, right?"

Even if you established on-the-record ground rules early in the interview (as you should), this last-minute statement creates a problem — use the story and you risk losing a source.

Every reporter has faced this dilemma, and you'll have to decide quickly which is more valuable, story or source.

Try to jolly the source: "C'mon, Mr. Mayor, you know it's on the record" or, "Hey, there's no dynamite in this interview."

If that doesn't work, and the source is of great long-range value, you might have to go off the record. But make the ground rules clear in the next interview, and stick to them.

In general, try hard to leave sources happy. You'll need them again.

COMPUTER-ASSISTED REPORTING

Beginner reporters typically misuse computer-assisted reporting.

Some ignore its enormous strength. Others plunge into cyberspace and don't emerge until overwhelmed by huge quantities of facts and figures, some relevant, some not; some reliable, some not.

In between such extremes lies the tremendous value of computer-assisted reporting (CAR). Keep two points in mind:

- American newspapers are overwhelmingly local in news orientation, and your job as a reporter, at least in your early years, will be to work Main Street with old-fashioned news-gathering techniques — interviews and lots of leg-work.
- However, CAR can help you frame your local story in national and even international terms and buttress it with facts and meaning that aid reader understanding.

To illustrate, let's say you're reporting on crime on your campus. The university police chief releases a bare-bones statement that violent crime is up 13 percent over last year. He refuses to elaborate.

Filling in the Holes

For good reason — such as fear of being fired — sources sometimes will demand anonymity in your story.

First, consult a senior editor on whether the source has justification for remaining unidentified, and, importantly, whether your newspaper will protect any pledge of anonymity that you make.

Second, devise language that will inform your reader of why you cannot identify your source.

Blaine Harden of the *New York Times* does that on a story about how an economic downturn is affecting the lives of rich people in New York City. A butler reveals he is pouring relatively cheap wine for dinner guests because his employer is cutting expenses. Harden passes that delightful fact to his readers — and protects his source:

(CONTINUES)

FILLING IN THE HOLES (CONTINUED)

The butler, who noted that he would be fired if he or his employer were identified by name, said he had stopped pouring '89 Chateau Palmer ($195 a bottle) at dinner parties, downshifting instead to a slightly more shallow and marginally less complex '89 Chateau Talbot (about $40 a bottle). Though if there is a connoisseur among the guests, the butler said, he pours the better Bordeaux.*

Maureen Dowd of the *Times* has an exclusive on turmoil in the Smithsonian Institution and attributes her information to "disgruntled Smithsonians (who) slip me a stunning in-house list."***

Jill Carroll and Antonio Regalado of The *Wall Street Journal* have a fascinating story on a U.S. Customs Service inspector who found smuggled goods on a ship. Readers naturally wonder how the inspector works, and the writers answer this way: "To protect agency techniques, (the inspector) insists that the precise details of what piqued the government's interest remain secret."****

A *New York Times* writer, Alison Leigh Cowan, reports how, in his last days in the presidency, Bill Clinton was pressured to pardon convicted felons. Cowan reports her story was "drawn from interviews with people directly involved and documents made public for Congressional hearings."[4]

That is how to fill holes in a story—and show readers that you did!

---

*"Some very Expensive Belts Tightened, but Just a Notch," April 1, 2001, p. A–1.

**"Tales From the Crypt," June 24, 2001, p. A–13.

***"Who Would Expect Korean Fish Imports to Contain Pork Fat?", June 22, 2001, p. A–1.

[4]"Rich Cashed in a World of Chits to Win Pardon," April 11, 2001, p. A–1.

SHOUT FOR HELP

With CAR, you can consult experts — and summon help — that magnify the clout you and your campus newspaper have.

For example, the Student Press Law Center (http://www.splc.org), funded by the Society of Professional Journalists, gives free advice on which police documents by law are open to inspection and makes available professional reporters who can counsel you on how to develop effective working relationships with police.[17]

The non-profit Security on Campus (http://campussafety.org) has university-related background, and the Cops and Courts Reporters Directory (http://www.reporters.net/ccr) gives you names of professional reporters in your region who can advise you. Associated Collegiate Press Discussion List (http://www.studentmedia.org) puts you in touch with other students facing similar reporting problems.

That is, CAR enables you to seek *distant authority* with reach and speed your predecessors in journalism never dreamed possible. Use that reach.

IDENTIFY TRENDS

To put that 13 percent increase in proper context, you need to flesh out your reporting in two ways:

Establish historical trends. Your story is *not* violence of yesteryear, elsewhere. But you establish crucial context for your local story if you obtain through CAR facts on campus crime elsewhere in the nation in years past.

Establish current context. What's happening right now on other campuses? Against that present-day reality, is your 13 percent increase high or low?

In reporting, *deviations from the norm* often are your first clue that news is breaking.

Think about it: If crime has been increasing by 6 percent annually on your campus and at universities nationwide, your 13 percent this year is news. It's also news if your 13 percent measures favorably against a nationwide average of 20 percent.

Use CAR to establish standards and averages against which to measure your story.

SEEK STATISTICAL SUBSTANCE

A crime story pegged solely to one number—13 percent—is shallow, unfulfilling and far short of the fact-filled, substantive reporting you owe your readers.

With persistence (and guidance from the Student Law Press Center) you should be able to crack the police chief's reticence and break down that 13 percent into rapes, dorm burglaries, auto thefts and so forth.

With CAR you can compare statistics for each category with breakdowns for crimes in, say, the surrounding "civilian" community or in universities elsewhere.

CRUNCH ORIGINAL DATA

Much newspaper reporting revolves around asking someone else what the news means. With CAR, you sometimes can arrive at independent judgment of its meaning.

Think about it: Government officials, special interest groups and spin artists of all types are eager to explain the meaning — as they see it — of the millions of documents stored in cyberspace.

Traditional reporting technique requires you to ask one informed source what those documents mean, then scurry around to ask a couple more for their views.

With CAR, you can go directly into the cyberspace storehouse and independently analyze the meaning of U.S. Census Bureau data, federal and state statistics of all sorts, polling data, business-world information . . . the list is endless.

Hugely important stories have been broken in recent years by newspapers that developed sophisticated teams of CAR specialists, then turned them loose on raw data. With proper career preparation (for a start, see the Recommended Reading note at the end of this chapter), you can join their ranks.

BUT, BEWARE!

CAR produces hugely important stories — revelations of pedophiles employed as teachers, bus drivers with DUI convictions, banks denying credit to minorities.

Many are CAR's benefits. Many, too, are dangers inherent in it:

- CAR opens to you *thousands* of Internet sites and sources and *millions* of words. That can be overwhelming and easily lead to loss of focus. Don't let your reporting wander so far from its local implications that meaning is lost.
- Lazy reporters try to avoid the unavoidable — the hard work of one-on-one interviewing and street-smart reporting. Some choose instead to stare at screens all day, which can produce dry writing that reads like an accountant's report and has no local flavor or whiff of human contact.
- Some reporters mistakenly let the marvelous *technology* of cyber-space lend automatic credibility to its *content*, which may or may not be reliable. Handle Web content with all the suspicion and double-checking you accord information from any source. And *always* question the motives and credentials of those who post information. The cloak of Web anonymity hides many scoundrels out there!

THE REPORTER'S SIX-FINGER CHECKLIST

Your interviews are over, your reporter's notebook is full, and you're ready to write.

Now what?

Now you run through the Reporter's Six-Finger Checklist: Whether you're writing a two-graf news brief or a 1,000-word blockbuster, tick 'em off on your fingers—who, what, where, when, why and how.

Don't start writing unless you can answer those questions. They are central to a strongly reported story, whatever your medium.

Then consider carefully how to place them in your writing, and the focus and emphasis you will give each.

"Who?" and "what?" frequently will be your starting point.

WHO AND WHAT

Whether they originate news or are subject to its impact, people — not issues, not things — are the core of most reporting.

A Professional's View

BY MICHAEL A. GIARRUSSO
NEWS EDITOR
ASSOCIATED PRESS, ATLANTA

Computer-assisted reporting is just that, reporting that is *assisted* by a computer. Computers cannot replace human reporting skills and news judgment. They are simply tools to gather information that can be turned into a story using the same journalism techniques that have been around for more than a century.

Computer-assisted reporting has permitted big enterprise projects involving government or corporate records that could not have been analyzed or obtained without the use of computers. But in the last decade, the World Wide Web, online phone and address directories, source-finding services and databases have become basic journalism tools that are as indispensable to reporters as the telephone, tape recorder or notebook.

While training a new AP employee, I realized that I spent nearly two days showing her reporting tools that didn't exist when I joined the company in 1992. I remember a newswoman showing me a huge three-volume reverse directory that could be used to find the phone numbers of Atlanta residents based on their addresses. The directory was out of date almost as soon as it was printed. Today, if police give us the address where a brutal murder took place, any reporter or editorial assistant can simply plug in the address and immediately get the phone numbers and names of neighbors and nearby businesses.

And services like ProfNet make it possible for reporters to send questions that only a handful of experts could answer to thousands of professors, college public information officers and corporate public relations staffs around the country with one click of the mouse. A decade ago, reporters would spend a day cold-calling professors hoping to find someone who could answer their question.

Most reporters have learned to use databases to make sense of the morass of statistics that come across their desk each week. I can't imagine how reporters covered the Census without databases.

But this technology is useless unless it is combined with solid reporting and writing. Even on large computer-assisted reporting projects, the raw statistics and other material can't be turned into a story without old-fashioned journalism skills.

(CONTINUES)

A PROFESSIONAL'S VIEW (CONTINUED)

Reporters can make mistakes by relying on technology too much. Sometimes, reporters come up with a thesis that they think can be proven by accessing information or crunching numbers. If the thesis is incorrect, some reporters are unwilling to let the story go, so they stretch or force the issue to make their story work the way they envisioned it.

Another problem occurs when reporters try to make the statistics tell the story instead of finding the real people behind the numbers. Who cares if drunk driving accidents are up 45 percent in a neighborhood where a new bar opened if you don't quote someone who was in an accident with a drunk? Who cares that 75 percent of football players don't graduate from State U. if you don't quote a former player who can't find a job?

Some of the more successful computer-assisted reporting projects for the AP involve government records that could not be analyzed without the help of computers. In 2000, Tim Molloy of our Pittsburgh bureau analyzed a year's worth of sentences in Pennsylvania and found that whites were getting shorter sentences than blacks convicted of the same crimes. He led with the perfect example, a black man and white man convicted of the same crime but given sharply different sentences.

In 1999, Martha Mendoza, a national investigative reporter for the AP, looked at all civil rights complaints made to the Justice Department in a four-year period and found that the agency took no action in 96 percent of all cases. The AP analyzed computer records of 1.4 million cases to do the story. And the Dallas bureau did a project, which inspired similar stories around the country, comparing the salaries of Texas high school football coaches to other public education employees.

Reporters who are open to using new technology are among the most valuable to editors. And their value will only increase as even more amazing gadgets enter newsrooms. Reporters are already using pocket-sized, handheld computers to transmit stories back to the bureau and do research on the Internet. Some reporters are sending digital audio files and even video back to the office for use in multimedia packages for online news sites.

However, a reporter who is savvy about technology but weak in basic journalism skills is a danger in the newsroom and is eventually going to make a costly mistake. As an editor, I would prefer a technological neophyte who knows how to report and write. I can teach some computer-assisted reporting skills in a week. It would take much longer to teach someone the rest of the job.

If a person originates or dominates your story, ask yourself: Is the name the story? The source's credentials? Or both?

Below, a reporter focuses on both a well-known name and the source's credentials (emphasis added):

Bogota, Colombia — *White House anti-drug czar Barry McCaffrey* on Monday predicted heavy fighting in an approaching U.S.-backed anti- drug offensive and warned that there would be repercussions for Colombia's neighbors.

The Associated Press[18]

Below, the "who" is the object, not the originator of news, and his name is secondary to the "what" — a stay of execution.

Raleigh, N.C. — The North Carolina Supreme Court issued a stay of execution today for a death row inmate whose lawyer admitted sabotaging his appeal after deciding his client "should be executed for his crimes."

In a unanimous decision, the high court sent the case of (Fred Smith) back to Forsyth County Superior Court for a new hearing and ordered the court to appoint new lawyers for (Smith.)

(Smith) had been scheduled to die Dec. 7 for the 1994 murder of a Kmart security guard . . . .

The ruling came after his attorney, (John Jones) confessed that he let his co-counsel miss a deadline for filing an appeal, a move he hoped would lead to (Smith's) death . . . .

The Associated Press[19]

When reporting the "who" factor remember that *people* are what news is all about. A shipwreck is not about a ship sinking; it's about people drowned in a shipwreck. An avalanche is not about snow; it's about skiers killed by it.

As the two stories above illustrate, the "who" factor often emerges automatically from your reporting — the drug czar gives a speech, and thus he is news; the death row inmate wins a stay of execution, and gets his 15 minutes of fame.

The "what" factor, however, frequently lies hidden, requiring you to think carefully how to locate and highlight it for your readers.

Note in the following how an AP reporter sorts through a host of issues and focuses on the real "what" — charges of murder.

Springfield, Mass. — A nurse murdered four patients at a veterans hospital because she liked the thrill of medical emergencies and wanted to impress her boyfriend, a prosecutor said in opening statements yesterday in Massachusetts' first capital case since the 1980s.

(Jane Smith), 33, is accused of murdering four patients at the Veterans Affairs Medical Center in Northhampton by injecting them with high levels of adrenaline. She is also accused of trying to kill three other patients . . . .

The Associated Press[20]

Sometimes, *two* "what" factors of almost equal importance emerge in a single story. Here's how a pro reports that (emphasis added):

In what would be the *single largest police misconduct settlement* in Los Angeles history, City Att. James K. Hahn on Monday proposed that the city *pay $15 million to a man who* *was shot in the head and chest*, then allegedly framed by two Rampart Division officers.

Tina Daunt
Los Angeles Times[21]

WHERE AND WHEN

These two factors on your Reporter's Six-Finger Checklist frequently slide into your writing smoothly, almost unnoticed (emphasis added):

Jerusalem — Israeli attack helicopters and antitank missiles pounded Palestinian rioters *yesterday* in an attempt to extinguish a three-day explosion of violence that spread from the West Bank and Gaza Strip to towns and cities inside Israel.

Lee Hockstader
Washington Post[22]

The "where" above, of course, is Jerusalem in the "dateline" — so-called though it frequently doesn't include the date. And, "when" is "yesterday."

Sometimes, both "where" and "when" require special treatment.

Below, a reporter is more precise than usual with "when" because for A's baseball fans the "when" is a moment in history.

The suspense ended at precisely *3:50 yesterday afternoon*. Only then, as Jason Isringhausen's curveball danced across home plate, did a stadium full of A's fans finally, gleefully exhale.

Texas' Frank Catalanotto chose not to swing, umpire Brian Runge raised his right arm and Isringhausen led 45,606 people in wild exultation. The strikeout punctuated a dramatic day of baseball, as the A's won 3–0 and clinched the American League West championship.

Ron Kroichick
San Francisco Examiner[23]

Below, a *Columbus (Ga.) Ledger Enquirer* reporter gives special first-graf emphasis to "where" — Newnan, Ga. — because it serves as a *locator*, a geographic point known to Columbus residents.

A 40-year-old Columbus man accused of stabbing his wife to death in their home in May and then dumping her body in an abandoned shack outside Newnan, Ga., was indicted Tuesday.

Eileen Zaffiro
*The Columbus (Ga.)
Ledger Enquirer*[24]

It's worth emphasizing: If the writer above had not highlighted the "where" factor in the first graf her story would have lost meaning for many readers.

Always include "where" and "when" in your reporting. They help readers locate events in time and place.

WHY AND HOW

"Why" and "how" are crucially important because although newspapers cannot be faster than electronic media, they can delve more deeply each day into what's behind the news and what it means.

Your reporting task isn't finished unless you return from the news hunt with a firm grasp of these factors.

Sometimes, the "why" is obvious and easily highlighted (emphasis added):

Washington — Three companies are recalling about 243,000 bicycle helmets *because they failed government impact testing.*

The Associated Press[25]

So, too, can "how" be isolated sometimes in tight focus to aid reader understanding (emphasis added):

Three men, including one wanted on murder charges, have been arrested on suspicion of attempted robbery after undercover San Francisco *police officers watched them cruise the city's jewelry trade centers in an apparent search for victims*, authorities said Friday.

Jaxon Van Derbeken
San Francisco Chronicle[26]

Frequently, however, true meaning — the "real why" and "real how" — are deeply hidden in a news story. To tug true meaning to the surface we use special in-depth reporting skills and interpretive writing. We'll turn to those in later chapters.

First let's work on precision and clarity in writing the basic news story. That's next, in Chapter Three.

SUMMARY

- *How* you write in journalism can vary but *what* you write always must be founded in accurate, factual, balanced and fair reporting.
- You'll sometimes have days to report a story but mostly you will need to report quickly and assemble facts *right now*, to meet a deadline *right now*.
- What readers want and what editors think they need from a "news mix" flowing from impact, proximity, timeliness, conflict, prominence and novelty.
- First consider *impact*—how many people a news event affects and how deeply — because all media give top priority to news crucial to large numbers of people.
- *Proximity* — how close to home a story breaks — always must be reported but this also can mean giving high priority to stories of compelling interest of your readers, wherever the news breaks.
- *Conflict* between people, armies, nations and ideas frequently frames news, but always seek the deeper meaning behind conflict.
- News by definition is new, current, timely, so *timeliness* — being first with news—is important, but don't let accuracy suffer in your rush to beat your competitors.
- *Prominence* — and, thus, newsworthiness — attaches to persons or things in the public consciousness, but don't let your reporting degenerate into mindless personality voyeurism.
- A story can be news if it is so unusual and such a radical departure from the expected that it fascinates readers.
- In the hunt for news, your most important tools are *people skills*, *interviewing and note-taking*, and *computer-assisted reporting*.
- People sources can lead you to news in the vast databank of cyberspace or the tons of documents in the courthouse basement, so

develop sources with authoritative credentials who are positioned to know what's happening.

- You'll succeed in interviewing only if you have a well-developed strategy *before* the interview, and only if you practice, practice, practice.

- Computer-assisted reporting gives you enormous reach for facts and figures that can lend meaning to your local story, but one-on-one interviewing and legwork on Main Street are your best tools.

- When you've finished your interviews and legwork, run through the Reporter's Six-Finger Checklist: Can you answer who, what, where, when, why and how?

- People and what happens to them — your "who" and "what"— are most important in reporting.

- "Where," the locale of your story, and "when," its timing, often slide almost unnoticed into your writing, but check to make sure they are there.

- "Why" and "how" — analysis of what's behind the news — are crucial to you in newspaper journalism because you cannot be faster than electronic media to report the news.

RECOMMENDED READING

As always in any study of journalism, you'll find excellent guidance through reading what great reporters do for great newspapers. Particularly impressive are reporters for the *Boston Globe*, the *New York Times*, the *Wall Street Journal*, the *Washington Post*, *Chicago Tribune*, *Dallas Morning News*, *Los Angeles Times* and *Seattle Times*, among others.

I discuss specialty reporting techniques in three books published by Iowa State University Press of Ames, Iowa: "Sports Writing: The Lively Game" (2001), "Bottom Line Writing: Reporting the Sense of Dollars" (2000), "Writing Opinion for Impact" (1999.)

Magazine reporting is covered in Conrad Fink and Donald Fink, "Introduction to Magazine Writing" (New York: Macmillan, 1993.)

The ethics of reporting is discussed in Conrad Fink, "Media Ethics" (Boston: Allyn and Bacon, 1995.)

For a definitive account of computer-assisted reporting, see Christopher Callahan, "A Journalist's Guide to the Internet: The Net As a Reporting Tool" (Boston: Allyn and Bacon, 1999.)

EXERCISES

1. Study all stories on the front page of today's *New York Times* (or another newspaper designated by your instructor) and, in about 400 words, discuss how reporters weave in elements of the news mix — impact, proximity, timeliness, conflict, prominence, novelty. Which elements are the central focus of stories?

2. Study the front page of a newspaper designated by your instructor. Which story on that page covers a news event with the widest impact on the most people? In about 350 words, discuss whether the reporter properly structured the story to emphasize impact. Is impact described in real-life terms, as discussed in Chapter Two? Did the writer make an obvious attempt to translate impact into language and scenarios that express the story in human terms?

3. This is an exercise in computer-assisted reporting. Go to the Student Press Law Center at http://www.splc.org and, in about 300 words, describe the types of legal advice that organization offers student reporters. In effect, write an editor's deskbook on how student journalists can use the center's help.

4. This is an exercise in computer-assisted reporting. Go to Cops and Courts Reporters Directory at http://www.reporters.net/ccr and find the names of professional police and court reporters near your university. Interview one, even if by e-mail or telephone, on how he or she decides what elements to emphasize in a news story lead. Report on your interview in about 300 words. Write your interview as a news story.

5. This is an exercise in computer-assisted reporting. Contact Student Journalist Discussion List (Stumedia) at http://www.journalism.sfsu.edu/www/internet/mail/stumedia.htm and locate a student journalist at another university. Interview that person by e-mail or telephone on how his or her newspaper develops professional relationship with local police officials. In about 300 words, describe how you could use that reporter's techniques in fashion-

ing your own relationship with news sources.http://www.journal-ism.sfsu.edu/www/internet/mail

NOTES

1. "MTA Strike's Full Impact to Hit Today," Sept. 18, 2000, p. A–1.
2. "Holden Criticizes Wachs Over Use of City Mailers," Oct. 18, 2000, p. B–2.
3. "Man Facing Charges of Forgery," Nov. 22, 2000, p. 2.
4. "Counterfeiting Probe Focuses on Middle School Students," Oct. 8, 2000, p. B–5.
5. "World," Oct. 18, 2000, p. A–7.
6. "Suddenly, New Foes to Waterfront Plan," Oct. 1, 2000, p. B–1.
7. "Silicon Valley Teachers Fight for More Pay," Nov. 20, 2000, p. A–13.
8. "CSU Course Focus of Pointed Debate," Oct. 18, 2000, p. A–1.
9. "Phila. Officer Shot and Wounded," Oct. 1, 2000, p. B–2.
10. Dispatch for Sunday papers, Oct. 8, 2000.
11. Dispatch for morning papers, Oct. 2, 2000.
12. Dispatch for Nov. 10, 2000.
13. "Jean Hill; Witness to JFK Assassination," Nov. 10, 2000, p. B–6.
14. Dispatch for Oct. 1, 2000.
15. "6-Year-Old Girl, Father Hurt by Falling Branch in Westwood," Sept. 18, 2000, p. B–3.
16. Dispatch for Oct. 8, 2000.
17. "Covering Campus Crime," second edition, Student Press Law Center, 1815 N. Fort Myer Drive, Suite 900, Arlington, VA 22209–1817.
18. Dispatch for morning papers, Nov. 21, 2000.
19. Dispatch for morning papers, Nov. 29, 2000.
20. Dispatch for morning papers, Nov. 21, 2000.
21. "$15 Million Urged to Settle LAPD Shooting," Nov. 21, 2000, p. A–1.
22. Washington Post-Los Angeles Times News Service dispatch for morning papers, Oct. 2, 2000.
23. "Green and Golden," Oct. 2, 2000, p. A–1.
24. "Husband Indicted in Wife's Death," Oct. 18, 2000, p. C–1.
25. Dispatch for Sunday papers, Nov. 18, 2000, p. A–12.
26. "3 Suspects in Jewel-Theft Ring Arrested in S.F.," Nov. 21, 2000, p. A–17.

PART TWO
Sharpening Your Tools

Sharpening Your Tools

Like a carpenter headed for work, you must check whether you possess the essential tools of your trade before proceeding further in your study of newswriting.

Your tools are strong language skills. Without them you will fail in journalism just as surely as the carpenter will fail without hammer and saw.

No matter how firm your grasp of Chapter One's definition of news or Chapter Two's principles of strong reporting, you cannot succeed as a journalist unless you can write in language that is open, engaging, vibrant and grammatically correct.

We'll rummage through your writer's toolbox in Chapter Three: Achieving Precision and Clarity, a refresher on grammar and writing to bring your story alive.

In Chapter Four: Becoming a Stylist, we'll rummage deeper for ways to develop a crisp writing style unique to your personality and to become not only an acceptable writer but a very good one.

3
Achieving Precision and Clarity

THE ENGLISH LANGUAGE IS a living, shifting, changing instrument of beauty and strength, and I hope this book frees your creativity to write with ease and independence that take fullest advantage of that beauty and strength.

But just as there is no complete freedom in other human endeavors, so is there no full freedom in *effective* writing.

To be effective, writing must flow from established style and traditions — a consensus, really — developed through the centuries to help us speak and write with precision and clarity and thus communicate well.

Yes, new words appear (*cyberspace, Internet*) and others fade into disuse (*buggy whip, butter churn*) as social customs emerge or fade. And, in journalism, writing styles and usages shift as life shifts.

But certain basics don't change, and to them we must turn now.

First, understand that journalists nationwide generally consult two authorities on language usage. One is "The Associated Press Stylebook and Libel Manual." It's the desktop bible for hundreds of newspapers and the core even of those other stylebooks written individually by newspapers. The other is Webster's New World Dictionary, widely viewed as the authority on spelling and meaning. Memorize the former and consult the latter. Do otherwise, and your writing will signal editors that you are an amateur.

Second, a disclaimer: You'll encounter in this chapter what may look like *rules* for good writing. Accept most only as guidelines, not fixed standards to measure your writing against. (You'll note the previous sentence ends on a preposition, which breaks a "rule" — but underscores my thinking that generally if your writing makes you and your readers happy, it is good writing.)

PARTS OF SPEECH

Quickly (because you encountered them in high school!) a review:

Nouns denote persons, things, places, ideas, qualities (Lincoln, car, England, conservatism, crippled.)

Pronouns take the place of nouns and assume their functions (you, I, his, they, it, us.)

Adjectives describe nouns and pronouns by modifying, limiting or qualifying them (*black* car, *tiny* England, *sturdy* house.)

Verbs tell what a noun or pronoun is doing or being and express action (Lincoln *criticizes*, the car *runs*, the house *falls*.)

Adverbs modify other adverbs, verbs and adjectives by expressing degree, time, manner (criticizes *quickly*, run *smoothly*, falls *slowly*.)

Interjections are emotional exclamations (wow! darn!)

Prepositions link a noun or pronoun to another element that follows in a sentence (*in* the campaign, *after* the collapse, *before* the fall.)

Conjunctions connects words, sentences, phrases, clauses to each other (Lincoln *and* Douglas, write well *or* fail, close to success *yet* not complete.)

PARTS OF A SENTENCE

A *subject* is a noun or pronoun substitute about which something is said; that is, it's the noun or pronoun doing the *acting* or *being* in a sentence (*Lincoln* criticized Douglas. The *politician* criticized medical care. The *car* costs more.)

The *verb* expresses action (Lincoln *criticized* Douglas.)

The *direct object* is direct receiver of the action of the verb and, thus, sentence (Lincoln criticized *Douglas*.) An *indirect object* indirectly receives the action; it's the person or thing to whom or which the action is done (Give *him* the car.) A *predicate objective* follows the direct object and restates it (The voters elected Lincoln *president*.)

Much writing in journalism takes the direct route of subject + verb + direct object because such simple sentences communicate clearly and (no minor consideration) they are easy to write on deadline. A steady diet of such simplistic sentence structures gets monotonous, however, so strive for a variety of forms.

For example, place something other than a direct object behind a verb (Lincoln retreated sadly. The politician was applauded by voters.)

Or, in pursuit of journalism's "who" and "what," open with the subject (Politicians stumped for votes. Cars sped north.)

Or, open a sentence with an adjective to achieve special emphasis (*Determined* were the politicians. *Saddened* was Lincoln.)

PHRASES, CLAUSES AND SENTENCES

Phrases are groups of words conveying a thought but lacking either a subject or predicate (Lincoln, *waving his arms*, attacked Douglas.)

Clauses are related words with both a subject and verb. *Independent clauses* form complete thoughts (Lincoln seeks the victory.) *Dependent clauses* are not complete thoughts (because he wants it.)

Sentences must express complete thoughts. They have at least one independent clause and may have dependent clauses.

NOW, MORE ABOUT NOUNS AND PRONOUNS

Nouns and pronouns change form in four ways — number, gender, person, case.

Nouns and pronouns can be *singular* (I, he, she) or *plural* (we, they, us.)

Gender can be masculine (actor) or feminine (actress) or neuter (people, children.)

In *person*, nouns and pronouns can be *first* person (I, we); *second* (you); *third* (he, they, it, one, she.)

How they are used in a sentence gives nouns and pronouns *case*. *Nominative* case is used when a noun or pronoun is the subject of a sentence (*He* leads the complaints.) *Objective* case is used when the noun or pronoun is the direct object (Assist *him* in the complaints) or indirect object (White helped *him* complain.) *Possessive* case shows ownership (*Lincoln's* supporters.)

Some beginner writers have these problems with nouns:

- Writing plural forms. If the noun ends in "o," add "s," as in piano (pianos.) But beware those that take "es," as in hero (heroes) and tornado (tornadoes.) The plural of some compound words takes an "s" at the end of the *first* word (fathers-in-law.) And, of course, some nouns and pronouns are the same in plural and singular forms (deer, sheep.)
- Usage of gender forms is changing with changes in societal attitudes. Thus *actor* is used in many stylebooks for women as well as men. *Aviatrix* for women aviators virtually has disappeared.[1]
- In forming the possessive case of plural nouns, some writers get confused. No need. Just add an apostrophe to the "s" (General Motors' employees numbered many.) For compound words, add the apostrophe to the word nearest the object possessed (fathers-in-law's attitudes.) If two people own separate houses it's *Fred's* and *Janet's* houses; if they jointly own one, it's *Fred* and *Janet's* house.
- Common or generic nouns (soda, tissue) are not capitalized but proper nouns (Coke, Kleenex) are. Companies spend billions of dollars developing brand names. Don't use them incorrectly.
- Don't use *abstract* nouns when *concrete* nouns are available. Abstract nouns name ideas, attributes, qualities (poverty, wealth) and you should be using concrete nouns that name something material (pots, pans, knives, forks.) That is, write not of a rich man's "wealth" but, instead, of his 50-foot yacht and his long, black limousine!
- Note that pronoun and antecedent (the noun or pronoun to which it refers) must agree in person, gender, number. Common error: "The students failed primarily because he or she was depressed and ill, and that angered their parents," Better: "The students failed primarily because *they* were depressed or ill, and that failure angered their parents."

AND, MORE ABOUT VERBS

Verbs deserve intense, loving study by any aspiring wordsmith.

Verbs express action or state of being, and if properly used will inject strength and life into your writing.

Improperly used, verbs will create dull, flat writing or, indeed, writing that misleads.

Let's take verbs step by step:

Verbs have *person*, which must be appropriate for each personal pronoun: first-person singular (*I* study); second-person singular (*you* study); third-person singular (*he/she/it/one* studies); first-person plural (*we* study); second-person plural (*you* study); third-person plural (*they* study.)

Verbs have *number* — singular or plural — that must be appropriate to the subject's number; be certain subject and verb agree (The student body (singular) *takes* the test — *not take*. The students (plural) *take* the test—*not*, of course, *takes*.)

Verbs have *tense*: present tense (I take, you take, he/she takes); past (I took, you took he/she took); future (I will take, you will take); present perfect (I have taken, you have taken); past perfect (I had taken, you had taken); future perfect (I will have taken, you will have taken.)

Verbs have tone in each tense: normal (I study, you study); emphatic (I *do* study, he *does* study); progressive (I *am* studying, you *are* studying); progressive-emphatic (I *am* studying, I *was* studying, I *have been* studying.)

Verbs have *voice*: *active* voice, when the subject of the sentence is the doer of action (The student *studied* the text); *passive*, when the subject is receiver of action (The text *was studied* by the student.)

Verbs have *mood*. Two are most important: *indicative mood* to state a fact or ask a question (They *study* the text. *Are* they *studying* the text?); *imperative mood*, to issue instructions or command (*Study* the text. *Complete* the reading.)

Pointers:

- Use strong verbs in present tense *when appropriate* to inject sparkle in your writing. ("The senator jumps to his feet and screams his demands." That's stronger than, "The senator rose to his feet and made his demands." But be certain he jumped and screamed!)
- Use active voice, not passive, when possible. ("The senator screamed his demands" is stronger than, "His demands were screamed by the senator.")
- For most stories, pick a verb tense and stick with it throughout (not, "senator *screams*" in first graf and "senator *screamed*" in second.) Note, however, that in some story structures it's effective to lead with present tense, then shift to past in subsequent grafs. More later on that.

- Don't misuse *helping verbs*, which accompany verbs (as in, "I *have* studied the text"). One common error is using helping verbs that imply volition when they shouldn't (as in, "He had three texts stolen," which implies he arranged to have three of his books taken. Better: "Three of his texts were stolen.")
- Ensure your verb agrees with the subject, even if a noun or pronoun is used between subject and verb (correct: "The text, with its graphs and photos, *is* a huge undertaking." *In*correct: . . . "*are* a huge undertaking.")
- Double-check subject-verb agreement anytime a subject follows the verb. Common error: "There's many issues before Congress." Should be, "There are" . . . , of course. Even better: "Many issues are before Congress."
- Remember that most *collective nouns* (university, crew, committee) take *singular* verbs (The committee *is* moving slowly.) Some *uncountable nouns* take singular verbs (guidance *is* given, courage *is* admired) but others take plural verbs (thanks *are* given.)
- Avoid using nouns as verbs. Don't write that "he *authored* the text" or "she *inked* the contract."
- Routinely double-check when you've finished your story. Do your verbs agree in tense, voice and mood? If not, edit or rewrite.

VERBALS FOR VARIETY

These are verbs used as parts of speech other than verbs.

Gerunds are present or past participial forms of verbs *used as nouns*, usually with *-ing* ending, or *-ed* or *-t*. (*Studying* can ruin a Saturday night. They were among the *saddened*.) A common error arises when a gerund is preceded directly by a pronoun or noun, and beginner writers forget the pronoun or noun must be in the possessive case. Correct: "He's worried about his *teammates'* drinking."

Participles are verbs, usually ending in *-ed*, *-ing*, *-t* or *-en*, in present or past participial forms and used as adjectives. Example: "Complaining, they walked into the room." *Complaining* describes *they*. Another example: "The irritated students left angry." Both *irritated* and *angry* describe the students.

Infinitives receive far more scrutiny from editors than they deserve. Infinitives are created most often when *to* precedes a verb: "He would like *to study*," Editors likely will complain if you split an infinitive: "He would like to *soon study*." (Yes, I know! That's the way we talk. But listen to all the grunts, the "ahs" and "wells" and grammatical errors in your roommate's speech, and you'll never again write like we talk. Like, you know, don't do it, man.)

WRITER'S MINEFIELD: ADJECTIVES AHEAD!

The tired, hollow-eyed, unshaven, ill-kempt, penniless, hungry student came into the room.

I stacked those adjectives like landmines in front of a pronoun to illustrate a danger: Unless you tread carefully, you'll find yourself lazily grabbing for adjectives in an effort to *tell* a story instead of tapping into your creative and descriptive energy to let your readers *see* the story.

Don't tell me the student is tired; describe how he hasn't slept in two days.

Don't tell me he is penniless; mention that he is down to his last $1.67.

Don't tell me he is ill-kempt; write that his sweater has holes in both elbows and that one pant leg is ripped.

Don't tell me he is hungry; let me know he hasn't eaten since breakfast yesterday.

Don't tell me; *let me see.*

A problem with adjectives, of course, is that they are too readily available (especially on deadline!) to grab for modifying a noun or pronoun and telling what kind, how many and so forth. Adjectives have three degrees of comparison in doing so: *positive* (The *hungry* student), *comparative* (The *hungrier* of students), *superlative* (The *hungriest* student.)

Aside from simply avoiding overuse of adjectives, you have another option: move them around in a sentence so they aren't stacked like landmines. For example, write, "The student, hollow-eyed and unshaven, came into the room."

Other problems with adjectives:

- Some don't have comparative or superlative forms — unique, perfect, complete, for example. Never write that something is *more* unique, *more* perfect, *most* complete. It's either unique, perfect, or complete or it isn't.

- *Coordinate adjectives* are two adjectives of equal importance that take either a *comma* or *and* in preceding a noun or pronoun. ("The short, heavyset student" or "The short and heavyset student.")
- *Compound adjectives* take a hyphen when they precede the word they modify ("The out-of-state student.") If in doubt about hyphens, rewrite: "The student from out of state." In writing ages, hyphenate if the compound adjective precedes the noun or pronoun. Thus, it's "19-year-old student" but the "19 year old."

ADVERBS: HANDLE GENTLY

Using adverbs properly is crucial to clear writing, yet many beginner writers overlook adverbs' importance.

Adverbs are formed mostly by adding *-ly* to positive-form adjectives: gradual—gradually; careful—carefully.

Construct adverbs in comparative form by using *more* or *less* in front of other adverbs: more or less gradually, more or less carefully.

Adverbs come in four types:

- *simple*, tightly tied to the word they modify: The student dressed *beautifully* (modifying the verb dressed). The *beautifully* dressed student (modifying the adjective dressed).
- *interrogative*, asking a question: *When* is the student finishing? (modifying the verb).
- *conjunctive*, linking a dependent clause to a sentence or previous clause: The student was planning his program, *though* he feared it might be too late.
- *parentheticals*, modifying a sentence or linking it to another: *Still* (or *nevertheless*, *yet*, *accordingly*), friends told the student there was time to prepare.

Caution:

- Don't use adjectives for -ly adverbs. Make it, "The student read smoothly (not *smooth*)" and "The student ran more quickly (not *quicker*.)"

- Don't use a hyphen after an adverb ending -*ly*: The student is beautifully dressed (not *beautifully-dressed.*)
- *However*, generally speaking, do use a hyphen in a compound modifier after -ly *adjectives*: The student was described as a beautifully-dressed person. Here a noun follows the adjectival phrase.
- Some adverbs modify a sentence: personally, frankly, sincerely. Editors will argue if you start a sentence with this one—"Hopefully, it will be an easy test." Who, alert editors will ask, is "hoping"? Only with experience will you understand when it's wise — or unwise — to argue with editors. I suggest you avoid this argument, and rewrite to, "I hope the test will be easy."
- Simple guideline on adverb placement in a sentence: Put them close to the word they modify. Example: "The student *only* has one test to pass" is confusing because it can mean only that student has a test to pass. What is meant is that, "The student has *only* one test to pass."
- Avoid attempting to inject emphasis by opening sentences with adverbs such as *personally*, *frankly* and so forth. "Personally, I think the test was tough" is redundant. "I think" obviously means "personally."
- *Conjunctive adverbs* are useful in leading readers between two sentences naturally related. Example: "The test was difficult. *However*, I aced it." Other conjunctive adverbs: also, for example, furthermore, hence, meanwhile, nevertheless, therefore. However, before using any, make certain the linkage is logical. This is *not* logical linkage: "The test was difficult. However, student fees are rising."

WOW! AVOID INTERJECTIONS, SLANG AND OBSCENITY

Those *interjections* you hear so frequently on campus — "wow!" and "man!" — have little or no place in journalism. *If* they are used by an interviewee *and* you consider them essential to a story, use interjections *in quotes*. Only in unusual circumstances, such as a light feature, should you use them otherwise.

Slang is acceptable to many editors under only similar circumstances — in quotes, if crucial to a story. But yesterday's slang can be today's King's English, particularly when you're writing features and a little zesty street-smart language fits your purpose better than something formal and stuffy.

Obscenity, *profanity* and *vulgarity* are banned from many newspapers and magazines. However, definitions of offensive language are changing. Suggestions: Don't write dirty (as some amateur writers do) to inject phony impact into your writing; use offensive language in quotes if there is compelling need to include it; discuss with your editors in advance what to use and how.

PROBLEMS AND PREPOSITIONS

They are easy to handle, those *simple prepositions* that relate a noun or pronoun to something else in a sentence (The room *in* the library. The shed *behind* the house.)

Also unthreatening are *compound prepositions* (in front of, because of, on top of).

But large groups (*battalions*) of editors out there are poised to hammer you if you misuse prepositions, particularly in two ways:

- If you end a sentence with a preposition. Yes, I know that "What are you studying for?" sounds better than, "For what are you studying?" But why should grownups fight over such things? Rewrite to avoid conflict.
- If you don't construct *parallel prepositional phrases*. Many editors demand this: "The student said the text was *on* reporting and *on* editing." Yes, you can get along without that second preposition. But aforementioned vigilant editors won't accept, "on reporting and editing."

Incidentally, don't write, "Mayor Fred Smith Tuesday said . . . ", and if you do, don't try to fix it by inserting a preposition to separate those two proper nouns (Mayor Fred Smith *on* Tuesday said"). Rewrite to, "Mayor Fred Smith said Tuesday."

CONFLICTS OVER CONJUNCTIONS

Conflict over conjunctions arises not out of what they are — linking words, like prepositions — but, rather, out of how they're used.

Coordinate conjunctions (but, for, and, now, or, yet) link words, phrases or clauses of *equal rank*. But how is equal rank judged?

Rule of thumb: A word equals another word (books *and* fees); a phrase equals another phrase (to be going *or* not to be going); an independent clause equals another (He is skimming the book, and he is not memorizing it); and a dependent clause equals another dependent clause (He said he would memorize the information if given time *or* if the instructor granted an extension).

Caution: Put a comma before a coordinate conjunction, one that connects two independent clauses (The student promised to read the text, but he didn't).

Correlative conjunctions are used in pairs, and this gives some writers trouble. Remember: It's "as well . . . as", "either . . . or", "neither . . . nor", "whether . . . or". (If you own this book, underline in ink "neither . . . nor" and promise to never write, "neither . . . or".)

Subordinate conjunctions (although, as, because, if, until, whether) link two *un*equal parts of a sentence, mostly independent and dependent clauses. A question frequently arises over whether a comma is needed before subordinate conjunctions. The answer is not usually, because most newspapers practice "open punctuation," meaning they insert punctuation only when clarity requires it—and subordinate conjunctions generally don't require it.

Now, where is this grammar review taking us? *Toward writing effective sentences and building engaging, informative news stories*!

EFFECTIVE SENTENCES: YOUR BEST TOOL

First (and quickly), the basics:

A sentence must state a complete thought and usually contains both a subject and verb. It must end with a full-stop punctuation mark — period, question mark, exclamation point.

Sentences have four functions:

- *Declarative sentences* state fact (Learning to write well is difficult.)
- *Interrogative sentences* ask questions (Why is writing well so difficult?)
- *Exclamatory sentences* express emotion (But what a delight writing can be!)
- *Imperative sentences* request or command (Please learn to write well. Sit down and write!)

You have four types of sentences to use, and varying the mix in a story can strengthen your writing.

- *Simple sentences* contain a single independent clause and frequently are written as subject + verb + object (The team expected victory.)
- *Compound sentences* have two or more independent clauses, each expressing a complete thought (The team has reached new strength, and fans expect victory.) Note my use of *both* a comma and a coordinating conjunction — *and* — to link those independent clauses.

Complex sentences contain an independent clause and at least one dependent clause. Note the subordinate clause depends on the main clause for meaning: (Because the team is "up" emotionally, the fans expect victory.)

Compound-complex sentences contain two or more independent clauses and one or more dependent clauses. Many are far too wordy for newswriting *unless* you write carefully. Yes: "Although the team was 'up' emotionally, injuries eliminated three key players, and fans may have been unreasonable in expecting victory." No: "The team talked itself into new emotional highs and an over-confident expectation of victory, but knee and ankle injuries to three key players, a linebacker, fullback and defensive end, sidelined the team's driving force, and fans were unreasonable in their own emotional highs and expectations of victory."

SENTENCES TO SHOOT ON SIGHT

I've noticed in my 45 years in journalism that a common writing error by beginner journalists is to construct ill-conceived *run-on sentences*, those that start out promising meaning and impact, but soon lose their zest because the writers lack mental discipline, and the sentences meander — like this one — first here, then there, until editors and readers alike scream for an end to it all.

Then, criticized for such journalistic felonies, the perpetrators of those outrages attempt to correct things by writing *sentence fragments*. Like this. Just bits. And pieces. That are easy to read. But don't hang together. And thus don't make sense.

We can't *really* shoot sentences, of course, and it's illegal to shoot writers, so what to do?

First, never fall in love too quickly with one of your sentences. Yes, you created it, and it indeed is a jewel. But even fine jewels must be cut, reworked and polished. Avoid premature emotional commitment to your creation. Treat every sentence as a work in progress that must be reworked and polished.

Second, make sure you diagnose the problem properly and think through the solution.

SENTENCE PROBLEMS AND SOLUTIONS

Reading your copy aloud and listening carefully to your sentences can provide an excellent early alert if something is wrong.

Running out of breath three times in the same sentence may indicate you have a *run-on sentence*. Reading jerkily in staccato outbursts may signal *sentence fragments*.

But don't trust only your ear. Methodically check structure, content and grammar.

FIXING RUN-ON SENTENCES

Run-on sentences simply run on too far. Even if grammatically correct, many fail because they include unrelated and irrelevant information. Many are created when writers try to link two or more independent clauses with a comma.

A comma simply doesn't create a pause long enough between independent clauses. Example: "The team is highly motivated, fans hope for victory."

That's the "comma-splice" problem, and it kills the writer's effort because words following the comma do not support, augment or complement what readers previously saw. The problem does not exist with *parallel clauses:* "Write coherently, write smoothly, write correctly."

Remedies for comma-splice include periods in place of commas (". . . highly motivated. Fans hope . . . "). Use semicolons *only* if the two thoughts in the run-on sentence are closely connected.

In the example, a comma with a helping conjunction would do (". . . highly motivated, and fans hope . . . ").

Many run-on sentences cannot be fixed with "and" if the independent clauses in the run-on don't reinforce the same point or follow one another in logical sequence. Example of illogical sequence: "The team is highly successful, and the university is constructing a new stadium."

You can rewrite and use a *subordinating conjunction* to fix the problem: "The university is constructing a new stadium *because* the team is highly successful."

FIXING FRAGMENTS

Sentence fragments are a single word or group of words that lack a subject and predicate or are dependent clauses.

You *cannot* fix fragments by inserting subject and verb *unless* the result expresses a complete thought and thus becomes a complete sentence.

For example, "Although she stated her views" has a subject (she) and verb (stated) but doesn't express a complete thought. Thus, it's a fragment.

Fixes: "She stated her views." Or, "Although she stated her views, no one listened." Note both fixes yield complete sentences.

Now, you'll remember that I opened this chapter by stating that some "rules" of grammar should be studied only as guidelines. That exception applies to sentence fragments.

Some writers intentionally create fragments to achieve special impact:

- In direct quotes, fragments can capture the way people speak. "I prayed," she said. Then, "All night." Or, he said, "Cute. Real cute. Why?"

- Fragments are acceptable to some editors if they answer a question: "Why did they fail? No team spirit."

OTHER PROBLEMS IN SENTENCES

Fused sentences result from punctuation errors that run together two main clauses.

For example: "The team got behind they could not win."

Reading aloud helps you spot fused sentences. (Don't you *hear* the need for a pause after "behind"?)

Fixes: Create two sentences ("The team got behind. They could not win.") Or, make it, ". . . behind, and they . . . . "Less frequently in journalism, use a semicolon (". . . behind; they . . .").

Warning: Guard against creating a comma splice with simple insertion of a comma (". . . behind, they . . .").

Improper parallelism creates chaos in a sentence — and confusion in readers' minds. *Proper* parallelism requires all ingredients in a series to be alike, all verbs to be in the same tense, voice and mood, and subjects to be in the same person and number.

For beginner writers, the biggest trap is in lack of parallelism in verb tense.

No: "She spoke (past tense) weakly, then she says (present tense), 'Hello.'"

Yes: "She spoke weakly, then she *said*, 'Hello.'"

Suggestion: When you've written a page or screenful of copy, run your eyes across your verbs, speaking them aloud: "He says . . . said" — oops, *there* is lack of parallelism.

Oversubordination of sentences is an error common in journalism (especially in sports writing.) Here's how it happens:

You suddenly realize you have created a jumble of sentence fragments or you have tried to jam too much information into a sentence and have created a horrible run-on sentence.

What to do? Ah, *subordinate* one idea to another — make it less important — and create a new sentence. Carefully done, subordination works well; haphazardly done, it can create a train wreck.

Example of sentence fragments:

The team won the game.
The team was suffering many injuries.

Good fixes:

The team, though suffering many injuries, won the game.
Although suffering many injuries, the team won the game.

*Over*subordination can create a problem worse than the one you were trying to fix:

The team, though suffering many injuries and losing a quarterback to academic ineligibility, plus suffering from a feud among coaches and lack of fan support, won the game, although not even supportive sports writers thought it would.

Read that aloud. The choking sound you hear is you trying to draw a breath (or two). Oversubordination is the villain.

The Sin of There Was and It Is must be avoided. Want to *kill* a sentence at birth? Start with "there was" or "it is."

No: There was a vote by team members to quit.

Yes: Team members voted to quit.

No: It was the team's intention to quit.

Yes: The team intended to quit.

Don't dangle modifiers. It is a rule broken, alas, throughout journalism. Ways to avoid problems:

Put *single-word modifiers* immediately in front of words they modify.

No: The team *only* spent $500.

Yes: The team spent *only* $500.

Position *modifying prepositional phrases* carefully to indicate what they modify:

No: A demonstration drew police attention *in the stands*.

Yes: A demonstration *in the stands* drew police attention.

Place *adjective clauses* next to the words they modify:

No: The team bought food in the stadium from a catering firm that cost $600.

Yes: The team bought food, which cost $600, from a caterer in the stadium.

Position *participial phrases* correctly.

No: *Discouraged by poor passing*, running the ball was logical.

Yes: Because the team was *discouraged by poor passing*, running the ball was logical. (Or, Discouraged by poor passing, the team said running the ball was logical.)

Rewrite dangling *phrases containing infinitives*.

No: Not able to pass, a coach suggested the team run the ball.

Yes: Because the team was not able to pass, a coach suggested it run the ball.

Rewrite dangling *elliptical adverb clauses* (those that imply words rather than state them).

No: Told the truth, nothing was said.

Yes: Told the truth, the team said nothing. (Or, When the team was told the truth, not one word was said.)

SPECIAL PROBLEMS

Skipping ahead (as I must in this single-chapter review), I'll identify special problems that plague beginner writers.

INADEQUATE TRANSITIONS

Don't labor dutifully over word choice, sentence construction and paragraphs, then fail to link those parts into stories that flow smoothly and lead readers gently from start to finish.

A transitional word or phrase can link ideas within a sentence:

Voters back the mayor, *but* the governor doesn't.
The mayor supports education *and* tries to raise money for it.

Avoid particularly writing stand-alone, self-contained paragraphs, then simply plugging them into a story without proper transitions. It's simple to build smooth flow:

The mayor supports education and has some support for that.
However, the governor opposes his plan . . . .
Similarly, conservative groups oppose the mayor . . . .
Indeed, it seems opposition is building rapidly . . . .

Transitional words have many uses:

- Linking thoughts (also, and, besides, furthermore, moreover).
- Comparing like ideas (also, as well as, similarly).
- Contrasting (although, but, however, despite, otherwise, still, yet).
- Illustrating time and sequence (after, before, during, earlier, following, simultaneously).
- Showing cause and effect (accordingly, because, consequently, due to, therefore, thus).
- Emphasizing (certainly, indeed, surely, truly, undoubtedly).
- Summarizing (finally, in short, in sum, to sum up).

IMPROPER SUBJECT-VERB AGREEMENT

As you know, the verb must agree with the number of the subject. But sentences presenting *false subjects* require specially careful handling:
The *record* (subject) of victories *is* (verb) improving (not *are*).
Winning (subject) games *is* (verb) the coach's goal (not are).
The *coach* (subject), along with his assistants, *was* (verb) (not were).
Think *singular* when you use these pronouns as a subject: each, either, anyone, everyone, much, no one, nothing, someone (*Each* of the players *has* his specialty).
Also think singular with measurements of money and time. (One hundred yards per game *is* the standard he set. Two hours of waiting in line *has* angered him.)

BETWEEN YOU AND I (OR IS IT "ME"?)

It's "me," of course. But many beginner writers have difficulty with *errors in pronoun case occurring in compound objects of a preposition*, such as "between you and *I*." In this example, both pronouns are objects of the preposition *between*. Therefore, "between you and *me*" is correct.

When I get hung up on such a dilemma I eliminate "and," and ask myself which sounds better, "I" or "me"?

Example: "The book is for a friend and I (or me)." "The book is for I" doesn't sound correct, does it? "The book is for me" does sound correct, however.

Sexist Language

Writers without a sexist bone in their bodies can slip easily and unthinkingly into using inappropriate language.

Don't write, "The average student . . . he." (Rather, make it, "Average students . . . they.")

Don't write man-made, man hours, mankind (use synthetic, work hours, humankind.)

Use *generic terms* when appropriate: postal carrier (for postman), firefighter (fireman), police officer (police man).

However, use specifics rather than the generic anytime you can. "Spokesman" or "spokeswoman," for example, tell your readers more than does "spokesperson."

A good rule: Don't use language that unnecessarily is insensitive to women, minorities, gays or other groups laboring for equality in our society. That does *not* mean you should give in to *political correctness*, an extremism that can shut down reasoned dialogue. For example, "he or she" is clumsy (go to plural, *they*) and using "s/he" is just plain awful. But you *should* practice journalism consistent with society's larger goals of equality and fairness.[2]

SUMMARY

- A journalist's tools are strong language skills, and without them you will fail in journalism, just as a carpenter will fail without hammer and saw.
- Your goal should be to free your creativity to write to the full advantage of the beauty and strength of the English language.

- However, effective writing can flow only from style and traditions — a consensus — developed through the centuries to help us write with precision and clarity.
- Two authorities on language usage are consulted frequently by journalists: *The Associated Press Stylebook and Libel Manual* and *Webster's New World Dictionary*.
- Most (but not all) so-called rules of writing should be accepted only as guidelines; measure your writing by whether it makes you and your readers happy.
- Master parts of speech and parts of a sentence as a basis for building your own writing style.
- Much writing in journalism takes the direct route of subject plus verb plus direct object, mainly because such simple sentences communicate well and are easy to write on deadline.
- However, a steady diet of simplistic sentences gets monotonous, so strive for a variety of forms.
- Verbs deserve especially intense, loving study by any aspiring wordsmith because they express action or state of being, and can inject strength into your writing.
- When possible, write in the active, not passive, voice and in the present tense, using appropriately strong verbs.
- Adjectives form dangerous minefields for beginner writers because if used improperly, they *tell* readers a story, rather than let them *see* it.
- Interjections (wow! man!) have little place in journalism and, along with slang, obscenity and profanity, should be used only in special circumstances.
- Two common errors committed by beginner writers are creating *sentence fragments* and writing *run-on sentences*.
- Sexist language can be used unthinkingly (as in, "The average student . . . he"), and it's wrong to practice a form of journalism that's inconsistent with society's goals of equality and fairness.
- But don't practice *political correctness*, an extremism that can shut down reasoned dialogue.

RECOMMENDED READING

Buy — and memorize — "The Associated Press Stylebook and Libel Manual."
Knowing AP style thoroughly is the mark of a professional.

Three sources are excellent on grammar, punctuation and the basics of
sound writing: Brian S. Brooks, James L. Pinson, Jean Gaddy Wilson, "Working
with Words," fourth edition (New York: St. Martin's Press, 1999); Lauren
Kessler, Duncan McDonald, "When Words Collide," fifth edition (Belmont,
Calif., 1999), and John C. Hodges, Winifred Bryan Homer, Suzanne Strobeck
Webb, "Harbrace College Handbook," thirteenth edition (New York: Harcourt
Brace Jovanovich , 1998).

EXERCISES

1. The intent of this exercise is to help you recognize effective use of
   verbs in newswriting. Using a newspaper designated by your instructor, find two news stories whose writers use verbs effectively
   and *appropriately*. Do the verbs bring stories alive? Do the verbs
   create what appears to be a true word picture? Use the wordage
   necessary to make your report.

2. Find examples of *inappropriate* verb usage. Look particularly for
   usage that *distorts* the story being reported. Recall the discussion
   in Chapter Three of verb usage that distorts a story being reported
   (a senator "jumps" to his feet and "screams" — but does he really?) Look also for passive verbs that should be written in active
   form, and for inappropriate shifts in verb tense. Use a newspaper
   designated by your instructor and write your report in the
   wordage required.

3. Examine a newspaper designated by your instructor. Do the writers rely heavily on use of adjectives? Do you find examples of
   writers who try to *tell* a story rather than let readers *see* it? In
   about 250 words, describe your findings. Quote examples of appropriate and inappropriate use of adjectives. Do writers "stack"
   adjectives, as discussed in Chapter Three? Or do they show cre-

ative use of options, such as moving them around in a sentence. Did you find any examples of incorrect use of superlative forms (*completely* destroyed, for example, or *more* unique)?

4. Recalling *sentence fragments* and *run-on sentences* discussed in Chapter Three, examine the writing in a newspaper designated by your instructor. Do you find examples of either type? Are many sentences structured simply as subject + verb + direct object? Or, is imaginative and creative sentence structure evident? Provide examples of sentence structures you rate as strong or weak. In general, is the writing effective in this newspaper? Discuss in about 300 words.

NOTES

1. I address this issue in more detail in Conrad Fink, "Media Ethics" (Boston: Allyn and Bacon, 1995.)

2. Ibid.

4

Becoming a Stylist

GET READY FOR a huge challenge in your personal journey toward learning to write well.

We're going for that elusive (but, never fear, attainable) goal of becoming a *stylist*, a writer with your own uniquely open, engaging and readable style.

Our launching pad for this Great Leap forward is Chapter Three's review of correct grammar and other minimal standards for *acceptable* writing. In Chapter Four we'll move beyond acceptable writing to look broadly at characteristics of *strong* writing:

- Clarity and simplicity that deflate pomposity and eliminate verbosity.
- Language that's lively and colorful, yet precise and accurate.
- Rhythm and structure that create smoothly flowing narrative.

Combine such writing with strong, accurate reporting, and you're off to a fast start on a career in journalism.

GOAL #1: CLARITY

A journalist's basic job is to *communicate* news and information, facts and figures. That requires, above all, writing that is clear.

USE SHORT SENTENCES

Here's a pop quiz: Read once (just once) the following, then quickly jot down its principal meaning:

Lima, Peru — President Alberto Fujimori, long the iron-fisted chief of one of Latin America's most tumultuous regimes, officially resigned Monday in a letter to Congress, brought down by a corruption scandal that threatened to haunt him as he remained holed up in a hotel room in Japan, his ancestral homeland.

Patrice M. Jones
Chicago Tribune[1]

You didn't cheat, did you? You didn't go back and read that twice (or three) times? I'll confess I did as I first tried to unwind its 48-word complexity of at least *seven* principal thoughts (Fujimori, iron-fisted chief, tumultuous regime, resigned in letter, corruption scandal, holed up in Japan, ancestors' homeland.)

Try this one:

Lima, Peru — Protected by the cover of night and a crisis-ridden government, Vladimiro Montesinos, Peru's top spy and right-hand aide to President Alberto Fujimori, fled aboard a private plane to Panama early Sunday, where he requested asylum.

Stephen Franklin
Chicago Tribune[2]

Reads more smoothly, right? Still, you must work your way through 35 words and, again, at least seven principal thoughts.

Now, try this:

After proclaiming his innocence for nearly 12 years, Earl Hampton received his first taste of freedom from a federal judge who ordered his release from prison.

Janan Hanna
Chicago Tribune[3]

Note the writer above takes you through just 26 words and three principal thoughts (proclaiming innocence, tastes freedom, ordered release.)

It's not true that 26-word sentences always work and 48-word sentences don't. But you can bet on this: Wander too far above 25–30 words per sentence and two or three principal thoughts, and you'll lose readers.[4]

Readers on average devote about 30 minutes to the *entire* newspaper. And it's easier to move to sports pages or comic strips at 6 a.m., over that first cup of coffee, than to labor through a sentence that requires three readings.

First lesson of clarity, then, is *simplicity*.

I don't mean to suggest writing sentences that are intellectually shallow, devoid of meaningful content or dull or flat in language. I *do* suggest that a sentence should yield its full meaning in one reading.

For certain, I don't suggest writing a series of 25-word sentences, then simply jamming them into a column of newsprint. Varying sentence length can create a rhythm that is pleasing to readers and, because it draws them deeply into your story, enhances communication.

Some hints:

- *Start* a sentence thinking short, with a goal of expressing one, maybe two ideas.
- Read your sentence aloud and, particularly if it runs more than 25–30 words, listen to its cadence. If you find a natural pause, plunk in a period, then test the effect of that by reading aloud once more.
- Revise, then revise again. Journalism's great wordsmiths may produce writing that looks from the start to be effortless and flawless. But even great writers seldom score on the first draft.

Do you think the following story, its rhythm, its *music*, emerged from a first draft?

The snow is so deep, the corner grocery store seems too far.

The dog won't set foot on the icy sidewalk; the car won't chug to life; just getting dressed is an ordeal.

Holiday shopping? Too much.

Shoveling? Too often.

A white Christmas? *Hmphft!*

Winter doesn't officially start until Thursday, but some area residents are already sick of snow. With almost 20 inches on the ground — and more on the way — weary commuters are cashing in sick days rather than face long traffic delays, homemakers are making do without that quart of milk rather than venture out into the cold, and city dwellers are leaving their cars in coveted curbside spots rather than risk losing them to a neighbor . . . .

John Yates,
Courtney Challos
Chicago Tribune[5]

Note above the wonderful mix of short, snappy sentences — simple declarative and complex — that gives this story life and vitality beyond its intrinsic news value. The story, after all, could be just another routine piece about the start of winter. But how the writing lifts this story beyond the routine!

Note, too, the generous use of typographical devices — semicolons, question marks, dashes and even an italicized exclamation, all of which will lead some purists to exclaim, *hmphft*! Not me! For me, this writing works.

In the Mideast, gospel music is sung in praise of the Rev. Martin Luther King Jr.

In Hungary, a children's art exhibit honors the slain leader of America's civil rights movement.

In Puerto Rico, panelists are exploring the social impact of the Nobel Peace Prize winner's life.

King Day, a national holiday in the United States has gone global . . . .

Mae Gentry
Atlanta Journal-Constitution[6]

Below, a writer strings together a three-sentence intro of short sentences (averaging just 15.6 words) and achieves reading rhythm with careful pacing (emphasis added):

USE SIMPLE VOCABULARY

The richness and diversity of the English language give you many choices when selecting words to use.

One choice to *avoid*: fancy language that merely displays your erudition.

Remembering — always — that your mission is to *communicate*, you'll seldom go wrong by selecting words that are short, rather than long; simple, rather than complex; of few syllables, rather than many.

But don't go too far in search of simplicity, as did many journalists some years back, in saying we should write for people with eighth-grade reading comprehension. That yielded writing quaintly similar to "See Jane run. See Spot run" and introduced into some newspapers an unmistakable note of condescension that even a fifth-grader could catch — and be offended by.

As discussed in Chapter One, newspaper and magazine readers are increasingly upscale in education, and for them your word choice must be somewhere between the two extremes.

But, whatever your audience's education level, don't puff up your writing with bloated language. Examples of word substitutes to use:

verbal altercation	argument
accelerate	speed up
apprehend	seize, catch, arrest
conflagration	fire
intoxicated	drunk
remuneration	pay
modicum	some
peruse	read, examine
purchase	buy
residence	house, home
self-confessed	confessed
vehicle	car, truck

BE CONCISE

Which of the following versions are best?

The board will give consideration to (will consider) the bill.

She gave encouragement to (encouraged) her students.

He gave instructions to (instructed) the players.

They said they have the belief that (they said) grades are not important.

No contest, right? So, make it a rule: If you can say it in one word, don't use two (or three or four or . . .).

And, be certain to eliminate those terrible phrases that clutter so much writing:

as a matter of fact	in terms of
as already stated	in the final analysis
as of this date	it appears that
at the present time	it is interesting to note that
frame of reference	it stands to reason
fullest possible extent	it should be noted that
goes without saying	needless to say
in a very real sense	to summarize the above

TRANSLATE JARGON

Do you know what a humerus is? Understand stock splits on Wall Street? How about "pump and dump"?

Don't feel bad if you didn't score 3–0 on that quiz. Most newspaper readers wouldn't, either.

Recognizing that many scientific and business terms are not understood by readers, newswriters striving for clarity must serve as *translators*. Examples:

Tony Saunders of the Tampa Bay Devil Rays baseball team (note I didn't assume you know the Rays are a *baseball* team) goes down with a fractured humerus. An AP writer translates that (emphasis added):

Dr. Koco Eaton, the Devil Rays' orthopedic physician, said the fracture occurred in the same general area of the humerus—*the bone running from the shoulder to the elbow*— that Saunders originally injured on May 26, 1999, against the Texas Rangers . . .

Fred Goodall
The Associated Press[7]

Neil MacFarquhar of the *New York Times* is on a great human-interest story — a 15-year-old accused stock market swindler. MacFarquhar nicely builds on the wonder of it all:

To help pass the time, (Fred), like many 15-year-olds, frequented World Wrestling Federation matches at the Meadowlands, went bowling, cheered the Mets and booed the Yankees.

Unlike most 15-year-olds, he also used the Internet to manipulate the stock market, racking up almost $273,000 in illegal gains, federal officials said.

Then, a full paragraph of essential translation:

Securities regulators said his scheme, known as pump and dump in the argot of the trade, involved buying obscure penny stocks, hyping them in a barrage of false E-mail messages to various Web bulletin boards that made the choices seem hot and then selling as soon as the price rose.

Neil MacFarquhar
New York Times[8]

That story was published in the *Times'* Metropolitan Section, aimed at general news readers, who especially need translation. But even when writing for sophisticated readers, such as Wall Street investors, you must translate.

For example, CNNfn, an Internet service aimed at investors, reports Amazon.com split its stock 3-for–2 — that is, gave shareholders three shares for every two they owned. The CNNfn writer hastens to point out:

> Usually, companies authorize stock splits in the hope that cheaper shares will lead to increased investor interest. A company may also authorize a split in a move to increase liquidity, reduce volatility and broaden its shareholder base, thereby diminishing the chances of a hostile takeover.
>
> *CNNfn*[9]

Your translator responsibilities kick in most frequently, obviously, when you are reporting on science, law, business, finance and other endeavors whose experts talk a language known mostly to themselves. You also need to translate bureaucratic terms favored by politicians and government officials.

For example, a mayor says two towns are in "growth modes," and a *Chattanooga Times* reporter lets it go at that. And readers are left wondering whether that's growth in population, construction, retail sales or what.[10]

Most bureaucratic jargon translates quickly and easily *if* you choose your words carefully, as does a *Boston Globe* reporter writing about city officials seizing private property under the right of "eminent domain." Under that process, the reporter writes, the city may seize property but "is obliged to pay owners 'fair market value' for their property."[11]

GOAL #2: SPARKLE

This is all too common in newspapers:

A reporter spends hours (days, even!) carefully reporting a story crucial to readers. Facts and figures so important to detailed, accurate reporting fill notebook after notebook.

Then, the reporter writes in dull, leaden language, chipping from hard stone a series of monotonous subject + verb + object sentences that squat menacingly on paper in defiance of all but the most persistent readers.

Lost is the readers' opportunity to absorb information crucial to their lives. Lost is the writer's chance to help them live better lives, surely the ultimate responsibility (and joy) of a journalist.

Want to Be a Writer?

We know of only three ways to grow as a writer. First you must read good writing. Then you must write. Then you must spend the rest of your life thinking and talking about good reading and good writing.

Roy Peter Clark and Christopher Scanlan, *America's Best Newspaper Writing* (Boston: Bedford/St. Martin's, 2001.)

To avoid that happening to you, write with *sparkle*, in language lively and colorful, yet precise and accurate.

WRITE IN ACTIVE VOICE

Writing in active voice almost always is more lively and less wordy than writing in the passive voice.

Here's a simple way to remember the difference: The voice of the verb shows relationship between the doer and the action. In the active voice, the *doer acts*; in passive, the doer *is acted upon*.

Thus:

> Police shot the suspect (active voice.)
> The suspect was shot by police (passive.)

> Catcher Fred Smith hit a homerun (active.)
> A homerun was hit by catcher Fred Smith (passive.)

Avoid shifting voice in the same sentence:
No: The team won the series, but the last game was lost.
Yes: The team won the series but lost the last game.

Now, an exception. Passive voice sometimes is best in news stories because it enables you to emphasize certain elements. For example:

> *Active*
> The New York Jets fired coach Fred Smith today at the end of a 13–6 losing season.

Passive (and preferable)
New York Jets coach Fred Smith was fired today at the end of a 13–6 losing season.

Another example: The president of the United States is big news. So is what he sees, hears and *is told*. Using the passive voice emphasizes that in the following.

Active
Military leaders in the Pentagon told President Bush today Islamic terrorists are a threat to national security.

Passive (and preferable)
President Bush was told today by military leaders in the Pentagon that Islamic terrorists are a threat to national security.

WRITE IN PRESENT TENSE

You've seen and heard the drama of present-tense reporting on television ("You can see, over my shoulder, the flames shooting from the building.")

Such reporting takes viewers to the scene, involving them in the story in a real-life way difficult to match in past-tense writing.

Unfortunately, because newspapers publish mostly the day after the event, we report *today* what happened *yesterday*, and in past tense ("Police arrested five suspects yesterday" . . . "President Bush said last night" . . .).

Nevertheless, even on routine stories you sometimes can write in present tense and avoid the dull "yesterday" time element:

Seaside, Monterey County — Police *are searching* for a teenage girl who was last seen Tuesday when she was picked up after school by her boyfriend.
Los Angeles Times[12]

Present tense is perfect for crafting a timeless, colorful intro on a story *that later shifts to past tense.*

For example, Michael Cabanatuan of the *San Francisco Chronicle* interviews a transportation executive who *said* (past tense) that train ridership shows no letup. That could make a routine past-tense lead:

Gene Skoropowski, director of the Capitol Corridor Joint Powers Authority, said yesterday there is "no letup" in train ridership.

I wrote that lead above to illustrate how dull such past-tense writing can be. The *Chronicle*'s Cabanatuan nicely avoids that trap and, instead, crafts a *present-tense* intro:

It is 5:10 in the morning and downtown Sacramento is cold, dark and empty — except for the steady stream of cars speeding down J Street to the train station.

The drivers park behind the depot, grab their briefcases and walk briskly to a five-car double-deck train, settling into blue upholstered seats or heading to the café car to grab a much-needed cup of coffee.

The 150 hardy souls aboard the 5:25 a.m. train to the Bay Area are among a fast-growing legion of commuters and travelers riding Capitol Corridor trains, making it the fastest-growing rail line in the nation.

Now a shift in tense (note the shift is so smooth you might not see it unless I called your attention to it):

Ridership aboard the trains, which run between the Sierra foothills and Silicon Valley, *has boomed* since 1998, when a eight-county authority took control from the state and BART began managing the service.

This year's growth in patronage *has been* particularly impressive. The number of passengers riding the train in the 12 months that ended in October—a total of 767,749—was up 41 percent over the previous year . . . .

Finally, that interview is reported in past tense:

"There's no letup," *said* Gene Skoropowski, director of the Capitol Corridor Joint Powers Authority. "It's gone up almost every month since February" . . .

Michael Cabanatuan
San Francisco Chronicle[13]

For Jack Warner, a distinguished cops reporter, present-tense writing is perfect for breathing see-it-now life into a story. With interviews and painstaking reporting, Warner reconstructs a shooting in a fast-food restaurant:

> The man steps out of the darkness into the Waffle House, a pair of white pantyhose pulled over his head, wrapped into a ball and tied off on top.
>
> He looks like someone bound for a costume party . . . But in his right hand he's holding a black-and-silver pistol.
>
> "Oh, no," a woman whispers.
>
> "You know what this is," the man barks. "Give it up!"
>
> The restaurant falls deathly silent. The sizzle of the grill becomes a roar.
>
> It is 6:01 a.m. on Friday, June 4. The robber doesn't know it yet, but he has made a bad mistake, the next to last of his life.
>
> There is a cop in the back booth.

Are you hooked by now on Warner's writing? Me, too. And, with judgment born of experience, Warner knows that. So he chooses this point to interrupt the present-tense narrative for background: The cop is Derrick Shean, off-duty and having a cup of coffee — with his Glock .40-caliber pistol stuck in the back waistband of his trousers. Back to the action:

> At 6:01 a.m., Derrick Shean puts down the spoon with which he has been stirring his coffee and reaches around to scratch his back. He hears somebody gasp "Oh, no."
>
> Looking up, Shean sees the gunman standing in front of the cash register. He recognizes the pistol in his hand as a 9mm Ruger . . . The gun is waving from side to side and employees and patrons are staring at it as though it is an angry rattlesnake.
>
> "Give me the ——money," the robber rasps, his voice muffled by the pantyhose. He is desperate. He has 66 cents in his pocket and an ATM receipt showing a bank balance of 75 cents.
>
> "Don't look at me!" he screams.
>
> Some of the customers lower their eyes and bow their heads.
>
> Shean drops his right hand from the itch on his back to the polymer grip of his Glock and slowly withdraws it, keeping it out of sight . . . .
>
> The robber . . . grabs a customer around the neck . . . with the Ruger pressing at the back of his head . . .
>
> Very slowly, Shean slides out of the booth into a crouch, holding his gun with both hands, pointed at the floor . . . .
>
> Shean has made up his mind. He will not let the gunman leave with a hostage. Shean has always worked hard on his marksmanship and gun-handling. He is calm and confident, running through possible scenarios. He is waiting for an opening, a distraction. "You don't gimme the money, I'm gonna kill this ——," the robber yells, backing away . . . .
>
> Shean has his opening . . . .

"Police!" he screams.

The distance is about 12 feet, and the little hollow circle on Shean's front sight is trained on the gunman's chest. His hands are steady. He doesn't hear the commotion of people screaming and diving for cover . . . .

The robber makes his last mistake. Instead of dropping his pistol, he swings it toward Shean.

Shean squeezes through the 5 pounds of pressure necessary to move the Glock's trigger. The report is deafening. Less than two seconds have passed since he got to his feet . . . .

He fires eight times . . . . At least six of the bullets find their mark. Some pierce the cash drawer the man is clutching. It crashes to the floor. The robber is backing through the door. Glass shatters all around him as one bullet after another finds its mark.

One round grazes his right chin, strikes his neck and pierces his voice box. Another, its momentum almost stopped by something, perhaps the door frame, barely penetrates the soft tissue of his abdomen. One strikes the right side of his chest, cracks a rib, tears through his right lung and strikes another rib.

A bullet hits his right chest, slides between ribs, pierces his right lung, rips open his heart and punctures his left lung. His lungs collapse. He cannot breathe. His heart is pumping blood into his chest cavity . . . .

He turns, falling, and a bullet pierces his left upper back, striking two ribs.

"Get down!" Shean yells. "Everybody down." . . . He . . . sees the robber, lying on his right side, soaked with blood, motionless. His hands are empty. The Ruger is behind him, unfired. Shean, his own weapon still at the ready, kicks it away.

"Call 911!" he yells, not taking his eyes off the gunman. "Tell them Signal 63, Officer Shean." Signal 63, probably the most universal police code, means "officer needs help." It is used only in the gravest situations.

It is 6:02 a.m. Sirens wail in the distance. In the stunned silence inside the Waffle House, the gunman — later identified as Jonathan Bartley—dies.

Jack Warner
Atlanta Journal-Constitution[14]

Note above the absence of flaming adjectives and any "stretch" by the writer for phony drama. Simple, straightforward present-tense writing is enough because it takes readers into that restaurant and lets them "see" the action.

That is how present tense can put sparkle into your writing.

Use Colorful Language

Sometimes, you can capture sparkle in just a few words *if* your choice isn't a stretch for phony drama.

For example, a *Boston Globe* reporter covers a bombing in Israel and can write that the bomb "went off" or "exploded" — or the following (emphasis added):

Hadera, Israel A car bomb *ripped through the heart* of this northern Israeli town at afternoon rush hour yesterday, killing two people, wounding at least 60, and *shattering storefronts* along an entire city block.

Obviously, "ripped through the heart" and "shattering storefronts" are the writer's personal and subjective interpretation of events. Does that language *properly characterize* what happened? The writer adds supporting detail that lets readers decide:

A large after-work crowd gathered on Hanansi street in Hadera, about 30 miles north of Tel Aviv, when the car bomb exploded at 5:20 p.m. The blast sent a passenger bus careening into a building and sparked fires in several apartments.

"I saw pieces of flesh on the ground, fingers and blood," said witness Lilach Moskowitz. "Then I fainted."

Many of the wounded were riding the bus when the bomb went off, including a woman whose legs were severed at the knees. Others were on the sidewalk or in nearby stores and restaurants . . .

Dan Ephron
Boston Globe[15]

A financial news writer's word choice plugs sparkle into a lead:

The Federal Reserve lowered interest rates Wednesday in a *surprise move* that *triggered a massive rally* on Wall Street and *buoyed hopes* the economy will escape a recession this year.

Tom Walker
Atlanta Constitution[16]

Again, the question: Does that language properly characterize the event? Walker backs up his choice by quoting an economist as saying the rate cut truly buoys hope — and that the "massive rally" is an unusual 299.60-point rise in the Dow Jones Industrial Average, a prime market indicator.

Note these stylists create colorful writing with careful word choice:

- A *New York Times* reporter describes "a millionaire businessman with the oratorical gallop of an evangelist" . . .
- A writer lifts an obituary out of the ordinary: "Under chilly, slate-gray skies, Vice President Al Gore buried his father today"
- Michael Wines of the *New York Times* describes Russians as "almost genetically suspicious of most government pronouncements"
- *Boston Globe* writers describe how "flames roared up from the basement" and killed two young boys
- A writer depicts a gambler "whispering intimately for effect."[17]

Now a warning: Unless careful, you can reach for colorful language and instead grab a cliche — flames "licking hungrily" at the building, shots "ringing out" (they don't ring; they have a dull, menacing sound); cars "careening" around curves.

> Except for the lips, which are as plump as a pair of cocktail wieners waiting to be wrapped up in their flaky little triangles of dough— *mmm*, so delicious, so . . . trashy— there is nothing about the way Sandra Bernhard looks, up close, to explain her status as a glamour puss.
>
> Cathy Horyn
> *New York Times*[18]

If colorful language comes to mind quickly that may be because you've read it so often (which is one definition of cliches.)

And sometimes, the search for colorful language leads to excess: Too much of a stretch? *Far* too much, for me.

Lessons:

- Reach (but don't stretch) for colorful language that makes your writing come alive.
- Support your word choices with detail proving to readers your choices accurately characterize the event or person.
- If you reach for colorful language but grab a cliche, throw it back and try again.
- When you start comparing lips to plump cocktail wieners, you've stretched too far.

GOAL #3: STRONG QUOTES

Here's a significant difference between amateur writers and highly skilled stylists:

- Amateurs tend to think what they see and hear while reporting must be paraphrased and written in their own thoughts, their own words.
- Stylists know when to back out of a story, plug in quotes *and let sources tell the story in their own words.*

Partial quotes are useful particularly when you must convey with absolute precision what is said. An example:

Washington — Republican Presidential nominee Dick Cheney suffered a "very slight" heart attack yesterday and will remain in a Washington hospital for at least another day after undergoing a two-hour procedure to keep blood flowing freely from his heart.

In the example above, the crucial news elements are 1) heart attack and 2) how serious? The partial quote characterizes the seriousness. But what's missing? *Attribution.* So the writer delivers that quickly in the second graf (emphasis added):

Doctors said Cheney, 59, is in good condition and *they expect* him to make a full recovery within a few weeks. *They said* there is no medical reason he could not assume the duties of vice president, or even president, if necessary.

Now, essential background and an expanded partial quote:

Cheney has experienced three previous heart attacks, the last one in 1988.

"I would expect him to return very rapidly to a normal and vigorous lifestyle without . . . restrictions," said Dr. Jonathan Reiner, a cardiologist at George Washington University Hospital Center,

Marc Sandalow
San Francisco Chronicle[19]

Warning: Don't use a partial quote, then fail to include later the full quote from which you've extracted the fragment or, at least, back up that partial quote with attribution and elaboration.

Quote marks can be used effectively on a word substitute for a lengthy legalistic term:

Laguna Niguel — A man facing a "third strike" prison sentence of 25 years to life for cocaine possession fled Tuesday from a courthouse in a pickup truck, authorities said.

"Third strike" is a term in general use as a substitute for full citation of a law requiring life sentences for persons convicted of three felonies. For a general newspaper audience, full citation is not necessary.

Full quotes can flesh out meaning — often with greater drama than can a paraphrased explanation. For example, the writers of the single-graf lead above followed immediately with this:

(Fred Smith), 45, of Mission Viejo was in the South Court Justice Center for arraignment when a judge granted his request to step outside the courtroom to talk with his attorney, said Sheriff's Department spokesman Steve Doan. Once outside, (Smith) fled to the parking lot and left in his truck, authorities said.

"He knew he was going away for the rest of his life and he didn't like it," Doan said . . . .

Theresa Moreau,
Stuart Pfeifer
Los Angeles Times[20]

Conveying properly and fully what is said sometimes requires the full quote.

For example, former President Bill Clinton and his lawyers negotiated long and hard over precisely which language he would use to admit he gave false testimony under oath, and thus avoid indictment. Bob Dart of the *Atlanta Journal-Constitution* decided (wisely, I think) to handle the story this way:

Washington — Less than 24 hours before leaving office, President Clinton struck a deal Friday with the independent counsel to avoid indictment and admitted he gave false testimony about his relationship with Monica Lewinsky.

"I tried to walk a fine line between acting lawfully and testifying falsely, but I now recognize that I did not fully accomplish this goal and that certain of my responses to questions about Ms. Lewinsky were false," the president acknowledged in a statement read by his press secretary.

Bob Dart
Atlanta Journal-Constitution[21]

Note the full quote conveys Clinton's language with a precision—and fairness—that would not be possible in a partial quote.

An AP writer handled the lead essentially the same way, but chose a different full quote as backup:

Washington — In a deal sparing himself possible indictment, President Clinton acknowledged Friday for the first time that he had made false statements under oath about Monica Lewinsky. He also surrendered his law license as part of an arrangement with prosecutors who had pursued him for six years.

"I hope my actions today will help bring closure and finality," Clinton said in a written statement that abruptly ended the wide-ranging investigation that had dogged him for most his time in office . . . .

Pete Yost
The Associated Press[22]

Sometimes, of course, quotes add sparkle to a story merely because they are funny:

Washington–Joe Lockhart, the president's combative spokesman, left the job officially yesterday and, after his last daily briefing was interrupted by his boss, turned over the duties to his deputy, Jake Siewert.

"Most people think Joe's leaving

for purely selfish, monetary reasons," President Clinton said. "but the truth is, he told me that I was no longer in enough trouble to make it interesting for him."

Sonya Ross
The Associated Press

If a quote is unclear, too long, ungrammatical, obscene or otherwise unprintable, eliminate the quote marks and paraphrase. *Never* change what's between quote marks.

What you write *outside* the quote marks can lend essential meaning to what is said *inside* them.

For example, the *New York Times'* Judith Miller interviews a young Muslim militant who says he has killed at least 100 people in a jihad, or holy war. Miller asks if he would "blow up women and children for Islam."

Miller quotes his reply with precision and adds chilling emphasis:

"Yes, I would do it," he said *quietly, without hesitation.*[24]

GOAL #4: WORD PICTURES

Capture detail, color, emotion in word pictures that take readers places they never go, that help them see and hear things they otherwise never experience.

Sketching word pictures is effective in, broadly, three ways:

- You take readers on a featurish ride, with a motive no more complicated than letting them experience vicariously what you have seen first-hand
- You capture a moment important in history – freeze-frame a memorable vignette.
- You create a word picture that contributes to reader understanding of an important event.

THE FEATURISH RIDE

Josh Getlin of the *Los Angeles Times* writes a newsfeature — a hard-news story with a timeless, featurish angle — on legalized betting in New York City restaurants. Getlin walks readers through one restaurant:

On a recent weekend, while people dined in a wood-paneled room out front, the mood in a smoky back lounge was raw: Clusters of men, many in black leather jackets, pored over racing forms. They stared hard at 10 TV screens beaming action from Aqueduct Raceway, and froze as horses broke from the gate.

Then, like popcorn popping, the men began to stir, first muttering encouragement, then rising to their feet and finally shouting at the horses in English, Russian and Chinese. When it was over, curses filled the room and losing tickets were tossed on plates of half-eaten cheeseburgers . . . .

Josh Getlin
Los Angeles Times[25]

Would you like to go along — and listen in — as a reporter lunches with a famous author at an exclusive New York City hotel? Bob Morris of the *New York Times* invites you along as he interviews Patricia Hearst Shaw, author of "Murder at San Simeon":

On a recent morning at the Edwardian Room of the Plaza, she raised an aristocratic, manicured hand and dug into her bacon and eggs. "I guess I'm supposed to pick at my food," she said, "but it looks *so good*."

Bob Morris
New York Times[26]

Above, the writer puts a highly readable angle on a newsfeature about Shaw, her background, her book.

CAPTURING A MOMENT

Historic moments can be captured in *hard-news* stories and lifted to new heights by stylists with an eye for detail.

Note the detail in a story on the inauguration of George W. Bush:

The noontime inaugural ceremony on the west side of the Capitol drew a crowd of thousands undeterred by persistent drizzle and temperatures in the low 30s. Applause, offered 14 times during Bush's speech, was muffled by gloves and mittens.

Moments after Dick Cheney took the oath as vice president, Bush stepped to the podium and faced Chief Justice William Rehnquist, who asked: "Governor, are you ready to take the oath?"

"I am, Sir," Bush responded.

Wife Laura and 19-year-old twin daughters Jenna and Barbara stood next to Bush, and he hugged them tightly after taking the oath of office.

Bush then sought his father's right hand and put his left hand behind the senior man's head. The president and the former president embraced. The elder Bush — who had predicted tears — wiped one away as his son's eyes also welled up.

Moments before Bush began his remarks, a tear trickled from one of his eyes.

Arthur Brice
Atlanta Journal-Constitution[27]

Note the guidance you can take from Brice's watchful reporting and precision writing:

- Amateur writers report there was applause. Stylists write there was applause 14 times and that it was muffled by gloves and mittens.
- Amateurs write that Bush said he was ready to take the oath. Stylists write that when asked, Bush responded, "I am, Sir."

- Amateurs write that Bush shook hands with his father. A stylist writes . . . well, read again that vignette in the word portrait above.

Listen and watch as another stylist captures an important moment (emphasis added):

Washington — At 12:43 p.m. Wednesday, Hillary Rodham Clinton answered her first roll call in the U.S. Senate. *"Here," she called gently from the back row of polished wooden desks* on the Senate floor during a routine parliamentary poll of the senators.

Here, indeed. Clinton's presence added celebrity crackle to a legislative body mired in *the musty, centuries-old customs* of Colonial America. Her *turquoise pantsuit* *stood out in the sea of conservative dark suits milling about the floor.*

It was all too much for the 98-year-old Sen. Strom Thurmond of South Carolina, the longest-serving senator in U.S. history. "Can I hug you?" Thurmond asked just seconds after Clinton had been sworn into office. He didn't wait for an answer, *grasping her around the waist with both hands and kissing her on the cheek.*

Scott Shepard
Atlanta Constitution[28]

HELPING READERS UNDERSTAND

Ever notice when talking with friends how their words can say one thing, their body language quite something else?

Of course you have. So, you listen, all right, but you also check for nods of agreement, frowns of disapproval, grins of encouragement and eye contact (or lack thereof).

It's the *totality of input* — words plus body language — that leads you to truly understand what your friends are communicating.

In newswriting, you can structure word pictures to convey such nuances and subtleties that lead readers to true understanding.

For example, shortly before leaving office, President Clinton travels to Moscow to negotiate with President Vladimir V. Putin of Russia on highly controversial missile defense systems. How did the talks go?

Elaine Sciolino of the *New York Times* reports the talks ended "with mutual praise, but without narrowing the differences" between the two countries. She adds:

Overall, senior administration officials described the atmosphere between the lame-duck American president and the new Russian president as correct and businesslike, though not necessarily warm. That was evident at their news conference.

That's where an amateur wordsmith stops. Not Sciolino. She adds:

Although the two presidents shook hands as they entered the hall, and Mr. Clinton gently nudged Mr. Putin to pose with him for the cameras afterward, they did not look or smile at each other during their opening statements or while answering questions.

Elaine Sciolio
New York Times[29]

Another example:

In his unsuccessful race for the presidency, Vice President Al Gore portrays himself as more vigorous than his opponent and launches a grueling 30-hour nonstop series of speeches. How is he holding up?

Kevin Sack of *The New York Times* duly reports that Gore *says* he's holding up well and will be campaigning "after my opponent's gone to bed."

Are Gore's assurances all that readers have to go on? No, because Sack paints a word picture that communicates more fully than Gore's words:

By the time he arrived this evening in Flint, Mr. Gore was punchy from exhaustion, his face puffy and pink with rivulets of sweat meandering down his cheek. He sucked on lozenges as he spoke, but they did little to soothe his hoarseness.

Kevin Sack
New York Times[30]

It's worth emphasis: Let your readers *see*.

GOAL #5: THE LIGHT TOUCH

Can a squirrel predict the weather?[31]

That lead graf gave thousands of readers a fun stopping point in a newspaper — the *Boston Globe* — otherwise pretty much filled that day with gloom and doom, death and destruction, war and pestilence.

Wordsmith Joanna Weiss, sentenced to do the predictable, routine winter-is-coming story, as were generations of grousing journalists before her, decides to not write it routinely.

Weiss launches into tongue-in-cheek reporting of old farmers' predictors of severe weather ahead:

Squirrels especially fat and frenzied in gathering nuts portend harsh weather, as do house invasions by mice, heavy acorn harvests and broad stripes down the backs of caterpillars.

Chipmunks get into the act, too. There definitely is something going on with them out at Cider Hill Farm, where a farmer says, "There are more chipmunks than we've ever seen before." They're fatter, too.

Important news? No. So, who cares? Editors and readers care because we all seek occasional light reading in newspapers too often focused on the dark and deadly side of life.

Lesson: Never pass up a light-hearted approach *when the subject is appropriate* (and sometimes it isn't, of course).

War offers little humor but its memory 25 years later yields for wordsmith Seth Mydans a light-hearted intro:

Ho Chi Minh City, Vietnam — For months, a giant portrait of Vietnam's revolutionary leader, Ho Chi Minh, stared out across a central square at a billboard showing the American fashion model Cindy Crawford.

"The glorious victory of Communism will last 1,000 years," the portrait of Ho proclaimed. Miss Crawford's portrait, offering for sale an expensive watch to count the

hours, smiled enticingly and said nothing.

The portrait of Miss Crawford is gone now as this raucous, bustling city — still known to almost everybody as Saigon — smartened itself up to celebrate the high point of Vietnamese Communism: What Hanoi calls the liberation of the nation, after 30 years of war, from foreign domination by the French and then by the Americans.

After that my-how-times-change approach, Mydans transits to serious recollection:

It was 25 years ago, on April 30, 1975, that the last fleeing helicopter lifted off the roof of the American Embassy and the first tanks of the North Vietnamese smashed through

the gates of the presidential palace a few blocks away.

Some 58,000 American soldiers were dead, along with an estimated 3 million Vietnamese, military and civilian, both in the north and south. The ruinous decade-long conflict known to Americans as the Vietnam War, and to Vietnamese as the American War, was over.

But in its way, a quarter of a century later, the war is still being waged here, even though more than half the population of 78 million was born after 1975.

Ho Chi Minh and the alluring faces of Western capitalism still confront each other, emblems of Communist Vietnam's celebrated past and of a more complicated future it has not yet decided to embrace . . . .

Seth Mydans
New York Times[32]

Imagine that story above starting, "It was 25 years ago . . . ." A dull, non-starter, right?

Well, you might say, there is at least one sector of journalism — obituaries — where the light-hearted approach doesn't work. Wrong. Catch a wordsmith on the obituary of a college professor, Peter Griffin, who became an expert in gambling at the card game blackjack:

Mr. Griffin had not even played blackjack until January 1970, when, to gain practical experience for a proposed course on gambling math-

ematics, he paid a visit to Nevada and *promptly got his clock cleaned.*

Robert McG. Thomas Jr.
New York Times[33]

Or, an Associated Press obituary on the death of a famous columnist:

Washington — Lars-Erik Nelson, a columnist who wrote for *both the street-smart New York Daily News and the highbrow New York Review of Books*, died at his home Monday

night, apparently of a stroke. He was 59.

Randolph E. Schmid
The Associated Press[34]

The light touch can be used effectively, also, on hard news:

Striking MTA drivers put the brakes on mass transit Saturday, stranding an estimated 200,000 bus and rail riders in and around Los Angeles and creating eerie pockets of calm in ethnic business districts that usu-

ally are jammed with weekend shoppers.

Douglas P. Shuit
Jill Leovy
Los Angeles Times[35]

Note the writers we've studied don't make fun of their subjects or the gravity of news being covered. Rather, they just play with words a bit to make their stories more open and engaging, to lighten the readers' burden.

Some writers, of course, draw crowds of readers because they regularly hide delightful little nuggets deep in their stories.

William Safire, a *New York Times* columnist, is renowned for that. And he comes through for his fans once again in a story on a real estate entrepreneur famous for his leveraged buyouts of other companies and who, at the moment, is in highly publicized divorce proceedings. Comments Safire:

The nation's most celebrated deal artist is working on a leveraged throwout of his wife, who betrayed his trust by turning 40.[36]

Sometimes, just a word or two injects light-hearted sparkle into your writing.

Thus, *Boston Globe* writers describe a man as a "sidekick" of a mobster, and that works.[37]

It works too, when a writer in the *Chicago Tribune* opens with:

We wuz robbed. That is what 49 million Americans will believe (about the Bush-Gore race for the U.S. presidency).[38]

But, does the following work (emphasis added)?

Carolyn Anderson has no big complaint about government in Oregon — in fact, *she kind of likes it.*[39]

Lesson: Pursue the light-hearted touch, all right, but don't plunge into slangy language inappropriate for the lead story on the front page of a newspaper (where that lead was printed).

SUMMARY

- Advancing beyond minimal standards for *acceptable* writing and becoming a *stylist* requires you to achieve clarity through simple, yet lively and colorful language.
- Clarity is Goal #1 in newswriting because a journalist's basic job is to *communicate.*

- Short sentences of about 25 words and one or two central thoughts help achieve clarity.
- Start a sentence thinking short, then read aloud what you've written — and rewrite if it sounds cumbersome.
- A simple vocabulary of short words helps you construct sentences that yield their meaning on a single reading (as all sentences should.).
- Translate jargon and scientific or business terms that are unfamiliar to most readers.
- Goal #2 in writing is to inject *sparkle* into your stories by writing in active voice and present tense, when possible.
- Colorful language captures sparkle when used appropriately, but don't inject phony drama into your writing and thus elevate a story beyond its intrinsic news value.
- Goal #3 in writing is use of strong quotes; stylists know when to back out of a story and let sources tell it in their own words.
- Never change what is between quote marks; if a quote is too long, ungrammatical or otherwise unprintable, paraphrase.
- Goal #4 is drawing word pictures to capture detail, color and emotion in your writing.
- Sketch word pictures to give readers a featurish look at your story or to freeze-frame a memorable vignette.
- Capturing how persons in the news walk, talk and act with each other can show readers the true meaning of an event.
- Goal #5 is to write with a light touch when it's appropriate (and it isn't always), and give readers welcomed relief from the gloom and doom that frequently dominate news.
- Even slang is appropriate for some stories but don't slide into street talk unacceptable on front pages.

RECOMMENDED READING

Valuable commentaries on newswriting appear regularly in these trade journals: The American Editor (journal of the American Society of Newspaper Editors); American Journalism Review (AJR), Columbia Journalism Review (CJR), and Editor and Publisher.

Note particularly Roy Peter Clark and Christopher Scanlan, "America's Best Newspaper Writing" (Boston: Bedford/St. Martin's, 2001), latest in an annual compilation of outstanding newspaper writing.

The Associated Press Managing Editors, 50 Rockefeller Plaza, New York, NY, 10020, publishes annual "APME Reports," a valuable analysis of writing by AP and newspaper staffers.

Also see Joseph M. Williams, "Style: Ten Lessons in Clarity and Grace," fifth edition (New York: Longman, 1996) and Carl Sessions Stepp, "Writing as Craft and Magic" (Lincolnwood, Ill.: NTC/Contemporary Publishing Group, 2001).

EXERCISES

1. Examine the front pages of today's *New York Times* (or another newspaper designated by your instructor) and *USA Today*. Compare writing styles found in both and, in about 350 words, describe similarities and differences. Note particularly *sentence length* and writers' *word choices*. Were any stories particularly open and engaging? Any overwritten and verbose? Which page *communicated* better? Why?

2. Study today's *Boston Globe* (or another newspaper business section designated by your instructor) and, in about 300 words, comment on whether writers adequately *translate* business terms and esoterica. Would non-experts be able to understand terms and descriptions found in this newspaper? Or, do writers fail to serve as translators and thus close their stories to all but expert readers?

3. Read the sports section of today's *New York Times* (or another newspaper designated by your instructor) and, in about 250 words, comment on the presence (or absence) of "sparkle," as defined in Chapter Four. Do writers use *colorful language, active voice writing, present tense*? Do any stories strike you as particularly full of "sparkle"? Why?

4. Read the "A" section of today's *New York Times* (or another newspaper designated by your instructor) and, in about 300 words, discuss how writers use (or don't use) quotes. Do you see many partial-quote leads? If so, do writers present the full quotes later in their stories and adequately back-up partial quotes with attribution and elaboration? Your assignment in this exercise is to report whether guidelines in Chapter Four on use of quotes are followed by the newspaper's writers.

5. Study today's *New York Times* (or another newspaper designated by your instructor) and report, in about 350 words, on whether writers draw "word pictures," as discussed in Chapter Four. Are you able to "see" and "hear" events being described? Do writers make an effort to take readers along, to places and events readers otherwise never would visit?

NOTES

1. "Peru's Fujimori Steps Down after 10 Years of Iron Rule," Nov. 21, 2000, p. A–1.
2. "Disgraced Spy Boss in Peru Flees to Panama," Sept. 25, 2000, p. A–1.
3. "Feed Man Awaits Next Step," Nov. 21, 2000, p. A–1.
4. Reader habits are discussed more fully in Conrad Fink, "Strategic Newspaper Management" (Boston: Allyn and Bacon, 1996).
5. "Just Scraping By," Dec. 20, 2000, Section 1, p. 7.
6. "Holiday Honoring Atlantan Goes Global," Jan. 14, 2001, p. C–1.
7. Dispatch for Sunday papers, Aug. 26, 2000.
8. "Stock Swindler's Profile: Likes Wrestling, Hates Yankees, Is 15," Sept. 22, 2000, national edition, p. A–23.
9. Dispatch at 12:05 p.m., EDT, April 29, 1999.
10. Stump Martin, "Rossville Mayor Seeks to Annex 3 Roads," Dec. 12, 2000, p. B–1.
11. "Bridgeport Bucks Restoration Trend," Nov. 26, 2000, p. B–8.
12. "Missing Teen Calls Home to Tell Parents She's Sick," Oct. 2, 2000, p. A–19.
13. "Capitol Corridor Ridership Grows Dramatically," Dec. 26, 2000, p. A–21.
14. "'Critical Incident,' Polite Term, Grisly Reality," Aug. 22, 1999, p. G–1.
15. "6 Killed in Middle East Bloodshed," Nov. 23, 2000, p. A–61.

16. "A Hedge Against Recession," Jan. 4, 2001, p. A–1.

17. Respectively, Barry Bearak, "Questions of Race Run Deep for Foe of Preferences," July 27, 1997, p. A–1; Katharine Q. Seelye, "Gore Eulogizes His Father As a Loving Teacher," Dec. 9, 1998, national edition, p. C–31; "Russian City Buries a Hero, Firm in Its Faith in The War," March 15, 2000, national edition, p. A–3; Rick Klein, Jama E. Watson, "Two Boys Killed in Mattapan House Fire," Nov. 26, 2000, p. B–1; Brett Pulley, "A Gambling Impresario Leaves Little to Chance," Dec. 6, 1998, p. A–1.

18. "Making a Meal of The Hands That Feed Her," Jan. 9, 2001, national edition, p. A–18.

19. "Cheney Has 'Slight' Heart Attack in D.C.," Nov. 23, 2000, p. A–1.

20. "Man Facing '3rd Strike' Flees from Courthouse," Oct. 18, 2000, p. B–3.

21. "Clinton Cuts Last-Day Deal," Jan. 20, 2001, p. A–1.

22. Dispatch for Saturday morning papers, Jan. 20, 2001

24. "Killing for the Glory of God, In a Land Far from Home," Jan. 16, 2001, p. A–1.

25. "More Than Ever, New Yorkers Eat up Off-Track Betting," Dec. 25, 2000, p. A–17.

26. "A Second Act on The Wicked Stage of Life," Oct. 17, 1996, national edition, p. B–1.

27. "Bush Asks Citizens to 'Seek Common Good,'" Jan. 21, 2001, p. A–1.

28. "Hello, Hill: First Lady Becomes Senator," Jan. 4, 2001, p. A–1.

29. "Clinton and Putin Unable to Agree on Missile Barrier," June 5, 2000, p. A–1.

30. "Gore Ends Marathon With Final Charge Around Nation," Nov. 2, 2000, national edition, p. A–1.

31. Joanna Weiss, "Skeptics Throw Cold Water on Quirky Winter Forecasts," Nov. 24, 2000, p. B–1.

32. "Vietnam Faces An Old Foe With New Allure," April 13, 2000, national edition, p. A–1.

33. "Peter Griffin, Solver of Blackjack, Dies at 61," Nov. 2, 1998, national edition, p. A–22.

34. Dispatch for morning papers, Nov. 22, 2000.

35. "No MTA Talks Set; Strike Expected to Disrupt Work Week," Sept. 17, 2000, p. A–1.

36. "Clear Writing," an analysis of newswriting, Associated Press Managing Editors, 1998, p. 7.

37. Shelley Murphy, Ralph Ranalli, "Bulger, Flemmi Charged with A String of Murders," Sept. 29, 2000, p. A–1.

38. Linda R. Monk, "Impasse of Congressional Proportions," Nov. 20, 2000, Section 1, p. 11.

39. Jeff Mapes, Harry Esteve, The Oregonian, "Tax-Revolt Fever Cools in Oregon," Sept. 24, 2000, p. A–1.

PART THREE
Capturing – and Holding – Their Attention

Capturing – and Holding – Their Attention

Picture the households where your readers live:

If it's morning, radio or television (or both) blaring. Breakfasts being wolfed down. People scurrying about, sleepily preparing for school or work.

If it's evening, people dragging home, exhausted by their day, seeking a quiet meal, maybe a bit of television, then bed.

And you want to entice those people into reading your story?

You want to pull those harried, time-deprived people into reading about the compellingly important social, political and economic issues of our time?

Believe it: You have a challenge.

To that challenge we now turn in Part III: Capturing — and Holding — Their Attention. We'll discuss writing with clarity, force and vigor that will catch readers, then lead them to the end of your story.

In Chapter Five, we'll study leads, which are single or multi-graf intros designed to snag reader attention. Many optional leads are available, and mastering them is considered throughout journalism to be a test of professionalism.

In Chapter Six, we'll look at story structures you must build to maintain the reading momentum of your leads. If you don't, if you fail to knit a whole fabric of your stories, any readers your leads attract will depart quickly for other parts of the newspaper — or simply drop the entire newspaper and get on with their lives.

Think of writing leads and building story structures that keep straight the cast of characters and time elements. You thus can create a *bridge of confidence* that carries readers from intro to conclusion.

5

Hey, Readers!
Look at This!

YOU'VE FINISHED REPORTING and interviewing. You're at the keyboard, ready to write your lead.

But your screen is blank — and so is your mind.

What to do? *Ask yourself two questions*:

- What is the single most-important fact you must convey to *readers*?
- What, in your reporting and interviewing, interests *you* the most?

If both answers are the same, if your interests coincide with perceived reader interest, happy times are here. Your lead, its angle and your story thrust are clear.

If not, always go with the likely interests — and news needs — of your readers, for it is *their* news interests, not *ours*, that we serve in journalism.

Now, a three-step process:

First, review quickly from Chapter Two the "Six-Finger Checklist" of elements essential to any news story: who, what, where, when, why and how. Whatever your lead, however you structure your story, those elements must be covered.

Second, run down in your mind the factors affecting news judgment. Is it an event's *impact* on readers that makes it news? *Proximity*? Or *conflict, timeliness, prominence*? *Novelty*?

Third, in selecting a writing approach, consider the *type of material* you must communicate. If financial, for example, a dollars-and-cents, hard-news approach may be best. Or, if this is a "people story," one that must focus on the human element, perhaps a softer, featurish approach is best. And always consider the *type of audience* you're reaching. A financial story must be written one way for general-news readers of the front page, quite another way for money-savvy readers of the business section.

Now — but only now — can you select a lead and story form.

THE INVERTED PYRAMID

Readers, obviously, ultimately control how much of your story is *read*.

Just as obviously, editors control how much is *printed*.

So, we've developed a hard-news story structure — the inverted pyramid — that gives editors and readers alike the option of bailing out of a story early on, but still catching its highlights, or plowing deeper into the story in search of additional facts that you deal out in declining order of news value.

In sum, editors should be able to trim an inverted-pyramid story from the bottom up, to meet the cruel constraints of limited newshole, and still print its most important facts.

Readers should be able to depart after the first paragraph or two with firm grasp of at least the story's single most-important meaning.

In addition to readers and editors, a third constituency is served by the inverted pyramid: writers. On deadline, this story form is relatively easy to write, and even though it may lack poetic ruffles and flourishes, it can communicate meaning clearly and quickly.

An example follows:

Note below the characteristics of the inverted-pyramid story:

- The six-finger checklist is met unobtrusively: who (Ivanov), what (ready to cooperate), where (Berlin in dateline), when (yesterday), why and how (told forum on European security.)

Berlin--Foreign Minister Igor Ivanov of Russia said yesterday that his country is ready to cooperate with the European Union's new military force.
"We consider it completely natural the effort by Europe with their own forces to provide for their own security," Ivanov told leading European policy makers and analysts at a forum on Europe."And in a crisis situation we are ready for constructive cooperation."
European countries announced this week that they would form their own rapid reaction force outside NATO, the Atlantic alliance that formed the West's primary Cold War buffer against the former Soviet Union.
EU countries said they would create a force of up to 60,000 ground troops from the union's 15 member states by 2003 to handle regional conflicts and humanitarian crises. "The possibility of a Russian contribution in the conduct of European Union operations in regulating crises will be studied," Ivanov said...
Ivanov's proposal could raise U.S. fears of losing influence in European peacekeeping operations.
Ivanov mentioned Europe's differences with Washington over the possible development of a U.S ballistic missile defense system; Russia opposes such a system as a violation of the Anti-Ballistic Missile Treaty, and the Europeans are wary of it.

FIGURE 5.1   Inverted pyramid illustration of story (Reuters[1])

- The lead graf contains a single, easily grasped idea: Russia is ready to cooperate. In a newshole crunch, with editors obliged to cut stories to one-graf "World News" briefs, that lead graf would stand alone and give readers at least the principal thrust of the story.
- The second graf is a full quote that *immediately backs up the lead* and is enlightening elaboration of the lead.
- The third and subsequent grafs, also presenting welcomed elaboration, are stacked in order of descending news value. Trimming from the bottom, editors first would eliminate lesser-important facts.

Here is an inverted-pyramid lead that gives readers a larger mouthful to swallow but still reads easily because it is written carefully:

Atlanta — West Nile virus, the mosquito-borne disease that appeared suddenly in the United States two years ago, has spread to 12 states and the District of Columbia and is probably here to stay, the Centers for Disease Control and Prevention said yesterday.

Note above *two* central ideas are packed into a single graf: the virus has spread and is probably here to stay. Now, in order of descending news value, the writer adds detail:

The agency reported that evidence of West Nile activity in mosquitoes or birds was found last summer as far north as New Hampshire and Vermont, as far east as eastern Pennsylvania and as far south as North Carolina. Sixty-five horses were found infected with the virus, as well as bats, cats, raccoons, rabbits and a skunk.

In a piece of good news, the CDC said that only 18 humans were hospitalized this year with neurological problems caused by West Nile virus, compared with 62 in the first year that the African virus arrived in the United States.

The agency warned, however, that those 18 cases may significantly under-represent West Nile's presence in the eastern United States. Serious neurological illness occurs in fewer than 1 percent of people infected — so there may have been up to 2,000 cases of infection this year, most of them not noticeable.

Cox News Service[2]

Anything strike you about that story above?

It's *dull*. Oh, the facts are there, all right — 65 horses, bats and cats, "18 humans" and "2,000 cases." And, it's strongly attributed to an authoritative source, essential in science writing.

But, lordy, how dull!

And that, young writer, is a major limitation of the inverted-pyramid story structure. Written properly, it delivers facts in digestible batches, but can do little more than make them palatable.

Indeed, inserting "color" descriptive into an inverted pyramid, though perhaps improving reader appeal, inevitably delays delivery of facts — and thus defeats this structure's basic purpose, which is fast, clear communication.

A second limitation of the form: It tempts writers to pack too much into the first graf or two and thus lose control of reading flow. An example:

Antlered deer season opens today in Pennsylvania and police throughout the region — particularly in areas in which houses encroach on long-favored hunting grounds — are bracing for an onslaught of phone calls from scared or angry homeowners.

In fact, the first shots in the annual hunters-versus-homeowners battle have already been fired — by a man hunting deer illegally in Wrightstown, Bucks County. About 7:30 p.m. on Nov. 18, three rifle shots struck a home, shatter-

ing a family-room window and ter-
rifying the occupants, who were
not injured.

Richard Sabatini
Philadelphia Inquirer[3]

Note the story above covers a *spot-news development* (deer season starts), which is the most common use of the inverted pyramid. But so much else is packed into the first two grafs that two or three readings are necessary to sort it all out.

A third limitation of the inverted pyramid: It's used too much.

News services such as AP, Reuters, Dow Jones and Bloomberg are heavy users because their writers aren't guaranteed a specific pre-set newshole. An AP writer covers a Chicago Bears football game, for example, knowing the story might run 450 words in the nearby *Milwaukee Journal* but be trimmed to a couple grafs in the distant *Dallas Morning News*. The inverted pyramid is the writer's only option.

With over-use comes a terrible sameness, a sort of 1–2–3 lockstep writing by formula. For example, here's a structure you'll recognize (just fill in the blanks.)

Memphis — ————ran for a career-high ——— yards and ———— kicked —— field goals as No. 23 Colorado State beat 22nd-ranked Louisville 22–17 Friday in the ——— Bowl.

The Associated Press[4]

When you do fill in the blanks (Cecil Sapp ran for 160 yards; C.W. Hurst kicked three field goals; it was the Liberty Bowl) you have a *one-graf summary* of the highlights but in a form so predictable!

Here's an AP writer who breaks free of the inverted pyramid:

Atlanta — LSU brought in Rohan Davey to spark its offense in the Peach Bowl. Georgia Tech couldn't call on Ralph Friedgen.

Note, however, the single-graf lead above cannot stand alone. It doesn't even report the score. So, this:

Davey, replacing Josh Booty at quarterback in the second half, threw three touchdown passes to lead LSU to a 28–14 upset of the No. 15 Yellow Jackets on Friday.

Adding the *second* graf isn't sufficient, either, because the first-graf reference to Ralph Friedgen isn't explained. So:

George Godsey and the Tech offense were lost without Friedgen, the mastermind of its point-scoring success over the last three seasons. He left to become the head coach at Maryland shortly after the final regular-season game . . . .

The Associated Press[5]

You'll note, of course, that although AP's writer above breaks free of the 1–2–3 lockstep inherent in the inverted pyramid, editors who want to use a one or two-graf summary are out of luck.

ANECDOTAL LEADS

Some writers (and editors and, we hope, readers) favor anecdotal leads *even if they subordinate a timely spot-news development.*

For example, a Staunton, Va., man, arrested days earlier, is denied bond on Friday (that's the spot news), and Saturday morning the *Staunton Daily News Leader* publishes this:

Staunton — Three days after he allegedly shot and killed his brother and 1-year-old nephew (Fred Smith) trudged through the Augusta County jail in shackles. His feet, in unlaced hiking boots, scuffed along the tiled floor.

"It was self defense," he said. Charged with capital murder, first-degree murder and two other counts, he faces the death penalty if convicted of the slayings.

Note the writer still hasn't gotten to the news — denial of bond. That comes only in the third graf:

(Smith) was denied bond Friday in Augusta County Juvenile and Domestic Relations Court, and appointed a public defender. A preliminary hearing had been set for Jan. 17 but was canceled, with a second date to be announced.

Kristie DiSalvo
Staunton (Va.)
Daily News Leader[6]

Beware: Some editors demand *first-day leads* on stories such as the one above. That is, they want hard, more timely leads on spot-news developments — bond is denied on Friday, and that's the news angle for Saturday morning.

However, anecdotal leads are perfect for *second-day leads*, those that report what's happening two days or more after the event.

For example, on *Saturday* morning, an earthquake hits El Salvador. That's the news for *Sunday* morning papers. Now, what's the angle for *Monday* morning? Niko Price of AP uses an anecdotal lead:

Santa Tecla, El Salvador — First there was a blood-chilling scream from atop the mountain. Within moments, a wall of earth was crashing down onto the middle-class neighborhood of Las Colinas below.

When the dust cleared, nothing was left of Las Colinas but a flat plain, its silence giving way to the wails of the injured.

As many as 1,200 people disappeared below the mass of dirt: A woman walking to the store for some eggs. A 12-year-old boy waiting at home for a phone call from his father in Kansas. Three 5-year-olds riding bicycles they received for Christmas.

Rescuers on Sunday frantically dug with earth-movers, with shovels, with their bare hands to extract mangled corpses—and at least three people who had miraculously survived.

It began at 11:35 a.m. Saturday. Julio Antonio Ramirez, a bodyguard for an American woman who lives in a columned white mansion at the top of the hill, was standing in the yard when he heard the scream.

The earth had begun to shake . . . .

Niko Price
The Associated Press[7]

Note above these characteristics:

- The anecdotal lead enables the writer to neatly dodge the ordinary second-day lead, the deadly dull, "Rescuers on Sunday frantically dug." That angle is predictable on every earthquake, just as "Homeowners mopped up today following" is predictable following floods.
- The time elements necessary in any story, whatever its structure, are subordinated to color descriptive. Read again the lead graf above. Do you want a Sunday time element substituted for "blood-chilling scream"? No way, right?
- After a timeless intro of three grafs, the writer sorts out the time elements. Yesterday (Sunday) is in the fourth graf; then the writer nicely transits to beginning a chronological description in the fifth graf ("It began at 11:35 a.m., Sunday . . .)

NECK-OF-THE-VASE LEADS

Do you understand Oregon's statewide controversy over anti-tax measures?
   More to the point, do you want to read about it?
   No?
   How about an 18-year-old who labors in a warehouse loading and unloading trucks, then sees his paycheck savaged by taxes? Now, *that's* an interesting story, right?
   So reasoned Harry Esteve when the *Portland Oregonian* assigned him to cover the story: He could write *about taxes* or write *about people affected by taxes*. Here is his lead:

(Fred Smith) took a look at his son's pay stub recently and became instantly disgusted.
   New to the work force, the 18-year-old earned $1,750 for two week's labor loading and unloading at a local warehouse. After taxes and other subtractions, however, the bottom line barely touched $1,100.
   "He works awful hard," (Smith), 45, said. "My whole feeling is, taxes are just too high."

With just three grafs, writer Esteve fashions a readable, engaging people-oriented intro. However, this story *is* about anti-tax sentiment in Oregon, so in his fourth graf, the writer widens to this (emphasis added):

(Smith), a truck driver. . .and bedrock conservative, represents a solid core of Oregonians who can be trusted to support tax limits in any given year. Convinced that the government wastes enormous amounts of money on unnecessary services and overly generous salaries, they jump at any opportunity to cut or limit taxes.
   Although most Oregon voters say they're satisfied with state government, a stubborn layer of anti-tax anger persists. (Smith) typifies the attitude that schools and public agencies could function just as well with less.

Harry Esteve
Portland Oregonian[8]

What's more interesting? Anti-tax sentiment or an 18-year-old working his heart out and seeing taxes bleed his income? No contest, right?
   Seth Mydans of The New York Times faces a hard sell: He wants you to read about public opinion in Cambodia 20 years after Khmer Rouge rebels ravaged the country. His lead:

Phnom Penh, Cambodia— "I'm just a small person," said Un Samath, a customs inspector, using a common phrase among Cambodians, "so I

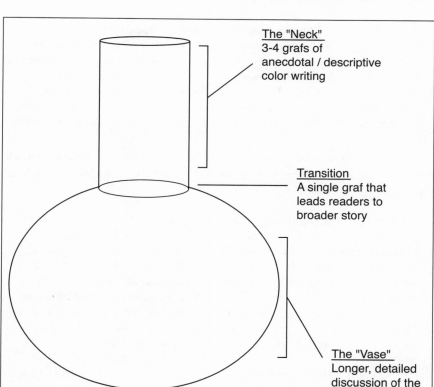

The "Neck"
3-4 grafs of
anecdotal / descriptive
color writing

Transition
A single graf that
leads readers to
broader story

The "Vase"
Longer, detailed
discussion of the
issue involved.

FIGURE 5.2   Vase illustration of story

dare not say."

But then he got angry, and he said it.

"I hate them," he said of defecting Khmer Rouge leaders who recently flaunted their impunity in a tourist trip around Cambodia. "So long as it doesn't cause a war, I wnat to see them on trial. Camboidans cannot be happy as long as they are happy."

And then, a like a man who has decided that the time has come to speak, Mr. Un Samth, 46, described the pain he shares with almost every other Camboidan of his generation— the killings of family member, the years of fear and hunger, the loss of youth and education, the continuing harshness of life.

With you now hooked on the tragedy of *one man*, writer Mydans makes smooth transition to where he wanted you all along — *the broader story in Cambodia*:

It was just one of countless unburdenings that taking place among Camboidans today as the country seems to be embarking, spontaneously, on a long-delayed national conversation about its traumatic past.

Here and in Battambang, the country's second-largest city, interviews with a score of people from market vendors to professors suggest that a common legacy of anger and pain is being shared in a new way. . .

Seth Mydans
New York Times[9]

A *Washington Post* writer has the unenviable task of getting readers into a story on unlawful eating in subway trains. She gets me into it with this intro:

(Jane Smith) had practically never been in trouble, let alone arrested. Then the officer clicked the metal cuffs on the 12-year-old's wrists and pulled the laces out of her tennis shoes.

She had been eating fries in a Metro subway station, and she was questioned, searched and taken away.

"We really do believe in zero tolerance," said Metro Transit Police Chief Barry J. McDevitt, who is unapologetic for such arrests.

Commuter complaints about unlawful eating on Metro cars and in stations led McDevitt to order a weeklong undercover crackdown on violators in October, and a dozen plainclothes officers cited or arrested 35 people, 13 of them juveniles. Only one adult was arrested . . . .

Petula Dvorak
Washington Post[10]

By now, you've probably picked up on the structure of neck-of-the-vase LEADS.

Consider these characteristics of the structure:

- It enables you to *personalize* a broader, faceless issue, to express in human terms a development readers otherwise might find complex, even mysterious. People love to read about people; issues are something else.
- The personalized intro should be detailed enough to create an understandable personality (a customs inspector) or an easily grasped word picture (a handcuffed 12 year old.)
- However, the personalized intro should be held to three or four grafs, or the balance of your story is ruined. Mydans' story is not about a customs inspector; it is about Cambodian opinion. Dvorak's piece is not about a 12-year-old; it is about police cracking down on unlawful eating in subways.

- The transition graf, leading readers from personalized intro into the broader issue, must be written and placed in your story with great care. Read again Mydans' smooth transition graf ("It was just one of countless unburdenings") and Dvorak's graceful "Commuter complaints about unlawful eating."

There are problems with neck-of-vase writing:

- It delays delivery of hard news and thus is unsuitable for important spot-news stories.
- It is used too much, forcing readers interested in *news* to sidetrack into conversations with individuals sometimes selected arbitrarily by reporters seeking the "average" or single representative person (who doesn't exist).

CONTRAST LEADS

Ever notice how great painters use contrasts to build vivid pictures? Black versus white, sharp edges versus blurred images, tall versus short . . .

Composers do it, too, with loud music versus quiet, fast versus slow, one instrument against another.

You can use contrasts to build vivid *word pictures.*

Note the contrast between brotherly togetherness and separation by death:

Wakefield — (Fred) and (Bill Smith), were as close as brothers can be. They lived together. They hung out together. They worked together.

But on Tuesday morning, they were forever separated by an assailant's bullet.

(Fred Smith), 26, arrived at Edgewater Technology late, delayed by an early-morning class. By the time he arrived, the building had been cordoned off with yellow tape, and his 29-year-old brother was dead inside . . . .

Michael Paulson,
Patrick Healy
Boston Globe[11]

Note below a writer skillfully contrasts fairy tale with reality, what was supposed to be with what is:

London — It was supposed to follow the dot-com fairy tale script. Two young entrepreneurs devise an idea for the next big e-commerce Web site, raise enormous sums of cash, spend lavishly on advertising, lose money on every sale, take the company public and make every employee a millionaire. (The company) . . . is insolvent and has been forced to call the liquidators, six months after its Internet debut . . . .

Andrew Ross Sorkin
New York Times[12]

Note the *rhythm* this writer builds in his first graf – they waved, they chanted, they applauded — then the contrast as they fell silent:

Urosevac, Kosovo — They waved tiny American flags, they chanted his name in an excited frenzy, they met his every word with thunderous applause — at least until President Clinton urged the Kosovo Albanians to try to forgive the Serbs. They the fell silent.

"You cannot forget the injustice that was done to you," Mr. Clinton told several hundred Albanians gathered at a sports arena here in southeastern Kosovo. "No one can force you to forgive what was done to you. But you must try."

Mr. Clinton finished making the point. The translator finished too. A stony silence settled on the crowd, and for a moment all the excitement seemed to disappear . . . .

Marc Lacey
New York Times[13]

Taking your readers in one direction, then jerking them in another is almost like playing *counterpoint* in music. Note below how a writer's rhythm takes you toward dogs of war, meat grinders, slaughter and warfare, then you are jerked the other way, toward peace:

Listen to the nightly news and hear the dogs of war growling as fiercely in this new century as ever: the meat grinder in Chechyna, religious slaughter in Indonesia and Kashmir, tribal warfare in the Congo, China rattling its giant saber.

Now hear this: It is peace, not war, that is on the march these days.

Implausible as it may seem, peace is advancing — fitfully but unmistakably — in the world. Consider these events since the start of the new year:

In Northern Ireland . . .

G. Pascal Zachary
Wall Street Journal[14]

Below, a writer draws vivid contrast in mid-sentence (emphasis added):

The Federal Reserve left interest rates unchanged Tuesday *but did an about-face* on its outlook on the economy, suggesting that the risk of a sharp slowdown now outweighs the risk of inflation.

Janet Kidd Stewart
Chicago Tribune[15]

Characteristics of the contrast lead:

- You need a sharp reporter's eye to catch *meaningful* contrasts. As in any newswriting, don't stretch for empty contrasts that carry no significant meaning.
- Write carefully to state precisely and clearly the contrast you see — fairy tale versus today's reality, cheers versus silence. Don't mask the contrast in nonessential verbiage.

"REAL-WHAT" LEADS

News seldom is what it initially seems to be on the surface. It frequently carries deeper meaning — and you must identify that clearly for your readers.

For example, the Federal Reserve cuts interest rates. That's the story's *what* (and you'll recall, *what* is one of the elements in the Six-Finger Checklist that must be in any news story, along with who, when, where, why and how.)

The *real what*, however, is not so obvious. But a skilled writer locates the real meaning (emphasis added):

Faced with eroding "consumer and business confidence," the Federal Reserve on Wednesday cut interest rates for the second time in a month. *The goal is to prevent a recession.*

Tom Walker
Atlanta Constitution[16]

The lead above is written for the *Constitution*'s *front* page and readers of *general* news.

On the same day, the same reporter writes the same story for the *Constitution*'s *business* section and its quite different audience of *money-savvy readers*. The writer assumes (correctly, I think) that business-section readers know the interest cut is designed to prevent recession. For this audience, the writer jumps the *real what* ahead to another dimension (emphasis added):

The same *stock market* that Federal Reserve Chairman Alan Greenspan blamed for causing economic "imbalances" in the 1990s *may be the quickest cure for the nation's current economic slump*, some analysts believe.

If the key to recovery is restoring consumer confidence — and spending — *a bull market rally would go along way in that direction.* That's what Rajeev Dhawan, director of the

Georgia State University Economic Forecasting Center, said following the Fed's half-point cut in short-term interest rates on Wednesday . . .

Tom Walker
Atlanta Constitution[17]

Israel cancels sale of a radar system to China. That's the *what*. A reporter quickly isolates the *real what* (emphasis added):

Thurmont, Md. — Israel announced today that it had canceled its sale of a sophisticated $250 million airborne radar system to China, *a decision timed for the second day of the Camp David summit meeting and aimed at improving the mood in Congress, where heated opposition to the deal had threatened aid to the Israelis.*

Jane Perlez
New York Times[18]

Below a writer finds a *diplomatic signal* — the real what — hidden behind the what of a story (emphasis added):

Washington — The United States and North Korea announced today that later this year they expect to begin their first joint effort to search for the remains of thousands of Americans soldiers missing from the Korean War.

The announcement, *which could signal a broad improvement in ties between the two countries*, means that Pentagon investigators could soon be wandering the North Korean countryside, searching for evidence of the burial sites of Americans missing since the war ended in 1953 . . . .

Philip Shenon
New York Times[19]

Two points about real-what leads:

First, today's world yields highly complex news stories, and you must dig deeply for true meaning, for the real what. Readers need your help.

Second, however, reporting what *you think* is true meaning can take you dangerously close to interpreting and analyzing news, which you may — *or may not* — be experienced enough to do. Whenever possible, let a recognized expert interpret the real what, as Tom Walker did by quoting Rajeev Dhawan in his second story above.

"REAL-WHO" LEADS

A Reuters reporter can lead a story by referring to Susan Rice. You remember her, don't you?

No? Well, that's why the Reuters reporter chose this lead:

Rumbek, Sudan — The *U.S. government's top official for Africa* met Monday with women freed from slavery in Sudan, and she called for action to end the "heinous" practice.

Now, you know the *real who* of this story — top U.S. official for Africa. The *who* — Susan Rice — is woven into the *second* graf:

On a rare visit by a senior American official to rebel-held southern Sudan, Assistant Secretary of State for African Affairs Susan Rice said Washington will work tirelessly to stamp out slavery in Africa's largest country . . . .

Rosalind Russell
Reuters[20]

In deciding whether to lead with the *who* or the *real who* of a story, you must judge whether the name or *what happens to the name is news.*

For example, Mr. Bing Quan Chung of San Francisco is not a high-recognition name. What happens to him, however, *is* news:

A fishing expedition at San Francisco's Baker Beach turned tragic early yesterday when a 77-year-old fisherman was suddenly pulled out to sea by a ferocious riptide and drowned.

Bing Quan Chung of San Francisco died after paramedics tried to revive him on the Golden Gate National Recreation Area beach . . . .

Carolyn Jones
San Francisco Chronicle[21]

Sometimes, what happens to the who in the news is so extraordinary that the name itself is subordinated even deeper than the second graf. An example:

Lake Elsinore, Calif. — A 68-year-old experienced skydiver died Sunday when her parachute apparently failed to open, authorities said.

"Witnesses said they saw the victim having difficulty during her jump and crashed to the ground," said Riverside County Sheriff's Sgt.

Mark Lohman.

Judy Bieloh of Long Beach was pronounced dead at the scene, said Lohman. She completed more than 1,000 jumps in eight years of skydiving, Lohman said.

The Associated Press[22]

Two pointers on "real-who" leads:

First, well-known names belong in your leads because readers instantly recognize and identify with them: President Bush, President Clinton, Mayor Fred Smith of your town, President Fred Smith of your university.

Second, however, what a relatively unknown person does (top U.S. official for Africa) or what happens to the person (tragically drowns) frequently must be the "news peg" for your lead.

ACHIEVING SPECIAL EMPHASIS

Ever raise your voice — or drop it to a conspiratorial whisper — to make a special point in talking to friends? Ever grab an elbow or grasp a shoulder to *really* catch their attention?

Sure you have, because those are effective communication techniques.

You have similarly effective techniques in writing leads to catch attention.

QUESTION LEADS

The business of journalists is answering questions, but *asking* them can be effective in catching reader attention.

Note these two examples:

Jerusalem — Is Israel using excessive force in its effort to quell Arab rioting?

Increasingly, that is the question from international critics and some Israelis themselves as Israeli troops use helicopter gunships and anti-tank missiles against Palestinian rioters . . . .

Barbara Demick
Philadelphia Inquirer[23]

St. Petersburg, Fla. — Remember the battleship Maine? In 1898, as the formidable American warship rested in Havana Harbor, it blew up and sank, claiming the lives of 266 sailors.

Whether the explosion was sabotage or accident was never determined. At the time, U.S. officials and the media blamed Spain, and used that as a reason to help Cuban revolutionaries overthrow Spanish rule — the Spanish-American War.

On Tuesday, a research team announced it had found the Main wreckage 3 miles off the Havana coast, two-thirds of a mile down.

Pat Leisner
The Associated Press[24]

Two points about question leads:

First, shout *at* me, and I'll probably ignore you. Ask me a question, however, and you've *invited my involvement* — and that catches my attention. So, *limited* use of question leads can warm up your writing for readers.

Second, however, don't use a question lead unless you rush to answer it (battleship Maine) or unless you hold the answer open (is Israel too tough?) by explaining that the answer is being debated without conclusive answer.

"You" Leads

"You" leads, like question leads, invite reader involvement and can lend warmth and openness to an otherwise dull story.

For example, a reporter is assigned to do another of those routine annual stories — Thanksgiving holiday travel problems. It's like doing the routine winter-is-coming story, and the lead can be written like this:

> The holiday travel season is in full swing, and millions of Americans are on the move.

Or, the travel story can be written like this:

> There you are this morning, standing in an endless check-in line at San Francisco International Airport, when over near the wall you spot a couple of passengers in front of an electronic kiosk, punching in a few numbers.
>
> Voila — out of a slot comes a ticket and boarding pass.
>
> Your line has not even inched forward in the three minutes it took for the passengers to get their tickets. Those travelers are well on their way to the departure gate and you're still fuming in a Thanksgiving holiday ticket line.
>
> With the holiday travel season in full swing, millions of Americans will be on the move and many of them may well be stuck in airports wondering if there's a better way to get through the preflight morass.
>
> And high-tech flying — or, rather, high-tech ticketing and boarding — appears to be a way.
>
> "These kiosks can do for airlines what the ATM did for banking," says Mary Beth Schubert, a spokeswoman for Northwest Airlines . . . .
>
> Michael Taylor
> *San Francisco Chronicle*[25]

As *you* can see, the "you" lead above is written for a *timely but timeless story* — that is, it's published two days before Thanksgiving and, thus, is timely. But it's not pegged to any specific day. Indeed, the story could be written one day — or three — before Thanksgiving.

"You" leads, therefore, are best on featurish stories (and we'll turn to them in depth in subsequent chapters.)

DASH AND COLON LEADS

Used judiciously — not too often, and only on appropriate stories — dashes and colons can lend special emphasis to your leads.

Two AP reporters get special punch with dashes:

Boston — Forget about pulling an all-nighter before an exam — a study suggests it's more important to get a good night's rest. Harvard Medical School researchers . . . .

The Associated Press[26]

Vatican City — The Vatican has blasted lawmakers for giving legal recognition to so-called de facto unions — including those between homosexuals — and said attempts to allow adoption by gays were "a great danger."

A 77-page document made public yesterday . . . .

Frances D'Emilio
The Associated Press[27]

A colon lead and second-graf dashes lend similar emphasis:

Washington — Here's something to be thankful for: The United States has had almost no major natural disasters this year.

The year 2000 dawned with apocalyptic fears — biblical, technological, meteorological — but so far has turned out to be downright benign.

Seth Borenstein
Philadelphia Inquirer[28]

Special problem with colon and dash leads: Used too often — particularly in setting off inappropriate material, like this — or repeatedly in the same sentence — like this — you end up with choppy, staccato writing that can lead readers to scream: stop!

SPECIAL PEG LEADS

Some things in life are recognizable "news pegs" for all of us, and "hanging" your lead on one can create connections with readers.

The *holiday peg* can inject special pathos into a story:

An 84-year-old man died and more than 100 tenants were left homeless on *the day before Thanksgiving* after a three-alarm fire, started by a space heater, at a Dorchester apartment building.

Mac Daniel
Boston Globe[29]

The *anniversary peg* gives you logical reason to revisit a story:

Dili—*A year after the rape of their land* for daring to choose independence, the East Timorese face the tough decisions of nationhood.

The Economist[30]

The *first-time-ever peg* is a wonderfully strong intro on significant stories.

Vail, Colo. — *For the first time ever*, a jury in the nation's No. 1 ski state has convicted a skier of homicide for a deadly collision on the slopes.

Robert Weller
The Associated Press[31]

The *shock lead* can be written to jolt readers with colorful (and smelly) descriptive:

Camden, N.J. — The sewers are backed up at Seventh and Elm Streets again, and pools of scummy liquid are collecting in the collapsing gutters and rutted street in front of the Bible Tabernacle Church. It stinks.

Iver Peterson
New York Times[32]

Or, the *shock lead* can be written, instead, to focus sharply on shocking details and let them speak for themselves:

The chief of a (nearby) fire company has been arrested in an investigation of a stash of child pornography found on a firehouse computer — images to which detectives were led by the man's wife, law-enforcement authorities said yesterday.

Erin Carroll
Philadelphia Inquirer[33]

COMMON PROBLEMS IN LEAD WRITING

Experienced editors can predict problems a beginner newswriter will have writing leads. Why not surprise your first editor by arriving on the job knowing how to avoid them?

In order of gravity, here are the problems:

- Missing the news peg.
- Writing choke-the-horse leads.
- Mishandling time elements.
- Mishandling sourcing.
- Writing without sparkle.

MISSING THE NEWS PEG

Only experience can teach you how to spot the true news in a story, and much of this book is devoted to giving you a head start.

You can begin — on every story — by asking yourself questions posed earlier in this chapter:

- What single fact likely is of greatest interest or importance to your readers?
- What single fact uncovered in your reporting interests you the most?

Another hint: Regularly read a major newspaper and watch closely how writers select news pegs. Watch particularly how they write leads on a story that continues for days or weeks.

Read newspapers not only to keep up on the world but also to learn how accomplished professionals structure stories. *Study* their techniques as you study a textbook — methodically, carefully.

WRITING CHOKE-THE-HORSE LEADS

Many beginners fail to write leads that, like this sentence, are understood easily.

Rather, burdened by the need to cover the Six-Finger Checklist — who, what, where, why, when and how — and touch base on prominence, impact, novelty and other elements that go into defining news, too many beginners write lead grafs that, like this sentence, would choke a horse.

It deserves emphasis: Especially in your beginner years, 1) focus your leads on the single-most important factor, 2) write leads in the 25–30 word range, 3) carefully parcel out secondary facts in subsequent grafs.

Be particularly alert when you must communicate crucial numbers. Too many in the lead graf will choke anybody, horses and readers alike.

For example, Amazon.com announces it is cutting workforce by 15 percent, or 1,300 employees. The company is $2 billion in debt, and has reduced its revenue estimates for 2001 to no more than $3.5 billion from an earlier $4 billion estimated. Fourth-quarter (October, November, December) revenue was $972 million, compared with $1 billion most analysts had been predicting.

All those numbers, *all* those facts belong in a news story. But note how two newswriting pros focus on a single element — the layoff announcement — and then parcel out other numbers carefully:

Amazon.com, the Internet site that defines e-commerce to millions of Americans, announced yesterday that it was cutting its workforce by 15 percent, or 1,300 employees.

"This was painful but very necessary for us to reach our goal of profitability in the fourth quarter," Warren Jenson, Amazon's chief financial officer, said in a conference call with reporters. That profitability, if achieved, would be on a "pro forma" operating basis, which doesn't take into account interest that must be paid on the company's $2 billion in debt.

Most of the staff cuts stem from the company's decision to shutter a distribution center in Georgia as well as its original customer-service center at its home base in Seattle . . .

Amazon, which started as a bookstore but now sells a broad range of products including wireless telephones and paper towels, also reduced its revenue estimates for 2001 to no more than $3.5 billion from $4 billion. Jenson cited the weak economy as the prime culprit.

Some evidence of a slowdown showed up in the fourth quarter. Amazon said today that its revenue for the period was $972 million . . . analysts had been predicting revenue or more than $1 billion . . . .

David Streitfeld,
Carrie Johnson
Washington Post[34]

MISHANDLING TIME ELEMENTS

We call them *news*papers for a reason: They deliver news. And that means, in major part, telling readers today what happened yesterday or last night.

Too many beginner newswriters ignore time elements in leads or misplace them.

In writing a *first-day lead*, you'll seldom go wrong by plunking the time element into your lead graf, next to the verb. Like this:

> The City Council voted last night to . . .

> Mayor Fred Smith said yesterday . . .

Do *not* misplace the time element like this:

> Mayor Fred Smith said five men would be charged with burglarizing City Hall in a press conference yesterday.

Writing *second-day leads* is trickier. Broadly, you need them in three situations:

#1. When competing media have informed your audience of the news *before* your paper hits the streets.

For example, if radio and television broadcast your college team's football game, and most everybody in dorms and barber shops listens or watches, you look pretty silly next morning with this *first-day lead*:

> Our Team defeated Their Team yesterday before 56,982 fans in Our Stadium.

Only by *advancing* the story through a *second-day lead* can you give readers the next day something new. For example, this:

> Inspired by a 14–0 victory over Their Team, Our Team heads into the second half of the season with high hopes of a conference title.
>
> "This win was an inspiration to Our Team," said coach Fred Smith after the shutout yesterday of Their Team.
>
> "We all think we have a good shot at the title," Smith said.

Note above the second-day lead is built on a present-tense first graf (team "heads") and drops the yesterday time element to the second graf.

#2. Another major need for second-day leads arises if you write for a weekly newspaper. Many news events you cover are even five or six days old by the time you get them into print.

Here's an example of how one weekly handles that (emphasis added):

> The alleged triggerman in the murder of Frank Arroyo in Middleburgh in May 1997 may once again face the death penalty.
>
> Judges from the state Supreme Court's Appellate Division *last week* threw out the guilty plea and sentence of (Fred Smith) who was sentenced in April 1999 to 25 years to life in prison for shooting Mr. Arroyo in a Middleburgh apartment in a murder-for-hire case . . . .
>
> David Avitabile
> *Cobleskill (N.Y.) Times-Journal*[35]

On another story, a *Times-Journal* writer decides the precise time element is irrelevant (emphasis added):

> If the Village of Cobleskill continues to grow as it has, it should have plenty of water for the next 20 years.
>
> Sewer capacity, though, could well be another story.
>
> Those are among the findings of a 35-page Village of Cobleskill Water Supply Study *just wrapped up* . . . .
>
> Patsy Nicosia
> *Cobleskill (N.Y.) Times-Journal*[36]

#3. Whether you're writing for a daily or weekly, a third major need for second-day leads arises on stories that continue over many day.

If lucky, you'll have new developments each day. For example, a horrible fire occurs Monday night in Beijing, and the *first-day lead* is just that — horrible fire occurs.

The *second-day lead* — published on Thursday morning — comes from an official announcement that advances the story:

> Beijing — Chinese investigators believe stray sparks from welding caused the blaze in a dance hall Monday night that killed 309 people, Xinhua news agency said Wednesday.
>
> Andrew Browne
> Reuters[37]

Sometimes, there aren't new developments — yet, public interest in the story remains high and, even though there's no "new news," your editors call for a story each day.

What to do? *Write with imagination!*

For example, a Washington Post reporter on a *three-day-old* double slaying shifts to a *mood piece*:

Hanover, N.H. — With authorities tight-lipped and a killer on the loose, the mystery surrounding the deaths of two beloved Dartmouth College professors is holding this quiet, cloistered town in watchful suspense.

Just three days ago, Half Zantop, 63, an earth science professor, and his wife, Susanne Zantop, 55, chair of the German Studies Department, were found lying in pools of blood on the floor of their home study. Police and the medical examiner's office here concluded they were murdered. Was their attacker a student in distress? A jealous associate, or a violent stranger? Friends and colleagues are loath to speculate, and investigators refuse to divulge even the most basic information, including how the couple died.

All police and prosecutors will say is that they have "no specific information" that anyone is targeted, and an arrest is not imminent.

Pamela Ferdinand
Washington Post[38]

Below, a writer adeptly revisits a slaying that's *more than three months old*:

Elberton, Ga. — Jimmy Webb, father, retiree and hobbyist, spent a lifetime collecting coins. In the end, it was the collection he took such pride in that cost him his life.

More than three months after the 67-year-old was found dead of gunshot wounds in his rural Elbert County home, his two 50-pound safes pried open and looted of $100,000 worth of collectible coins, investigators are no closer to catching his killer. A $5,000 reward posted by the governor's office and the Elbert County Commission has brought forth little useful information.

It's frustrating," said Darren Scarborough, the Elbert County sheriff's investigator . . . .

Stephen Gurr, *Athens (Ga.)*
Banner-Herald and Daily News[39]

Avoid writing empty second-day leads that are predictable:

Investigators probed the smoking ruins today of a (plane crash, house fire, you name it.)

Of course, investigators are probing ruins. The always do.

Investigators also always launch inquiries:

New Delhi — India is to conduct two inquiries into a guerrilla attack on an army camp in New Delhi's Red Fort in which three people died, an army spokesman said yesterday.

Narayanan Madhavan
Reuters[40]

MISHANDLING SOURCING

The lead in a university newspaper went like this:

An 18-year-old visitor was raped Monday night by a stranger in a Married Student Housing apartment.

The abject backdown the very next day in the same university newspaper went like this:

Campus police on Tuesday arrested an 18-year-old visitor on charges that she falsely reported being raped.

The lesson goes like this: *Always* source such stories to officials. It's easy:

An 18-year-old visitor *told police* she was raped Monday night . . . .

Or:

An 18-year-old visitor *reported being raped* Monday night . . . .

Such attribution in the initial story would have saved the newspaper enormous embarrassment.

Two sourcing problems seem to bother beginners:

- Sourcing simply is overlooked (which is inexcusable) or is deemed obtrusive and is withheld to "make the lead read better." As in the example above, sourcing need not be obtrusive.
- Conversely, some beginners throw unnecessary attribution into a lead and that, of course, *does* become obtrusive.

For example, this is way overdone:

An 18-year-old visitor told campus police Lt. Fred Smith and Sgt. Helen Waters she was raped Monday night . . . .

Note how *un*obtrusively attribution can be inserted (emphasis added):

In charge of the city schools by virtue of a court ruling, Mayor Stephen R. Reed *said yesterday* he will move quickly to establish a board of control, bring on better leadership and begin a top-to-bottom overhaul of a school district *he described* as deeply troubled.

John Luciew
Harrisburg (Pa.) Patriot-News[41]

Two years after states and tobacco companies reached the largest legal settlement in history, *health advocates give* the deal a mixed report card, *expressing disappointment* that it has not more radically changed cigarette marketing.

Scott Shane
Baltimore Sun[42]

Below, a skilled professional is close to pinning down a big story—but he doesn't quite have it. Note how he qualifies his first, second and third grafs, then cites a firm source in the fourth graf (emphasis added):

Four years *apparently* are enough for Rick Pitino.

The Boston Celtics head coach and team president *reportedly* told his players after a demoralizing 24-point loss to the Philadelphia 76ers Monday night that he would leave the team at the end of this season.

Pitino is in the fourth year of a 10-year contract that is one of the most lucrative coaching deals in the history of professional sports. He would leave nearly $30 million on the table *if he did indeed walk away.*

A *source very close to Pitino said yesterday* that the coach is frustrated with his inability to get the team to perform better . . .

Will McDonough
Boston Globe[43]

WRITING WITHOUT SPARKLE

Some in journalism (and I'm one) hold that there are no dull stories, only dull reporters.

Don't count Ben Deck among the dull. Look what he does with a routine vice squad raid:

Two Athens spas will wind up in court next week for rubbing their customers the wrong way.

After a month-long investigation, members of the Athens-Clarke County Police Department's drug and vice unit wrote citations against spas for violating the government ordinance on massage parlors.

Ben Deck
Athens (Ga.) Banner-Herald[44]

How a dull reporter would groan if assigned a story on children's backpacks! Not Diane Loupe:

Pound for pound, soldiers carry lighter loads than third-grader (Freddie Smith).

The 51-pound student at Dekalb County's Briar Vista Elementary School routinely carries a 21-pound backpack, or more than 40 percent of his body weight.

During Army infantry training, soldiers may carry backs up to only a third of their weight.

"At the end of the day, by back hurts," complained (Frank Jones), a 69-pound fifth-grader at Briar Vista who carries a 15-pound pack. "I just lay on my bed for like five minutes."

Chalk it up to an increased emphasis on learning, but schoolchildren today are hauling heavy loads.

Diane Loupe
Atlatnta-Journal Constitution[45]

Look at the drama here:

Anantnag, India — Peace, given a chance, lasted about 14 1/2 hours. India's unilateral cease-fire, an olive branch extended to militant groups waging war in Kashmir, began at 12:01 a.m. today in honor of Ramadan, Islam's holiest month. The tranquility endured until 2:30 p.m., when a booby trap blew apart an army vehicle, killing three soldiers and wounding a dozen more. . . .

Barry Bearak
New York Times [46]

Burma, East Timor — the soldiers of Battalion 745 greeted Sept. 21, their last full day in East Timor, by torching the barracks where they had spent the night.

As flames danced on the roofing timber of the cement buildings, the soldiers clambered into their trucks and rumbled away from the coastal town of Laga. In a few minutes, just a few miles down the road, the killing would begin.

Cameron W. Barr
Christian Science Monitor[47]

And, see what a little play on words will get you (and your *delighted* readers):

New York — The father gets bounced out of office after the economy tanks. Then the son bounces the bouncer to reclaim the seat in an era of prosperity.

George W. Bush wrote the original script. Now Andrew M. Cuomo wants to write the sequel.

Cuomo, 43, filed papers today to run in the Democratic primary for governor of New York, a job once held by his equally loquacious father Mario M. Cuomo. The current occupant is Gov. George E. Pataki (R), who ousted the elder Cuomo in 1994 and has said he will likely run for a third term . . . .

Christine Haughney
Michael Grunwald
Washington Post[48]

Even a seemingly routine business story can be made enormously reader-friendly:

Columbus — RC Cola's latest slogan is "We Make Beverages Exciting."

Tapping your toes yet?

Not many in the cola-drinking public are, either. Which helps explain why the Royal Crown Co.— one of the most innovative companies in Georgia history—is packing its concentrate mixers and quitting this town after nearly a century . . . .

Dan Chapman
Atlanta Journal-Constitution[49]

Now, any discussion of injecting sparkle into writing must contain a warning against excess. Don't stretch too far, as does this writer:

Carlisle — Cumberland County President Judge George E. Hoffer can officially consider himself a hanging judge.

He earned the right yesterday when the county Bar Association — following a tradition that dates to 1901 — presented an oil portrait of him to the county.

Most likely, it will end up hanging on a wall in Courtroom No. 1 in the county's main courthouse . . . .

Matt Miller
Harrisburg (Pa.) Patriot-News[50]

And, don't start guessing what many people might guess:

Many people might guess "Los Angeles" if asked where the recent sculpture showing in "Mise-en-Scene" originated. The exhibition, which opens today, comes to the California College of Arts and Crafts in San Francisco from the Santa Monica Museum of Art.

Kenneth Baker
San Francisco Chronicle[51]

Finally, don't overstate a story that's inherently dramatic; let compelling detail convey drama:

Terre Haute, Ind. — With the sting of a needle in his right leg, Timothy J. McVeigh was sedated, injected with poison and executed today by the government he so despised, a quiet end for the man who sent 168 people to their deaths in screams, flames and crushing concrete.

Mr. McVeigh, who was pronounced dead at 7:14 a.m. in the execution chamber of the federal prison here in Terre Haute, died unrepentant, without offering one word of regret for the bombing of the Alfred P. Murrah Federal Building in Oklahoma City on April 19, 1995. In fact, he did not say anything at all.

Relatives of his victims, both in the viewing room in the death chamber here and in a closed-circuit television broadcast of the execution in Oklahoma City, searched his gaunt, hollow-eyed face in his final minutes for some kind of apology or answer for the worst terrorist attack in United States history.

"We didn't get anything," said Paul Howell, 64, whose 27-year-old daughter, Karan Shepherd, was killed minutes after Mr. McVeigh parked a yellow rental truck loaded with a 7,000-pound homemade bomb just steps from the federal building, and walked away . . . .

Rick Bragg
New York Times[52]

SUMMARY

- Your readers live busy lives, and your challenge is to capture their attention with clear, forceful leads.
- Before writing leads, ask yourself which single most-important fact you must convey to readers and what interests you the most.
- If your interests and the perceived interests of readers are the same, that's your lead; if not, write to the readers' interests, not yours.
- Then review the Six-Finger Checklist (who, what, where, when, why and how) and factors affecting news judgment (such as impact, proximity, conflict.)
- Next, consider the type of material you must communicate; a financial story, for example, might best be told in a hard dollars-and-cents lead, whereas a "people story" might take a featurish lead.
- Inverted-pyramid leads are designed to quickly transmit the Five Ws and How—and permit editors to chop stories from the bottom and still preserve the most essential news elements.

- Unfortunately, inverted-pyramid leads restrict your creativity and, instead, force you into a sort of 1–2–3 lockstep writing style.
- Anecdotal leads permit colorful, personalized writing but often require you to subordinate spot-news developments, so this type lead is best restricted to featurish writing.
- Neck-of-vase leads use a single individual or incident to introduce readers gradually to a larger more complex issue.
- Contrast leads can build vivid word pictures if you carefully sketch differences — brotherly togetherness versus death, fairy tales of business success versus reality of failure.
- "Real-what" leads dig beneath the obvious and tell readers what really is behind the news.
- "Real-who" leads force you to decide whether a person by name is the lead or whether to focus on what the person does.
- To achieve special emphasis you can write "you" leads that invite reader involvement.
- Question leads also warm up your writing by inviting reader involvement — but rush to answer questions, which is the mission of journalism.
- Using dashes — like this — serves to emphasize material in a lead; so do colons.
- Many beginner newswriters have problems writing leads, particularly if they miss the news peg or deal out material too rapidly to be "digested" by readers.
- Other major problems include mishandling time elements, incorrect sourcing and writing without sparkle.

RECOMMENDED READINGS

Your best sources of great leads to study are major newspapers, including the *New York Times*, *New York Daily News*, *New York Post*, *Newsday*, *Boston Globe*, *Atlanta Journal-Constitution*, *Chicago Tribune*, *Los Angeles Times*, *Dallas Morning News*, and *Miami Herald*.

For annual compilations of great newswriting, see Roy Peter Clark and Christopher Scanlan, "America's Best Newspaper Writing" (Boston: Bedford/St. Martin's).

EXERCISES

1. Study today's *New York Times* (or another paper designated by your instructor). Find an example of an inverted-pyramid lead and, in about 250 words, comment on whether the story adequately answers the questions of the Six-Finger Checklist: who, what, where, when, why and how. Which of the factors affecting news value — prominence, impact, proximity, and so forth — is the news peg for this story? In your opinion, is this story structure suitable for the type of material being communicated?

2. Study today's *New York Times* (or another paper designated by your instructor.) Find an example of an anecdotal lead and, in about 250 words, discuss whether the writer is successful in creating an open, engaging and readable story. If so, why? If not, why? Are compellingly important facts subordinated to colorful, anecdotal writing? If so, would a first-day, hard-news lead have been better for the type of material being communicated?

3. Study today's *New York Times* (or another newspaper designated by your instructor) and locate a neck-of-the-vase lead. In about 250 words, discuss whether that style lead attractively personalizes the broader issue discussed in the article. Does the "neck" fully establish the personality of the person described? How well is the transition graf written? Is it well placed in the story? Does this writing structure delay hard news too long? Is this writing approach suitable for the information being communicated?

4. Study today's *New York Times* (or another paper designated by your instructor) and find an example of the contrast lead described in Chapter Five. Precisely which news elements are selected by the writer for the contrast? Is the contrast clearly stated? Is it described in vivid language? Does the writer select a meaningful contrast for a story peg or is the lead empty of meaning? Write your report in about 250 words.

5. Read today's *New York Times* (or another paper designated by your instructor.) Locate examples of *real-what leads*. In 250–300 words, discuss whether the writers properly contribute to reader understanding by digging beneath the *what* to find the *real what*. Do the writers maintain their balance and objectivity or does explaining the real what take them dangerously into subjective interpretation and analysis? Based on your study, do the writers walk the fine line between in-depth reporting and analytical writing?

NOTES

1. Adam Tanner, Reuters dispatch for morning papers, Nov. 26, 2000.

2. Cox News Service, dispatch for morning papers, Nov. 26, 2000.

3. "As Deer Hunters Take Aim, Officials Prepare for Complaints," Nov. 27, 2000, p. B–1.

4. Dispatch for Saturday papers, Dec. 30, 2000.

5. Dispatch for Saturday papers, Dec. 30, 2000.

6. "Accused Killer Faces Death Penalty," Dec. 30, 2000, p. A–1.

7. Dispatch for morning papers, Jan. 15, 2001.

8. "True Government Skeptic," Sept. 24, 2000, p. A–11.

9. "20 Years On Anger Ignites Against Khmer Rouge," Jan. 10, 1999, p. A–1.

10. Washington Post-Los Angeles Times News Service dispatch for morning papers, Nov. 19, 2000.

11. "Within Seconds, Lives Are Shattered," Dec. 28, 2000, p. B–7.

12. "Boo.com, Online Fashion Retailer, Goes Out of Business," May 19, 2000, p. C–4.

13. "Clinton, Saluting Kosovo Albanians, Urges Forgiveness," Nov. 24, 1999, p. A–1.

14. "Doves Marching," March 27, 2000, p. A–1.

15. "Fed Calls Risk of Slowdown No. 1 Threat," Dec. 20, 2000, p. A–1.

16. "Fed Gives Economy a Nudge," Feb. 1, 2001, p. A–1.

17. "Market May Be Economic Lifesaver," Feb. 1, 2001, p. D–1.

18. "Israel Drops Plan to Sell Air Radar to China Military," July 13, 2000, p. A–1.

19. "U.S. and North Korea Agree to Search for Missing," May 19, 1996, p. A–1.

20. "U.S. Official Hears Sudanese Tell of Slavery, Urges and End to Denial," Nov. 21, 2000, p. A–10.

21. "Fisherman Drowns at Baker Beach," Nov. 20, 2000, p. A–15.

22. Dispatch for morning papers, Sept, 18, 2000.

23. "A Question of Force for Israel," Oct. 2, 2000, p. A–1.

24. Dispatch for morning papers, Nov. 23, 2000.

25. "Parting the Ticket Thicket," Nov. 23, 2000, p. A–25.

26. Dispatch for morning papers, Nov. 22, 2000.

27. Dispatch for morning papers, Nov. 22, 2000.

28. "Few Major Natural Disasters in 2000 Have Kept Aid Down," Nov. 22, 2000, p. A–13.

29. "Dorchester Apartment Fire Kills 1, Leaves 120 Homeless," Nov. 23, 2000, p. D–3.

30. "East Timor's Birth Pains," Aug. 26, 2000, p. 29.

31. "Skier Guilty of Homicide," Nov. 18, 2000, p. A–2.

32. "Stricken Camden Is to Become a Ward of the State," July 17, 2000, p. A–1.

33. "Fire Chief Arrested in Pottsdown Child Pornography Probe," Nov. 22, 2000, p. B–2.

34. "Amazon.com Cutting 13,000 Jobs," Jan. 31, 2001, p. E–1.

35. "Murder Plea Nixed by Judges," July 26, 2000, p. A–1.

36. "Plenty of Water for Cobleskill," Aug. 23, 2000, p. A–1.

37. Dispatch for morning papers, Dec. 28, 2000.

38. "Murder of Two Professors Shakes Ivy League Town," Jan. 31, 2000, p. A–3.

39. "Few Clues in Elbert Case," Jan. 14, 2001, p. A–1.

40. Dispatch for morning papers, Dec. 25, 2000.

41. "Court Gives Reed Control," Dec. 16, 2000, p. A–1.

42. "Limited Success Seen in Tobacco Pact," Nov. 26, 2000, p. A–6.

43. "Pitino Seen Going at Season's End," Nov. 22, 2000, p. A–1.

44. "Health Spas Caught in Licensing Flap," March 17, 1998, p. B–1.

45. "Texts are Heavy Load for Schoolchildren," Oct. 19, 1998, p. C–1.

46. "India's Truce Over Kashmir Is Shattered As 3 More Die," Nov. 29, 2000, p. A–15.

47. Special reprint of series run in *Monitor* March 13, 14, 16, 17, 2000.

48. "Ex-Housing Chief Cuomo to Run for N.Y. Governor," Jan. 31, 2001, p. A–5.

49. "Goodby, Columbus," Dec. 31, 2000, p. C–1.

50. "President Judge Immortalized in Oil Painting," Dec. 16, 2000, p. A–3.

51. "Just Look at The Sculpture And There is Los Angeles," Jan. 27, 2001, p. B–1.

52. "McVeigh Dies for Oklahoma City Blast," June 12, 2001, p. A–1.

6

Lead Readers
Gently by the Hand

WELL, YOU'VE WRITTEN a brilliantly engaging lead that catches reader attention.

What now?

Now, you must pull your readers — gently but firmly — deeper into your writing, past that first graf and into the elaborating detail necessary to communicate the full story.

Pulling readers along with you requires weaving a whole fabric to tell your story, rather than simply writing stand-alone paragraphs and plugging them indiscriminately into a column of type.

In Chapter Six, we'll look at how you can weave such a fabric.

First, you need to plan your writing, roughing out, even if only generally and only in your mind, how you will structure your story.

Then, you must ensure logical flow of detail — fast enough to maintain reader attention but not so fast that you choke off readability. Careful use of linkage words will help tie one thought to another, one graf to another.

You'll need also to maintain tight control of the who, what, when and where elements of your story, giving readers clear warning anytime you switch from one to another.

Let's look at these and other writing tricks.

FIRST, THE STORY PLAN

When you've completed your lead, you'll be tempted to just bang away, plugging facts, color and other stuff into your story as it comes to mind. Don't.

Now is the moment to briefly but carefully take stock:

- After that first graf, where should your story go? Which facts, detail and color rank second in importance, and how will you pull readers out of the lead and into the second graf?
- Then, in order of descending importance, which facts and details must form the core of your third, fourth and subsequent grafs?
- Considering your audience and its likely interests, plus your material and its degree of complexity, will human-interest anecdotal writing work best or fact-filled, hard-news writing?

Blocking out your *story plan* on paper will be helpful. As you gain experience you'll be able to do this in your head while running to the keyboard.

After you've fashioned a lead, write toward concrete objectives.

OBJECTIVE #1:
FULFILL YOUR LEAD'S PROMISES

A lead is your promise to readers of things to come, facts to be revealed, a story to be told.

Start immediately revealing those facts and telling that story *in your second graf*.

Build logical flow directly out of the first graf and into the second.

Link first and second grafs with irresistible continuity, a tug and pull readers can't escape.

Note below a teaser lead that takes you down a rural road. Then comes a *linkage word* that takes you into the second graf — and into a house of horrors:

The 16-year-old runaway took police down a rural two-lane road that cuts deep into the forests of south Fulton County.

There, she said, in a modest ranch-style house far from the seedy urban bars and motels where girls like her often end up, she was sold for sex.

Now, a single graf of background, followed by smooth transition into the wider story — teenage prostitution:

For more than a year, the girl told police, she was forced — sometimes at gunpoint — to have sex for money with adult men and women. And many times, she said, the acts were captured on videotape.

In the latest effort to combat teenage prostitution in metro Atlanta, authorities on Friday arrested two residents of a house in the 5800 block of Butner Road. Atlanta police spokesman John Quigley said (Fred Smith), 29, and (Nancy Jones), 33, were charged with pimping, kidnaping, enticing a child for indecent purposes and cruelty to children . . . .

Stacy Shelton,
Alan Judd
Atlanta Journal-Constitution[1]

Reflect on your own reaction in reading that story above. Didn't the writing *require* you to continue out of the lead and into the second graf? And, didn't the second graf literally *force* you to go deeper.

That writing probably carried thousands — maybe *tens of thousands* — of readers deep into a compellingly important story, teenage prostitution. And that, of course, is why the writers wove an enticing fabric, complete with linkage words and thoughts.

Note below how skillfully a writer links first graf (killer) to second graf (the culprit):

Scientists at the University of Pennsylvania believe they have discovered what triggered the massive immune-system response *that killed* Jesse Gelsinger, 18, in a gene-therapy experiment at Penn in 1999.

The culprit, the Penn team has found, appears to be the protein coat of the disarmed cold virus, known as adenovirus, that was used to shuttle new genes into Gelsinger's liver . . . .

Huntly Collins
Philadelphia Inquirer[2]

Here, a writer cleverly creates linkage with a conversational technique ("Just ask" . . .) you might use in talking with a friend:

Forget love and war. All's fair these days in something even more crucial: finding a legal parking space in Boston.

Just ask (Fred Smith), who lords over a 25-car lot behind the Louis Boston clothing store in the Back Bay — Ground Zero of the city's parking crisis.

"I'd say at least once a week people are trying to pay me to let them park here," said (Smith), whose job is as clear as it is difficult: reserve spaces in the free lot for customers of the ultra high-end establishment. "It's ridiculous. I've actually had to chase people down the street who lied. They whine. They beg. They say they'll only be here a second" . . .

Raphael Lewis
Boston Globe[3]

Note that writers of the three examples above seized on a *human element* as the theme to achieve continuity. Readers will follow willingly a gripping tale about an identifiable person.

But how can you achieve linkage that pulls readers ahead on other, more impersonal stories? Like this (emphasis added):

Fresh evidence emerged yesterday that continuing weakness in the manufacturing sector *may have finally brought an end to the record expansion of the U.S. economy.*

For the sixth month running, factory production continued to shrink in January, even as inventory continued to build up in warehouses and the pace of new orders declined, *the National Association of Purchasing Management reported.*

As a result, the closely watched NAPM index fell to 42.7, it lowest point since the 1991 recession and a level that, in the past, has always coincided with an overall national recession.

Steven Pearlstein
Washington Post[4]

Note above how the writer, in a readable 25-word lead, emphasizes the news ("fresh evidence") and *characterizes its meaning* ("end to the record expansion.") The lead is tied to the second-graf mention of the source (the association report) and the reader is led by linkage words ("As a result") into elaborating detail in the third graf.

Below, a writer — in a *tight* 23-word lead — isolates the news development ("judge has declared") and *immediately* ties his second graf to that:

A federal *judge has declared* that a Los Angeles County ordinance that bars day laborers from soliciting work from passing drivers is unconstitutional.

In a 30-page opinion made public *Thursday*, U.S. District Judge George H. King found the law too broad, unduly vague and in violation of the 1st and 14th amendments . . . .

David Rosenweig
Los Angeles Times[5]

Below, a writer establishes rhythm in the first graf ("In Pennsylvania" . . . "In Cambridge" . . .), and achieves linkage with the second graf by maintaining that rhythm ("And in one of" . . .)

In Pennsylvania, researchers are documenting how religion keeps young people from drugs and delinquency. *In Cambridge*, professors are pondering how faith propels environmentalism and inner-city economic development.

And in one of the world's most religiously diverse laboratories — Southern California — scholars are visiting such sacred sites as Sikh gurdwaras, Chinese Buddhist temples and Armenian apostolic churches to scrutinize the powerful role that religion plays in the lives of new immigrants.

Now, the story widens:

Across the nation, scholars have begun to promote a new paradigm in academia: Religion matters . . .

Teresa Watanabe
Los Angeles Times[6]

OBJECTIVE #2:
MAINTAIN READING MOMENTUM

OK, your readers are on a roll. Your lead captures them and your linkage into the second graf pulls them along with you.

Now, *maintain that reading momentum.*

Four techniques are useful:

- Continue linking thoughts and paragraphs *deep* into your story.
- Insert quotes, always a reader draw.
- Inject authoritative detail, color and sources to create credibility in your writing.
- "Juice" your writing with anecdotes or humor.

CONTINUE LINKAGE

You'll note the linkage here between first and second grafs ("impressive resume" . . . "As a journalist and editor". . .):

Angola, La. — By any measure, Wilbert Rideau has *compiled an impressive résumé* during the last two decades.

As a journalist and editor, he has been honored with some of the most coveted prizes, including the George Polk Award and the Robert F. Kennedy Journalism Award. A collection of his reporting was published in 1992 and is now in its seventh printing . . .

Next comes further detail: Rideau works in radio and filmmaking and has been nominated for an Oscar. Now, deep in the story, shocking linkage:

Everything Mr. Rideau touches, it seems, turns to gold.

Everything, that is, except for the iron bars surrounding his spare dormitory at the Louisiana State Penitentiary here, where Mr. Rideau has entered the 38th year of a life sentence for one of the most vicious murders ever committed in Calcasieu Parish . . . .

Kevin Sack
New York Times[7]

Below, note linkage deep in a story on the trial of a man accused of forcing a teenager into prostitution — yes (more linkage), the girl mentioned in an earlier example:

It's a rare trial *exposing child prostitution* in Atlanta in which pimps put girls barely out of elementary school on the street to turn tricks, control them with death threats and ship them to cohorts in other states to keep families or friends from helping them.

It also exposes the unpleasant truths of solving crimes. The defendant is described in the case's police report as a well-known pimp of young girls. But homicide detectives looked on him as an ally in solving murders . . . .

Steve Visser
Atlanta Journal-Constitution[8]

Sometimes, a single word nicely links two grafs. For example, a *Chicago Tribune* foreign correspondent describes Kinshasha, Congo, as calm after the assassination of President Laurent Kabila. Then, linkage:

Yet that eerie calm belies the explosive problems that Kabila has bequeathed to one of Africa's largest and potentially richest nations — and to his eldest son, Joseph, who was tapped Wednesday as temporary leader of the country.

Paul Salopek
Chicago Tribune[9]

Other words that will link thoughts and paragraphs:

but	nevertheless	meanwhile
additionally	this	meantime
also	that	simultaneously
however	for example	of course
or	moreover	still

And (linkage, again!), note how easily I direct your attention to examples "above" and "below" in this book.

USE QUOTES AS READER DRAWS

A *Washington Post* correspondent takes readers on a trip:

San Cristobal, Mexico — Chickens strut along the dust-blown streets, pecking for scraps among newly laid paving stones. Goats and cows wander lazily down freshly poured concrete sidewalks, past smartly painted houses and shiny new utility poles carrying phone lines and electricity to a village not accustomed to such amenities.

Now that one of its native sons, Vicente Fox, is Mexico's president, and especially now that President Bush is coming for lunch next Friday, this little crossroads in central Mexico has been transformed like Cinderella, without the midnight deadline.

Great color, don't you agree? Still, something is lacking — reaction by local residents. A quote catches that beautifully:

"Everyone is walking around very pleased," said Ignacio Savedra, a local worker wearing a Los Angeles Dodgers baseball cap . . . .

Kevin Sullivan
Washington Post[10]

Note above how the third-graf position of that quote boosts the story along. No paraphrase of local sentiment in the writer's own words would have quite the same effect.

Another writer must sort out facts and testimony in the trial of a man accused of a double-murder — and catch the mood of the courtroom.

That mood is caught in a quote allegedly uttered by the accused killer as he pulled the trigger: "I don't care . . . I'll do my time."[11]

Should the writer have summarized testimony with, "The alleged killer said coldly that he didn't care about going to prison"? The "I-don't-care" quote wins hands down.

A 7-year-old girl is molested and slain. Her body is found after a massive search, and *San Francisco Chronicle* writers produce several thousand words that grip a city. Deep in the story they let the girl's aunt express the profound tragedy:

> "Little girls are supposed to laugh and play and run and giggle at the silliest little things," she said. "They're supposed to smile and twirl and chase pretty butterflies. One thing we can rest assured now is that Xiana is doing all these things and that she is safe and warm in heaven" . . . .
>
> Kevin Faganm, Stacy Finz,
> Matthew B. Stannard,
> Michael McCabe
> *San Francisco Chronicle*[12]

Peter Sleeth of the *Portland Oregonian* has a gripping tale about a former police officer whose son is killed by another policeman. Step by step, readers follow the father's investigation of the tragedy — and his return home with a friend to tell his wife.

Writer Sleeth builds the tension:

> As they drove down Canyon road and onto U.S. 26, past the Portland Zoo toward the city, tears worked their way out. How to tell MaryAnn? God, he wondered, how do I say this?
>
> Sitting at her computer when Cal walked in the door, MaryAnn knew instantly their world had collapsed. It showed in her husband's every feature. Cal lost track of his rehearsed lines.
>
> Then, the quote:
>
> He just blurted it out: "Adam is gone. Adam is gone" . . .
>
> Peter Sleeth
> *Portland Oregonian*[13]

It's early in George W. Bush's presidency, and reporters are trying to describe his program *and catch the essence of the man.* In a story on his income tax plan, *Washington Post* reporters describe the President's argument that a tax cut will stimulate the economy. Then, several hundred words deep in the story, this:

"A warning light is flashing on the dashboard of our economy," Bush said. "We just can't drive on and hope for the best" . . . .

Mike Allen, Glenn Kessler
Washington Post [14]

Note the quote above lets Bush explain the rationale for tax cuts and, for readers, lets his picturesque language say something about the man.

Deep in a story about education reform, a reporter lets a school superintendent explain in his own words just how complicated reform will be:

"You are not going to make life better for kids in school with just a silver bullet program," (The superintendent) said at a news conference in Rockville. "You're going to make life better for kids in school with a good teacher in a supportive environment, with enough time to do their job and reasonable numbers of children focused on academic achievement."

Manuel Perez-Rivas
Washington Post [15]

Lessons:

- *Perfect* quotes come along infrequently but when they do, put aside your writer's ego, step back *and let the quotes tell the story*.
- The real words of real people often inject drama into your writing better than can your paraphrase or descriptive language.
- Inserted with care in early grafs, at midpoint of a story and near the end, quotes will boost reading momentum.

INJECT DETAIL TO CREATE CREDIBILITY

What does your reporting and writing ask readers to do? *Believe you.*

And, in turn, what do readers ask? *Why?*

You answer readers' "why?" by presenting facts that support the central thrust of your article.

You let readers "see" what you have seen with carefully drawn color descriptive.

You build credibility in your writing by citing authoritative sources.

Writing based in fact and colorful descriptive plus authoritative sources will maintain reading momentum, pulling readers along and not letting go.

For example, *Chicago Tribune* reporters write about special-interest lobbyists showering state officials with gifts. Readers are drawn deeper and deeper into the story by stunning facts laid out one by one: a $349.52 dinner for one official, "thousands of dollars" spent on cocktail parties, a $217 fruit basket for an official's wife, lobbyist spending more than $1 million in one year, calendars handed out to lawmakers—"a pocket version worth $7.21 and a wall version, which cost $5.32."[16]

Inescapable conclusion: These *Tribune* writers have the facts locked up. Their credibility soars, and no reader need ask why they should be believed.

Another *Tribune* story addresses late arrivals and departures by airliners, and the hard facts are clear:

At O'Hare International airport, for example, considered a key link in the nation's aviation system, only 48 percent of the more than 2,400 daily flights arrived within 15 minutes of their scheduled arrival time. Nationwide, only 62.8 percent of the industry's flights arrived on time — considered by the U.S. Department of Transportation to mean within 15 minutes of their scheduled arrival . . . .

John Schmeltzer,
Jon Hilkevitch
Chicago Tribune[17]

Sometimes, of course, you'll not have all the facts. Nevertheless, you can build credibility in your writing and maintain reading momentum by explaining frankly what you *don't* know.

For example, President Laurent Kabila of Congo is assassinated by a bodyguard and the official account of what happened is full of holes. A *Los Angeles Times* writer explains:

(The) account, though allegedly firsthand, leaves many questions unanswered.

It fails to shed light on why a once-honorable bodyguard with no apparent history of mental disorder would suddenly decide to undertake an inevitably suicidal mission alone. It does not explain why several residents in the vicinity of the palace attested to hearing up to 30 minutes of gunfire from within the presidential compound around the time Kabila was known to have been shot. It does not answer why the other bodyguards would have opted to kill the assassin rather than capture him for interrogation . . .

Ann M. Simmons
Los Angeles Times[18]

A reporter has a moving story — Sri Lanka rebels are sending teenage girls into combat. Here is the setup:

Palali, Sri Lanka — Renuka, a 13-year-old wisp of a girl, said she is afraid she will be scolded because she chose not to swallow her cyanide capsule.

Recruited at age 11 by ethnic Tamil rebels to fight for a separate state, she lay wounded on the front lines of Sri Lanka's civil war six days ago . . . .

But rather than kill herself to avoid capture as her superiors in the Liberation Tigers of Tamil Eelam had ordered, Renuka said she wrapped her bloody chest in a sarong and waited for the soldiers from the Sri Lankan Army. "I didn't want to die," she said in a thin, quavering voice during an interview at an army detention camp here. "And I'm not going back to the L.T.T.E. They will threaten me and scold me and ask why I didn't take the cyanide" . . . .

Another rebel girl, Malar, also 13, is interviewed. Still, the reporter isn't sure there is *proof* of girls being enlisted as rebel fighters, so this:

The girls' stories could not be independently verified, though their wounds and scars were consistent with their accounts, as were the circumstances of their confinement. Army officials, happy to score propaganda points against the Tigers, readily agreed to allow Renuka, still in their custody, to be interviewed. Her last name was withheld by The New York Times out of concern that the rebels would punish her for turning against them.

A district magistrate in Jaffna permitted an interview with Malar, who unlike Renuka is still a true Tiger believer. Captured in July, she is now in judicial custody and is incarcerated in the rundown jail in Jaffna. Officials stood listening to both interviews.

One other thing also suggests that the Tigers are using child soldiers: the youthfulness of the rebel dead found after a Sept. 3 battle here on the Jaffna peninsula. Six of the 36 dead rebels whose bodies were picked up by the Sri Lanka Army and returned to the Tigers appeared to have been girls between ages, 12 and 16, said an international official who inspected them . . . .

Celia W. Dugger
New York Times[19]

Lessons:

- Precise factual detail and color descriptive inject *believability* into your writing. Note the difference between asking readers to believe an official was given a free "expensive" dinner and reporting the dinner cost "$349.52."

- No journalist is required to have all the answers. Every journalist, however, *is* required to explain which answers are missing — and why. Note again how writers of the examples above took readers behind the scenes in Congo and Sri Lanka to explain sourcing.

"JUICE" YOUR WRITING

Nothing maintains story momentum like a sparkling anecdote or a bit of humor inserted carefully to tug readers ahead.

Waugh said (after an illness) he was losing his concentration, but denied that drink was to blame. He had nine wine cellars in his home and apparently rejected a doctor's suggestion that he go easy on the claret.

He also never bothered to give up his 40-year habit of chain-smoking, despite having only one lung. Waugh lost the other in 1958 while doing his National Service in Cyprus when he attempted to unblock a jammed Browning submachine gun while standing in front of the weapon and shaking the muzzle. He took six bullets in the chest, losing several ribs, a lung and his spleen, which he nonetheless continued to vent against the deserving pompous . . . .

Majorie Miller
Los Angeles Times[20]

Deep in a rollicking obituary on Auberon Waugh, a British editor and writer "who made a career out of being wickedly funny — and sometimes just plain wicked," a writer juices things along with this:

Those anecdotes (and Miller's clever writing) boosted me along until I finished every word of that obituary.

Terrance Gainer, controversial No. 2 officer in the District of Columbia police force, is profiled. The story moves — slowly — through departmental politics and details *about* the man. But no picture *of* the man emerges. Then this:

Gainer, the son of a milkman and a lover of fine wines and mystery books, is of average build and serious mien. He has a push-broom mustache and a close-clipped fringe of salt-and-pepper hair. He can be brusque but said he does not see himself as harsh, just forthright. "I don't have any problem calling you in and saying, 'You haven't done your job. Here's what you need to do, and here's how you need to comport with what . . . I want.'"

He seems somewhat perplexed that he is controversial . . . .

Petula Dvorak, Allan Lengel,
Arthur Santana
Washington Post[21]

Reconstructing a dramatic moment can add momentum to your writing flow.

For example, as George W. Bush and Vice President Al Gore fought it out in the 2000 election, Gore conceded defeat, then retracted his concession. Two *New York Times* pros caught the moment:

> . . . after a flurry of phone calls, Mr. Gore placed his second call of the evening to Mr. Bush, this one at about 2:30 a.m. central time. In a holding room with family members and dozens of exhausted, red-eyed aides listening, Mr. Gore told Mr. Bush that circumstances had changed in the last 45 minutes, that the race was now too close to call, that there would be an automatic recount in Florida, and that he was going to wait it out.
>
> "You mean to tell me, Mr. Vice President, you're retracting your concession?" Mr. Bush asked, his tone incredulous, according to one aide. Mr. Bush, after all, had already begun preparing his victory remarks, and the crowd in front of the white-draped stage at the state Capitol was well into a wild celebration.
>
> "You don't have to be snippy about it," Mr. Gore responded, according to several of those present . . . .
>
> Kevin Sack, Frank Bruni
> *New York Times*[22]

Note above how tightly the writers attribute the you-see-it-now detail ("according to one aide" . . . "according to several of those present"). *Tell readers how you know.*

Capturing even a routine moment can add zest to your writing. Two *New York Times* pros win an exclusive interview with President Bush shortly after his election. Many hundreds of words are devoted — rightly — to what Bush says about policy and politics. Then:

> Throughout the conversation, Bush looked relaxed. He was clearly enjoying a day of puttering around his ranch, brewing coffee for visitors and interrupting the conversation repeatedly to admonish his two friendly but occasionally disobedient dogs, Spot and Barney. But he leaned forward and turned intent when the subject turned to his choice for attorney general, former Sen. John Ashcroft (R-Mo.), a religious conservative who he said he knew "could end up being a lightning rod" for criticism . . . .
>
> David E. Sanger,
> Frank Bruni
> *New York Times*[23]

Note above how nicely the writers move you out of the word-picture of Bush relaxing and back into more substantive matters. (The transition starts with, "But he leaned forward" . . .)

An AP writer interviews a survivor of a ship sinking that killed nearly 800 persons long ago. The survivor has difficulty talking about it . . .

The 1942 disaster so haunted (Smith), now 78, that he spoke of it only rarely over the decades. He never told his first wife about it, through 16 years of marriage.

"This event in my life has been one of the worst. So remembering it . . . ."

Stoliar pauses, collects his emotions.

"I tried for so many years to forget it."

He tries to explain.

"You feel like you did something wrong by surviving. It comes back to the question, 'Why me?' And of course there is no answer to that"

. . . .

The Associated Press[24]

Understand the man's trauma? Of course, you do — and that anecdote helped you, didn't it?

One writing device available for maintaining reader momentum is posing a question to readers deep in a story. For example, a writer for *Investor's Business Daily* goes on . . . and on . . . about money being made in e-commerce. My attention is caught by this:

Who are the players in this explosive market?[25]

That question involves me personally because it addresses what I had been wondering about: Are real people behind this industry and if so, who are they?

OBJECTIVE #3:
KEEP WHO, WHAT, WHERE, WHEN STRAIGHT

Think of the challenges you thrust at readers when you write about people they don't know, in places they've never been, on issues they don't understand.

How can readers sort it all out?

They can't — unless you do it for them.

Sorting out news complexities requires you to dole out in logical, understandable ways the key elements of any story — who, what, where, when. Lose control of those elements in your writing and you'll lose readers.

HANDLING "WHO"

Your first challenge is to ensure smooth flow of "who" identifiers as you lead readers out of your first graf and into the second.

Take particular care when more than one person is involved:

Durham prosecutors are reviewing their much-criticized method of going after *criminals the law labels habitual felons.*

District Attorney Jim Hardin Jr. and Assistant District Attorney Jim *Dornfried*, who specializes in prosecuting *such repeat offenders*, confirmed Friday that a review is under way.

John Stevenson
Durham (NC) Herald-Sun[26]

Note above how open and understandable is the linkage: *Durham prosecutors* ties to *Hardin* and *Dorfried*; *habitual felons* ties to *repeat offenders*.

Washington — Former President Clinton's library foundation received an estimated $450,000 in donations from Denise Rich, the former wife of a fugitive financier who received an 11th-hour pardon from Clinton, *a Democratic source says.*

The disclosure late Friday came hours after a congressional committee investigating Clinton's pardon of Marc Rich decided to subpoena records from Clinton's presidential library fund.

The Democratic source, who spoke on condition of anonymity, said . . . .

The Associated Press[27]

Take special care with "who" references separated by intervening material:

Note above that AP's writer uses the same identifier in the second reference — *Democratic source*. A reader can tie that back to *Democratic source* in the lead graf and easily follow the flow of the story.

Once you've identified a "who" element *stick with the identifier*. AP's writer would have been mistaken to switch in subsequent references to "informant," "high-ranking official," "Washington insider," "anonymous source" or other synonyms that would force readers to stop and puzzle out who was meant.

Limited switches in identifiers will work, of course:

Theo Ratliff will undergo surgery on his fractured right wrist tomor- row and will miss at least another month, the 76ers said yesterday.

The 6-foot–10-center has been out since scoring 14 points in the Sixers' loss to the Houston Rockets on Feb. 7 . . . .

Ratliff had been wearing a light

cast with the hope that his stress fracture would heal on its own . . . .

Ashley McGeachy
Philadelphia Inquirer[28]

Maintaining control of "who" sometimes looks more complicated than it is. For example, an AP writer must sort out for readers a prison escape by a convict whose father is charged with providing the getaway car. Easy:

. . . investigators believe the *elder* (Smith), 61, furnished the money to buy the Suburban . . . .

The *younger* (Smith), 38, was

serving a life sentence for paying a hit man $2,000 to murder his wife . . . .

The Associated Press[29]

HANDLING "WHAT"

In handling "what" you don't have an identifiable person to serve as linkage to pull readers deeper into your story.

Rather, you have an *issue*, a *development*, a *plan*, an *agreement*, and pulling readers ahead can be tricky.

Just remember one rule: Identify the "what" early in your story, then stick with that identifier throughout.

Here's how an AP pro does that:

Greensboro, N.C. — Passing a *patient's bill of rights* that has garnered support from both Republicans and Democrats would be an affirmation of the bipartisanship that President Bush is seeking, Sen. John Edwards says.

Edwards, D-N.C., visited Greensboro on Friday to . . . discuss *the Bipartisan Patient Protection Act* he and Republican Sen. John McCain of Arizona introduced this week.

Now, subsequent grafs:

Edwards called *the bill* a workable compromise . . . .

The bill would guarantee . . . .

Edwards said *the bill* has more . . . .

The Associated Press[30]

Don't worry that repetition of identifiers — the bill . . . the bill . . . the bill — is monotonous and must be avoided. It's *clarity of transition* from one graf to another you must seek, and if repetition ensures that, repetition is OK.

Nevertheless, you can use synonyms *if the linkage is unmistakably clear*:

Washington — President Bush on Monday moved to speed up the effect of the *tax cut* he will propose this week . . . .

Prospects for a *big tax cut* have improved dramatically in recent weeks . . . .

"This is the right size *plan*. It is the right approach. And I'm going to defend it mightily," he said.

The plan which would cost . . . .

James Gerstenzang,
Janet Hook
Los Angeles Times[31]

This varied usage also works because the transition is unmistakably clear:

Los Angeles teachers and the district on Tuesday trumpeted a *far-reaching contract settlement* that averts a threatened strike and gives teachers more than 15% in pay and benefit increases.

The three-year agreement, which

is expected to get school board approval . . . .

If ratified by the union membership and the board, *the pact* will . . . .

Doug Smith
Los Angeles Times[32]

So far, we've looked at single-element "what" factors — a bill, a tax cut. What if a story blossoms with *multiple* "what" elements? Proceed very carefully.

For example, Keith Bradsher of the *New York Times* has a story about the troubles of a car battery manufacturer and notes the company's problems "draw further attention to business practices in the auto and auto parts industries." Bradsher writes carefully that (emphasis added) the car battery problems "coincide with the *separate controversy*" over faulty car tires.[33]

A *San Francisco Chronicle* writer reports a leading utility is in financial trouble. But there is more, and it's so complicated that the writer breaks out additional "what" factors in dash matter:

Also yesterday:

—Reports circulated that an in-

dependent audit of the utilities' books . . .

—Shares of the parent companies gained ground . . .
—Federal regulators ordered . . .

David Lazarus
San Francisco Chronicle[34]

It's not pretty, that dash matter. It's not poetry. But it sure helps readers sort out multiple and very complicated "what" factors.

HANDLING "WHERE"

Many news stories require switches in *geographic locators* — the
"where" elements.

Write those switches carefully, and you'll lead readers to the destination, the end of your story. Make switches carelessly, and you'll get
everybody lost.

Below, a writer leads readers gently by the hand through multiple
switches in location. First, we're in Libya:

Tripoli, Libya — A smiling Moam-
mar Khadafy warmly embraced a
Libyan acquitted in the 1988
Lockerbie bombing, who returned
home yesterday, shaking his fist in
victory and chanting "God is great."

Now, a second-graf switch in "where":

In the Netherlands, the other
Lockerbie defendant, a Libyan intelligence agent, considered
whether to appeal his conviction for
multiple murders in the downing of
Pan Am Flight 103.

Now, back to Libya:

Under renewed scrutiny for links
to terrorism after the verdicts, *Libya
said* it would consider paying com-
pensation to the families of the 270
victims of the bombing . . .

Yet another switch, back to the Netherlands:

*A Scottish court sitting in the
Netherlands* sentenced Abdel Bas-
set Ali al-Megrahi to life imprison-
ment, with no possibility of review
for 20 years, for planting the device
that exploded in the plane over
Lockerbie, Scotland . . . .

Once again, a switch:

Lamen Khalifa Fhimah, acquitted and freed by the court, *arrived in Libya from the Netherlands* yesterday, to be greeted by a crowd of relatives and friends at Tripoli's airport who chanted: "Justice has triumphed! Down with America" . . . .

Sarah el Deeb
The Associated Press[35]

That's five (count them, *five*) switches in five grafs. But the writing so smoothly signals each switch that readers easily follow.

Note how nicely a Reuters reporter leads readers from inside to outside a conference hall:

Clinton, speaking to about 10,000 people at a conference . . . received a lukewarm welcome when he was introduced . . . . A majority of the attendees stood and applauded, but many sat silently in their seats. *Outside*, a dozen protestors carried signs attacking the ex-president . . . .

Jeff Franks
Reuters[36]

Below, a *Boston Globe* writer signals a geographic switch *and* a switch in story scope. The lead is focused on a local university:

The hope that some common pain drugs may prevent or delay the ravages of Alzheimer's disease has prompted a massive, seven-year clinical trial being launched today at *Boston University School of Medicine* and three other US medical centers.

Now, in the third graf, a switch to nationwide scope:

Nationwide, the study aims to recruit 2,600 volunteers aged 70 or older, with a family history of Alzheimer's, who will be randomly assigned to take the anti-inflamma- tory drugs or a placebo for seven years . . . .

Richard Saltus
Boston Globe[37]

A *Chicago Tribune* writer focuses on a local motorist consumed by road-rage who causes a fatal accident by chasing down another driver after a fender-bender accident. In the fourth graf, a switch in "where" and story scope:

In Illinois and around the nation, police say they are seeing an in- crease in accidents involving motorists who try to chase down other

cars they feel have broken the law.   *Chicago Tribune*[38]
          Rogers Worthington

The obvious is worth emphasis: You can lead readers through multiple geographic switches *if*, when you conclude one graf and intend to switch the "where" in the next, you *open the next graf* with the switch signal (as in, "In Illinois" . . . "Nationwide" . . . "Outside" . . .)

Handling "When"

Here's a simple (and frequently violated) rule: state the time element in your lead and you need not repeat it.

That is, do *not* do this:

The City Council voted 6–4 *last night* to . . .

With its vote *last night*, the Council . . .

Once is enough unless you introduce another time element after your lead. Then, you must write with all the care accorded switches in "who," "what," and "where."

Note the careful handling of these multiple switches in time element:

For years, (Mary Smith) had the habit of paying her taxes at the last possible moment. *In September* 1999, she waited a moment too long.

Early one morning that month, on the day she thought that her Main Line home and nearby office building in Narberth were about to be sold at a Montgomery County sheriff's auction, (Smith) went to Norristown to settle up.

But she was two days late. Both her home and the office building had already been sold—auctioned off to real estate bargain hunters for a small fraction of their actual value, which a local Realtor pegs around $1.4 million.

Now, (Smith's) family and lawyer are arguing that the 74-year-old woman should not be deprived of almost everything she owns just for misreading a date on official warning notices . . .

    Patrick Kerkstra
    Philadelphia Inquirer[39]

"When" switches should be written with clear up-front signals, at the *opening* of paragraphs:

Oxnard — *Six days later*, (Jane Smith) was still wishing she hadn't looked.

Last week, hunkered down in the Hueneme High School cafeteria after a young gunman took a student hostage, (Jane) stole a glance at the drama just as an Oxnard SWAT officer shot and killed Richard "Midget" Lopez.

On Tuesday, the first day school was back in session since the incident, the 14-year-old was trying to wipe away the memories of the gunfire, the blood, and Lopez as he collapsed on the campus quad . . . .

Katie Cooper,
Jenifer Ragland
Los Angeles Times[40]

Deep in a lengthy story, you can keep time elements straight with a variety of signals: Earlier . . . In the meantime . . . Meanwhile . . . In recent years . . . In days past . . . Shortly before . . . Shortly afterward.

However, note: in their preferred usage, "meanwhile" and "meantime" mean *during the intervening time* or *interval*. But, they're also used to mean *at the same time*. So, understand that "meanwhile" and "meantime" used to signal switches in time elements may mean different things to different readers.

In most news stories, the time element need not be terribly precise, and it's enough to report the city council voted "last night."

However, if the council debated through the night, it's news the vote didn't come "until 4:52 a.m., just before dawn broke."

Raphael Lewis of the *Boston Globe* decides — rightly, I think — that precise time elements are necessary for this story:

In what Boston police are calling the most violent 24-hour period of the year, one man was killed and five people were injured in four separate stabbings Friday and Saturday . . . .

In the most serious violence, a 38-year-old Mattapan man was stabbed *around 11 p.m. Friday* on the staircase of his home . . . .

About 30 minutes later, two groups of teenagers spilled out of a house party . . . and engaged in a melee that left three youths, ages 18, 17, and 16, with stab wounds . . . .

At 2:10 a.m., police found a man with a knife wound in his back . . . .

As dawn broke, busy detectives . . .

Raphael Lewis
Boston Globe[41]

And onward flows the terrible chronology . . . .

OBJECTIVE #4: TRANSLATE MEANING CLEARLY

You keep up on happenings in Mississippi, don't you? You're up to date on Yugoslavia?

No? Well, not everyone does, and for all who don't, two writing pros translate — characterize — developments in both places (emphasis added):

Jackson, Miss. — Stepping into *one of the most volatile issues of the day*, six of Mississippi's eight statewide elected officials have stood together to declare their support for a new state flag.

After Gov. Ronnie Musgrove on Friday signed legislation setting an April 17 referendum to decide whether to retire the state's *controversial flag*, Secretary of State Eric Clark, Attorney General Mike Moore, Treasurer Marshall Bennett, Insurance Commissioner George

Dale and Agriculture Commissioner Lester Spell joined the governor in declaring their intentions to vote for the new flag design.

The present flag, with its use of the Confederate battle emblem, has ignited passions like few other issues in recent years. So, the spectrum of officials taking such a public stand against it was remarkable . . . .

Reed Branson
Scripps Howard News Service[42]

Belgrade, Yugoslavia — Conceding a *stunning defeat* in Serbian parliamentary elections, a close aide to deposed leader Slobodan Milosevic said yesterday that a phase in the

Socialists' era was over but that the party would try to make a new beginning.

Katrina Kratovac
The Associated Press[43]

Note AP's writer uses just two words — "stunning defeat" — to characterize the election. On the flag story, Scripps Howard's writer devotes more wordage, including the entire third graf, to translate meaning for readers.

Lesson: It's a complicated world out there, and your busy readers need your help in understanding *the why and how* — the deeper meaning — of news developments.

HELP THEM ON LAW AND SCIENCE

Two sectors of newswriting particularly demanding your translation are science and law.

On law stories, avoid getting wrapped up in legalisms and, instead, go directly to basic meaning. Here is how to do that:

Washington — The Supreme Court handed *a major tactical victory* to the Microsoft Corporation today when it rejected the government's pleas to hear the appeal of its landmark antitrust case immediately and instead returned the proceeding to a lower court.

The decision gives Microsoft greater breathing room to pursue its appeals, relieves the company of any pressure to return any time soon to the bargaining table and, in the absence of a settlement, could have the effect of prolonging a final court judgment by a year or longer . . . .

Stephen Labaton
New York Times[44]

Here is CNNfn's translation of the same court decision:

New York (CNNfn) — The United States Supreme Court declined the government's request to hear Microsoft's appeal of the federal and state antitrust case against the company Tuesday, instead sending it to a lower court.

The decision is seen as a procedural win for Microsoft . . . .

CNNfn[45]

In science writing, you must translate the language of science for us ordinary mortals who don't understand it. Use illustrations we *do* understand (emphasis added):

The human genome, the sum of all genetic material encased in nearly every cell of the human body, is very, very long — at least three billion chemical letters long, *as many letters as you would find in a thousand copies of an entire Sunday issue of The New York Times.*

The human genome is pithy. The English alphabet has 26 letters; the Russian, 33 letters; and the Japanese, 1,850 symbols. *Yet, with just four distinct characters at its disposal, four nucleic acid bases, the human genome has given rise to the creators of every language uttered, every ballad sung, every Pokémon card traded.*

Natalie Anger
New York Times[46]

Biologists have *for the first time* deciphered the full genetic programming of an animal, a *landmark achievement* both in its own right and as a *milestone* toward understanding the human genome.

The animal is a microscopic roundworm known as *Caenorhabditis elegans* and used in laboratories throughout the world as a means to explore biology at the genetic level. *Its genome, or full DNA, has now been found to consist of 97 million chemical units and is predicted to contain 19,099 genes. If printed in ordinary type, the DNA sequence would take up 2,748 pages of this* newspaper.

Nicholas Wade
New York Times[47]

Frankly, I had never heard of *Caenorhabditis elegans*, and when biologists deciphered their genetic programming I was happy that Nicholas Wade characterized the meaning as a "landmark achievement" . . . a "milestone."

TRANSLATE POLITICAL NUANCES, TOO

Like law and science, American politics has its subtleties, which you must catch and translate.

Sometimes, full explanation is needed:

Washington — President Bush pitched cooperation across party lines to congressional Democrats and Republicans on Friday . . . .

Bush carried his effort to "change the tone" in the nation's capital and manage political disputes "in a way that respects one another" to a private gathering of Senate Democrats in Washington and a get-together of House-Senate Republicans in Williamsburg, Va.

Bush's charm offensive reflects not only his personal strength but also a cold political calculus. For the president to get anything through Congress — including features of the $1.6 trillion tax cut plan he proposes to Congress next week — *he must enlist Democrats* . . . .

Stewart M. Powell
Hearst Newspapers[48]

Sometimes, just a few words suffice — as when Rev. Jesse Jackson acknowledges an extramarital affair, and a key political question is whether his black political base will desert him:

A subdued Rev. Jesse Jackson emerged Sunday from three days of seclusion after admitting he fathered a child in an extramarital affair, taking to the pulpit to praise his wife before 3,200 parishioners at a Far South Side church.

"After 38 years, five children later, Jackie, we're still here. I love you so much," Jackson said looking at his wife and two of their children as the Salem Baptist Church congregation *roared with approval* . . . .

Mickey Ciokajlo
Chicago Tribune[49]

Even when you must delay full translation to deeper in your story, a few words in your lead can snag reader attention for what is to come:

Sacramento — A push by Indian gambling proponents to open casinos in urban areas of California could present a *sticky political situation* for Gov. Gray Davis.

Julie Tamaki
Los Angeles Times[50]

HANDLE NUMBERS GENTLY

Understand this about numbers: Many readers, and not just those with "math fright," have difficulty absorbing their true meaning.

Guidelines for newswriters:

- Although your reporting may produce notebooks full of numbers, use only those *crucial* to your story.
- Parcel out numbers carefully, feeding them to readers at a pace they likely can handle.
- Whenever possible, express a number also in percentage.
- *Always* characterize the meaning of a number.

For example, former President Clinton agrees to pay (and charge U.S. taxpayers) $85 to $90 a square foot for an office suite in New York City. Is that a lot? It's an "eye-popping $650,000" annually, says the *New York Daily News*.[51]

An Internet-based company loses $7.6 billion in one year, and a *Philadelphia Inquirer* writer translates that:

That's about as much as ExxonMobil or Microsoft earns in a year. It's enough to run the City of Philadelphia for three years.

Joseph N. DiStefano
Philadelphia Inquirer[52]

Do you know how much power is in one kilowatt-hour? *Los Angeles Times* writers don't assume you do:

Under a plan announced by (Gov.) Davis, the state would ... buy power from the wholesalers at a rate of 5.5 cents per kilowatt-hour .... One kilowatt-hour, which currently costs 30 cents on California's open

market, *is enough to power a computer and monitor for seven hours.*
Nancy Vogel, Bob Drogin,

Nicholas Riccardi
Los Angeles Times[53]

Note above the comparison — 5.5 cents versus 30 cents. Good rule: In newswriting, a stand-alone figure often is meaningless; compare it to another number.

A New Jersey politician spends $34 million on an election. What does that compare to?

A rumpled Wall Street mogul named Jon Corzine made political history of a sort in June by plunking down a record $34 million of his own fortune to win the Democratic primary for the U.S. Senate in New Jersey. Corzine's investment worked out to *an astonishing $141 per vote.* By contrast, Bill Clinton won the presidency in 1996 at *the bargain rate of $2 per vote.*

Paul Taylor
Mother Jones[54]

Expressing numbers in percentages can translate true meaning for readers.

For example, a company plans to lay off 450 workers. On a workforce of 25,000 that's a negligible percentage. But it's quite something else on a smaller workforce:

Bridgestone/Firestone Inc. plans to lay off 450 workers at its Decatur plant — about *25 percent* of the plant's workforce — and cut tire production at its plant in La Vergne, Tenn., and Oklahoma City for 28 days, company officials said Tuesday.

Melita Marie Garza
Chicago Tribune[55]

Note how this writer deals out numbers in manageable batches 'and establishes context and meaning with percentages:

New York — AMC Entertainment Inc. said yesterday that it would lower the curtain on as many as 548 screens, or about 80 of its 186 theaters . . . .

The fourth-largest U.S. theater operator, based in Kansas City, Mo., said . . . it had targeted 307 mostly underperforming screens for disposal by early 2004 and is putting an additional 241 on "watch" for possible closure.

The 548 screens represent 20 percent of AMC's total of 2,802. The 80 theaters represent 43 percent of the total . . . .

Jonathan Stempel
Reuters[56]

Whenever possible, relate numbers to something all readers understand. And all understand their food costs:

Washington — Here's something to be thankful for: A traditional Thanksgiving Day dinner will cost less this year than last, a farm group says.

A dinner for 10 people this year will cost $32.37, down $1.46 from 1999, according to an annual survey by the American Farm Bureau Federation . . . .

The drop reflects a decline in the cost of a wide range of food items, including milk, sweet potatoes and the turkey itself. *A 16-pound turkey dropped an average of $1.71 to $12.52.*

Los Angeles Times[57]

Another *Los Angeles Times writer* examines toll charges on private expressways and breaks out the bottom line:

Tolls on the private lanes . . . have gone up twice in the last year and six times in the last four years *and can cost peak-hour commuters as much as $146 a month.* On a per-mile basis, the tolls are among the highest in the nation. For many drivers, the economics of paying to drive are starting to make less and less sense.

Monte Morin
Los Angeles Times[58]

Finally on numbers: If any commonality unites journalists it might be poor math skills. When your story is finished, go back over your numbers. Add once more, subtract, figure percentages. Double-check!

ANALYZE POLLS AND SURVEYS CAREFULLY

Before you evaluate numbers yielded by a poll or survey, you must establish this:

First, who sponsored the poll? What is their political or special-interest affiliation? What is their likely motive in releasing the results?

Second, is valid survey methodology followed and what is the margin for error?

Believe it: Some polls are conducted for partisan reasons; results sometimes are skewed, if not misrepresented; and even pollsters with the best intentions can follow invalid methodology.

Below, the *Chicago Tribune* carefully advises readers of the source of the source of a survey and its methodology:

New York — Teenage marijuana use has dropped for a third straight year, but a jump in the use of the "club drug" ecstasy raised new concerns for parents, according to *the Partnership for a Drug-Free America's* annual report.

The *non-profit group's* 13th survey, being released Monday, questioned *7,290 students in 7th through 12th grades nationwide. The margin of error is plus or minus 1.5 percentage points . . . .*

Chicago Tribune[59]

The *Los Angeles Times* reports a survey finds "a whopping 73.4%" of college freshmen "want to be very well off financially." The *Times* elaborates:

"It used to be that money and status went together," *said Alexander W. Astin, a UCLA professor who founded the survey* in 1966. Not anymore.

The annual American Freshman Survey, a joint project of the American Council on Education and UCLA's Education Research Institute, is the *nation's oldest* and *most comprehensive* assessment of student

attitudes and behavior.

The survey, conducted last fall, is based on the responses of 269,413 students at 434 four-year colleges and universities. *The data have been statistically adjusted to be* representative of 1.1 million freshman entering these traditional four-year institutions . . . .

Kenneth R. Weiss

Los Angeles Times[60]

As in all newswriting, put polling results in proper context. Note how this writer does that with television ratings:

. . . "The Early Show" has added about 100,000 viewers a week — from about 2.15 million to about 2.25 million — in the four weeks since "Survivor" began, over its totals for the four previous weeks. *That is a modest number, but still notable* because the four previous

weeks were mainly within the regular television season and viewing has declined since then. "Today," for example, has lost about 170,000 viewers (off a base of more then 6 million) a week since then, *a typical summer development.*

New York Times[61]

OBJECTIVE #5:
HIDDEN INSIGHTS AND DELIGHTS

Your readers are travelers on a long journey: They'll tire of the trip unless hidden delights occasionally are found just around the next corner.

You can weave insights and delights into a pull-ahead fabric of your story, luring readers ever onward, *if* you develop a keen reporter's eye.

Adam Nagourney of the *New York Times* has that eye. Deep in a story about former President Clinton, Nagourney inserts this sparkler:

"It must be a slow news day in New York if you have to cover me," Mr. Clinton declared, chuckling at the sight of the reporters — *a fairly small bunch, if truth be told, compared with the old White House crowd* — who had come out to chronicle his first day as a private citizen . . . .

Adam Nagourney
New York Times[62]

A writer depicts a small Indiana town, half in one time zone, half in another:

"Here," says Mike Danner, the hardware story owner, *with a wink,* "we don't ever know what time it really is."

Pam Belluck
New York Times[63]

Seth Mydans of the *New York Times* reports an extraordinary story:

Suan Phung, Thailand—Between them, the 12-year-old twins say, they command 400,000 invisible soldiers. If anybody shoots at them, the bullets just bounce off. And they can kill their enemies simply by pointing a rifle at the ground and concentrating really hard.

These might be the fantasies of a million schoolboys. But they are the beliefs that have led grown men into battle — the legends that surround two child warriors who lead a ragged ethnic insurgency called God's Army, just across the border in Myanmar, the former Burma.

Then, with keen insight, Mydans puts it all in perspective:

Last week, one of the twins, Luther Htoo . . . spoke with The New York Times by satellite telephone — *a fidgety child with a little-boy voice* who answered many of the questions by turning to his followers and asking, "What shall I say?"

After some discussion, some of his answers were these: He wants freedom for his people, the Karen minority. He is invulnerable to land mines and bullets. His favorite toys are real guns and ammunition. And he misses his mother and father . . . .

Seth Mydans
New York Times[64]

Be alert to weave into your writing insights that you, a reporter on the scene, can catch but that are not communicated automatically in straight, objective reporting. Again, Seth Mydans (emphasis added):

Phnom Penh, Cambodia — A top leader of the Khmer Rouge muttered an apology today, saying he was "sorry, very sorry" for the suffering he had caused the Cambodian people.

His apology, in English, *came only after aggressive questioning at a news conference.* At the insistence of Cambodian reporters, he repeated it in the Khmer language: "Knyom som tos."

Seth Mydans
New York Times[65]

Another *Times* reporter interviews a man who claims to have come out of North Korea and to have seen American prisoners there, 40 years after the Korean War. The story sounds fishy, and the *Times* reporter insightfully signals that:

The reports of American P.O.W.'s were first published this week by Asia Times, a Bangkok-based daily whose reporter spoke with Mr. Oh Young Nam. During the (New York Times) interview on Wednesday, Mr. Oh said that he had not realized that his conversation with that reporter would be published in a newspaper, and he tried to avoid talking about American prisoners.

"I'll talk about anything else in North Korea, but right now I can't tell you about the American prisoners," he said. "Some time later it may be possible."

Asked if American officials had ordered him not to discuss what he had seen, he refused to say, *but he squirmed a lot.*

Nicholas D. Kristof
New York Times[66]

And always try for a "kicker"

A "kicker" is a dramatic or humorous bang at the end of your story, a snappy conclusion that prevents your tale from just sort of petering out.

A bit of drama:

Vera Atkins, who recruited, trained and watched over the legendary British secret agents who parachuted into France to sabotage the Nazis in World War II, died on Saturday in Hastings, Sussex. She was 92.

(During the war), Ms. Atkin's heart was with her 400 secret agents. She stood on the runway to watch each take off to parachute into France.

Now, a last-graf kicker:

She traveled a great deal, but settled in a cottage left her by an aunt at Winchelsea, *from which, on a clear* *day, you can see France.*

Douglas Martin
New York Times[67]

An AP writer leaves 'em laughing with an Athens, Ohio, story about a university professor, Mel Helitzer, who retires after years of teaching a course titled, "Humor Writing 488." The writer recounts final plaudits by students, then the kicker:

When his student had finished, Helitzer delivered a standup routine.

"One of the things I'm going to miss about Athens, I guess, is the signs," he said. "Remember a couple years ago they had that big sign 'Hicks for Sheriff.' I said, 'Why brag about it.' Then you go out to farmland and they have this big sign, 'Lots for Sale,' and there's nothing there."

As always, he got the last laugh.

Andy Resnik
The Associated Press[68]

SUMMARY

- After your lead catches readers, pull them deeper by weaving a whole fabric to tell your story.
- Plan your story by considering where it must go after the first graf and which facts, in order of descending importance, must follow.
- Consider your audience and your material's complexity, then decide which story structure is best.
- Objective #1 must be to write second and subsequent grafs that fulfill your lead's promise of things to come, facts to be revealed.
- Draw readers ahead by carefully linking one graf to another, one thought to another.
- Objective #2 should be to maintain reading momentum, once your lead catches reader attention.

- Insert quotes, always a reader draw, and detail and color to "juice" your writing and give readers incentive to continue.
- Create credibility in your writing by demonstrating your firm grasp of essential details and by quoting authoritative sources.
- Objective #3: Keep Who, What, Where and When straight, clearly signaling readers each time you switch time elements, for example, or geographic references in a story.
- Once you've identified the "who" element — "Democratic source," for example — stick with that identifier rather than switching to confusing synonyms, such as "informant," "Washington insider."
- If you switch geographic identifiers, signal readers clearly by opening a subsequent graf with, "In Washington" . . . "In New York," for example.
- Objective #4: Translate meaning of events readers might not follow closely, describing a politician's defeat in a distant election as "stunning," for example.
- Be alert particularly to characterize the meaning of law and science stories, and use lay language to explain technical terms used by experts.
- Numbers require special handling because many readers have difficulty absorbing their true meaning.
- Guidelines on numbers: Use only those crucial to your story; parcel them out at a manageable pace; whenever possible, express numbers also in percentages; and always characterize their meaning.
- In reporting polls and surveys, always describe the political or special-interest affiliation of their sponsors and survey methodology and margin for error.
- Objective #5: Weave insights and delights throughout your story, otherwise readers will tire of the journey.
- Strive for "kickers" — dramatic or humorous bangs at the ends of your stories—rather than let your writing simply peter out.

RECOMMENDED READING

Wordsmiths of the type discussed in this chapter are at work at major newspapers, particularly the *Los Angeles Times*, the *New York Times* and *Boston Globe*.

As in study of any form of newswriting, disciplined reading of those newspapers will be most helpful.

Writing hints in Chapter Six are discussed further in my "Introduction to Professional Newswriting" (New York: Longman, 1998) and "Introduction to Magazine Writing" (New York: Macmillan, 1994).

Also see Bill Walsh, "Lapsing into a Comma" (Lincolnwood, Ill.: Contemporary Books, 2000), a wonderful collection of writing hints by the copy desk chief of The Washington Post's business desk.

EXERCISES

1. Examine today's *New York Times* (or another newspaper designated by your instructor) for examples of writing that creates smooth continuity from lead to second graf. In about 300 words, discuss writing styles and techniques reporters use to fulfill the promise of their lead graf, as discussed in Chapter Six. Do you find examples of writing that does *not* provide such smooth continuity and thus fails to fulfill a lead's promise?

2. Study a longer story from today's *New York Times* (or work from an example of writing provided by your instructor) and discuss the presence — or absence — of the linkage factors mentioned in Chapter Six. What devices and techniques does the writer employ (or not employ) to pull readers out of the lead and deeper into the story? Does the writer weave a *whole fabric* of the story? If so, how? Write your findings in about 250 words.

3. Search today's *New York Times* (or another newspaper designated by your instructor) for examples of how writers insert color descriptive, factual substance and authoritative quotes deep in their stories. Do the writers thus achieve reading momentum and credibility? Can you find pull-ahead writing techniques, as discussed in Chapter Six? Write your findings in about 300 words.

4. Search today's *New York Times* (or another newspaper designated by your instructor) for examples of writers translating legal or scientific terms into lay language. In about 250 words, discuss how

successful writers are in characterizing technical terms and developments in terms appropriate for general newspaper audiences. Can you read stories of legal and scientific developments and understand them?

5. Study today's *Wall Street Journal* (or another newspaper designated by your instructor) for examples of how writers handle numbers. In about 300 words, discuss examples of writing that expresses numbers in percentages to aid reader understanding and numbers whose meaning is characterized in understandable lay terms. Are numbers dealt out in manageable batches or do writers overwhelm readers with vast quantities of hard-to-understand numbers?

NOTES

1. "Teen Helps Officers in Pimping Arrests," Feb. 11, 2001, p. C–1.
2. "Penn Team Finds Clue to Gene-Drug Death," Jan. 26, 2001, p. A–1.
3. "A Tight Spot for City Drivers," Jan. 26, 2001, p. A–1.
4. "Economic Expansion Appears to be at End," Feb. 2, 2001, p. C–1.
5. "Federal Judge Voids Ban on Soliciting by Day Laborers," Sept. 15, 2000, p. B–1.
6. "The New Gospel of Academia," Oct. 18, 2000, p. A–1.
7. "For a Lifer, An Oscar Offers Faint Hope," March 1, 1999, p. B–1.
8. "Girl Says Pimp Trial Defendants Sold Her Sex Services at Age 12," Feb. 3, 2001, p. E–1.
9. "Congo Says Kabila Succumbs to Wounds," Jan. 19, 2001, p. A–1.
10. "Fox's Town Dresses Up for Bush," Feb. 9, 2001, p. A–22.
11. Petula Dvorak, "Ex-Friend Says Alleged Killer Didn't Care," *Washington Post*, Feb. 9, 2001, p. B–3.
12. "Suspect Taken to Xiana Site," Feb. 5, 2001, p. A–11.
13. "A Father's Quest," Jan. 28, 2001, p. A–1.
14. "Bush Sends Tax Cut Plan And Economic Warning," Feb. 9, 2001, p. A–1.
15. "Montgomery Deal Raises Teacher Pay," Feb. 9, 2001, p. A–1.
16. Jeff Zeleny and Joe Biesk, "From Feasts to Floss, Lobbying Largess Surfaces in Reports in State," *Chicago Tribune*, Feb. 2, 2001, Section 1, p. 7.
17. "1 out of 4 Airline Flights Late in 2000," Feb. 2, 2001, p. A–1.
18. "Killer Approached Kabila Calmly, Then Fired, Aide Says," Jan. 22, 2001, p. A–1.
19. "Rebels Without a Childhood in Sri Lanka War," Sept. 11, 2000, p. A–1.

20. "Auberon Waugh: Acerbic Writer, Satirist and Editor Was Son of Novelist Evelyn Waugh," Jan. 18, 2001, p. B–9.

21. "Ramsey's No. 2 Ranks No. 1 in Unpopularity," Jan. 29, 2001, p. A–1.

22. "How Gore Stopped Short on His Way to Concede," Nov. 9, 2000, p. A–1.

23. New York Times Service dispatch for Sunday, Jan. 14, 2001.

24. Dispatch for Sunday papers, Jan. 21, 2001.

25. Murray Coleman, "Searching for E-Commerce Profits," Feb. 13, 2001, p. A–1.

26. "D.A. Reviewing Habitual-Felon Prosecutions," Feb. 11, 2001, p. B–1.

27. Dispatch for morning papers, Feb. 11, 2001.

28. "Ratliff Faces An Operation After Examination of Broken Wrist," Feb. 20, 2001, p. E–1.

29. Dispatch for morning papers, Feb. 3, 2001.

30. Dispatch for Sunday papers, Feb. 11, 2001.

31. "Bush Calls for Faster Relief in Tax Cuts," Feb. 6, 2001, p. A–1.

32. "Contract Accord May Avert Teachers Strike," Jan. 24, 2001, p. B–2.

33. "Exide Says Indictment Is Likely Over Its Car Battery Sales to Sears," Jan. 11, 2001, p. C–1.

34. "1.3 Billion PG&E Default," Jan. 30, 2001, p. A–1.

35. Dispatch for morning papers, Feb. 2, 2001.

36. Dispatch for morning papers, Feb. 20, 2001.

37. "Drugs That May Delay Alzheimer's Face Test over 7-Year Period," Jan. 29, 2001, p. A–3.

38. "Some Drivers Take Law, Lives into Their Own Hands," Jan. 18, 2001, p. A–1.

39. "High Cost for Pushing Tax Deadline," Jan. 26, 2001, p. A–1.

40. "Students Still Shaken, 6 Days After Shooting," Jan. 17, 2001, p. B–1.

41. "Spate of Violence in Boston Leave 1 Dead, Several Injured," Jan. 28, 2001, p. B–3.

42. Dispatch for morning papers of Jan. 15, 2001.

43. Dispatch for morning papers of Dec. 25, 2000.

44. "Microsoft Scores Tactical Victory in Antitrust Case," Sept. 27, 2000, p. A–1.

45. Dispatch at 11:29 a.m. ET, Sept, 26, 2000.

46. "A Pearl and a Hodgepodge: Human DNA," June 27, 2000, p. A–1.

47. "Animal's Genetic Program Decoded in Science First," Dec. 111, 1998, p. A–1.

48. Dispatch for morning paper, Feb. 3, 2001.

49. "Out of Seclusion, Back in The Spotlight," Jan. 22, 2001, p. A–1.

50. "Gov. Davis Faces Push for Indian Casinos in Urban Areas," Dec. 25, 2000, p. A–3.

51. Quoted in an AP dispatch for Sunday papers, Jan. 14, 2001.

52. "Web-Driven Merger is a Billion-Dollar Bust," Feb. 20, 2001, p. C–1.

53. "Energy Players Deeply Divided on Rescue Plan," Jan. 15, 2001, p. A–1.

54. "Beyond Excess," September/October 2000, p. 28.

55. "Firestone to Lay Off 450 People in Decatur," Oct. 18, 2000, p. A–1.

56. "AMC to Shut The Door on up to 20% of Movie Screens," Jan. 26. 2001, p. C–1.

57. "Drop in Food Prices Trims Cost of Thanksgiving Dinner," Nov. 18, 2000, p. A–13.

58. "Express Commuters Hit With Toll Hikes," Jan. 16, 2001, p. B–8.

59. "Fewer Teens Using Marijuana, But More Are Trying 'Ecstasy,'" Nov. 27, 2000, p. A–5.

60. "College Freshmen Rate Money as Chief Goal," Jan. 22, 2001, p. A–4.

61. "At CBS, Lines Between News and Entertainment Are Fuzzier," June 26, 2000, p. C–11.

62. "Hail to The Former Chief, Picking Up a Sandwich at the Deli," Jan. 22, 2001, p. A–16.

63. "Indiana Considers Synchronizing Its Watches," Jan. 30, 2001, p. A–1.

64. "Burmese Rebel Chief More Boy Than Warrior," April 10, 2000, p. A–1.

65. "Under Prodding, 2 Apologies for Cambodian Anguish," Dec. 30, 1998, p. A–3.

66. "A New Account in Tales of Korean War P.O.W.'s," Sept. 8, 1996, p. A–8.

67. "Vera Atkins 92, Spymaster for British, Dies," June 27, 2000, p. C–28.

68. Dispatch for Sunday papers, Nov. 19, 2000.

PART FOUR
Getting Started in Specialty Writing

Getting Started in Specialty Writing

Expect this question early in any job interview: "Where are your clips?"

Clips! They are evidence of commitment to journalism, proof that you don't just talk about writing some day, but that you write, *now*.

Before an interview, hiring editors know roughly who (and what) you are — young, college-educated, eager for an internship or first newsroom job. What those editors don't know is whether you've mastered the basics of accurate reporting and clean, clear writing.

You won't know, either, unless you start — now — doing it for real by writing for publication.

In Chapter Seven, we'll discuss how to get started building experience and your clip file. We'll cover how to formulate story ideas, then how to report and write for print media on and off campus. We'll concentrate on three writing specialties that offer enormous opportunities on any campus:

- Sports. It's a wonderful news sector for beginners in journalism, and if you develop skills, you'll be in demand at student and non-student newspapers and magazines.
- Science. Somewhere on your campus, right now, somebody likely is engaged in scientific research with solid newsworthiness. Reporting on-campus research is a great way to develop stringer relationships with off-campus papers.
- Business. We'll define the term loosely, concentrating on how-to stories that affect the pocketbooks of your fellow students—how to get a loan, how to buy a car, how to read an apartment lease. Great fun—and service to readers—await you in this news category.

7

Sports, Science, Business

SMART PLANNING INCREASES enormously your chances of getting published. Two steps are key:

First, carefully study the newspaper or magazine you will target, its reader audience and its own newsroom staffing.

Second, focus your story idea on a news angle that truly is within your capabilities *and* likely will interest your target editor.

PICKING A TARGET PUBLICATION

Whether you're aiming at a publication on campus or off, study its pattern of coverage. Note particularly the types of stories assigned its own staff writers.

For example, your on-campus student publication and nearby metropolitan newspapers undoubtedly assign permanent staffers to cover your school's football team. Offering "to cover next Saturday's game" will be a non-starter.

However, a paper with a limited staff on football might be open to your ideas for *sidebar stories* — a team trainer coming up on 30 years of fixing bruises and broken bones; a first-string player who makes the dean's list consistently; players who volunteer at a local children's hospital.

Almost certainly, covering intramural sports is wide open for you.

College newspapers frequently are so short-staffed they have trouble covering all major sports, let alone intramural games. Offering to start on intramurals is a marvelous way to *create a staff job for yourself.*

Nearby metros won't be interested in regular coverage of intramural sports. But how about pitching a story idea on that extraordinary goalie on the women's soccer team who has held opponents scoreless for 20 games? Or the running back on a flag-football team who is good enough to play varsity?

Once you understand how a newspaper covers the news, and the (always limited) staff it has for the job, story ideas will start emerging.

PITCHING YOUR IDEA

Whether you pitch your idea in person or in writing, do two things:

First, focus the idea tightly on a story element that truly is news — *as the target newspaper defines news* — and that you can convince an editor you can deliver. A common error among beginners is to suggest stories that are too broad — "A piece on intramural sports." That's too vague; it highlights no true news value, and, as any editor knows, even a full-time experienced staffer would take days (weeks?) to survey an entire sports program.

Second, state precisely how you will get the story, including sources you will interview, and roughly what the story structure will be (hard-news Five Ws and How? Or, a feature?) And, when (*exactly*) you will deliver the story. *Promise nothing that you're not certain you can deliver.* To miss a deadline is a journalistic felony, and will label you as an unreliable amateur.

WRITING THE IDEA

Structure your pitch something like this:

> (Your address)
> (Your telephone number)
> (Your e-mail address)

(Editor's name)
(Title and address)

Dear _____

I want to offer you a story on Fred Smith, lead trainer for Our College's football team, who in four weeks will mark 30 years of fixing bruises and broken bones.

Smith is a colorful character widely respected (not to say, *loved*) by generations of varsity players and coaches. He is full of anecdotes about past and present player greats and the team's memorable wins and losses.

I have interviews scheduled with players and coaches during the week of Oct. 1–7. I'll interview Smith on Oct. 9.

I can e-mail the completed story by 4 p.m., Oct. 12. Smith's 30-year anniversary is Oct. 24, so we would have plenty of time for consultation prior to publication. I envisage a feature — an extended personality profile — of about 600 words.

If you want to assign a photographer to this story I will be happy to help coordinate shooting. Alternatively, I can arrange for a fellow student photographer to shoot on a stringer basis.

I'll telephone you in a few days to discuss this idea.

Sincerely,

Note this about the story idea:

- It doesn't mention money. A beginner has little leverage in negotiating stringer fees. But take a couple assignments at low (or no) pay, *then* you'll have some wiggle room.
- The written offer reserves to *you* the followup. Editors get busy; they may put aside or lose correspondence. By telephoning — with gentle pushiness — you may break things loose.
- The story idea estimates wordage, although it's nearly impossible to judge story length in advance. If the story develops strongly, write longer; if not, chop down the wordage. *Never write beyond a story's intrinsic news value.* Seasoned editors hate gaseous writing.

STARTING ON SPORTS

Start by understanding three things:

- Sports coverage is hugely popular with readers. For many on-campus papers, sports is the single-largest reader attraction; off-campus, research shows at least 78 percent of all adults—88 percent of men, 68 percent of women — read newspaper sports sections. Consequently, editors accord sports large newshole — 20 percent or more of available space.[1]
- Sports readers/fans are discerning, as expert in their news specialty as are readers of financial news or science news or any other news category. You must *know your game* as a sportswriter, as expertly as a financial correspondent must know Wall Street.
- The best sportswriters today are hard-headed about sports, are objective and dispassionate, and they cover sports as *news*. Boosterism, the unthinkingly supportive (and thus distorted) journalism of the past, is out of fashion today. Don't let your love of game or team sway you from your first mission, which, as in all journalism, is service to readers.

THE BASIC GAME STORY

We define sports news as we define any news — in terms of proximity, timeliness, impact, conflict, prominence.

One huge difference: In sports, if you're covering a major (and sometimes even minor) event, television or radio likely will reach your audience before you do.

Therefore, in sports, more so than in other news, even a straightforward spot-news story must have an analytical or otherwise *exclusive* angle that your electronic competitors don't have.

Key elements of a basic game story:

- People. Focus on them; they're what sports is all about.
- What happened. Conflict — who won, who lost — drives sportswriting.

- Statistics. Your story must be heavy with numbers. Sports readers devour them as accountants devour balance sheets.
- Look-ahead angle. Every game, win or lose, sets up the next game; every season is a prelude to the next.

THE PEOPLE ANGLE

A *Boston Globe* hockey writer has a serious challenge: Before her story on the Boston Bruins hits the streets tomorrow morning, most fans will know the outcome of tonight's game. Indeed, many will watch on television as the writer watches from the press box.

How can the writer compete? *By focusing on the people angle.*

Here's how it looked in the *Globe* the next morning:

Panthers 2
Bruins 1

Sunrise, Fla. — They ripped backhanders. They fired forehanders.

Hard shots, slow shots, low shots, high shots.

They even changed goaltenders. They threw everything but the kitchen sink at the Florida Panthers last night, but in the end, the Bruins *were foiled by the remarkable performance of young goalie Roberto Luongo.*

Once the netminder of the future for the New York Islanders—he was taken with the No. 4 pick overall in the 1997 draft—Luongo is the goaltender of the here and now for the Panthers.

The high point for Boston was Bill Guerin potting his 30th goal of the season, tying his career best.

Guerin's goal at 14:14 of the middle period started a surge of pressure that lasted the rest of the game, but Luongo, who was acquired in a trade last June, was even more dominant than the Bruin's relentless attack.

Note above the writer's quick fifth-graf transition from opposing goaltender to Boston's star scorer — another people angle — then back to the central people angle, goaltender Luongo, in the sixth graf.

Now, transition into play-by-play:

The Bruins couldn't get anything going in the first period . . .

Nancy Marrapese-Burrell
Boston Globe[2]

Note below how a spot-news story on a basketball game subordinates everything — including score — to a people angle:

Seattle — Upon further review, *Jim O'Brien sees plenty of room for improvement.*

That observation may be one of the most encouraging aspects of Boston's 108–88 dismissal of Seattle Thursday night. It also may be one the strongest indications the resurgent Celtics are here to stay.

The Celtics want more. No, correction. The Celtics expect more . . . .

Now, after a hundred or so words of game details, back to the lead's people angle:

But for Boston to meet its expectations, the players must continually perfect their approach.

"The thing that I noticed more than anything when I watched the tape was that we have a lot of room for improvement in a lot of areas," said O'Brien . . . .

Shira Springer
Boston Globe[3]

Obviously, not all games will be broadcast. Then, your writing must focus on outcome — who won. Nevertheless, you can (and should) weave in the people angle.

Note how Associated Press pros do that (emphasis added):

Columbus, Ohio — *Sean Connolly's three-pointer* with 30 seconds left tonight gave Ohio State a 63–61 upset of No. 3 Illinois, opening up the race for the Big Ten title.

The Associated Press[4]

Kelly Mazzante scored 18 points and *Lisa Shepherd* had 17 last night as No. 19 Penn State upset No. 5 Purdue, 75–65, in State College, Pa.

A *three-point play by Rashana Barnes* stopped a Purdue run and gave the Lady Lions (19–7, 11–4 Big Ten) a 66–58 lead with 2 minutes 57 seconds left. Penn State hit 7 of 8 free throws in the last 1:10 to secure the win.

The Associated Press[5]

How about this for a pre-game story:

North Carolina State takes on Duke today at 3:30 p.m., in Cameron Indoor Stadium.

A real loser, right? Now, try this:

It's Game Day, and Duke's Shane Battier will be juiced up for this afternoon's shootout against ACC rival N.C. State at Cameron Indoor Stadium.

By the time the 3:30 p.m. tipoff rolls around, the Blue Devils standout will have guzzled 64 ounces of Gatorade, which has been part of his pre-game routine since he was a high school freshman.

Duke's Nate James also will be pumped — from pumping iron. Before each game, the muscular Blue Devil senior lifts weights, a ritual he has followed for several years.

State's Damien Wilkins will spend time relaxing in a hot tub and the Wolfpack's Anthony Grundy will try to get loose by watching a funny movie on the VCR before making the bus ride to Durham.

Players get psyched up in different ways. Anybody who has a pulse feels an edge before every game, but especially in frenetic February before a clash like this one . . . .

A. J. Carr
Raleigh (N.C.) News & Observer[6]

I wrote the dull lead above to illustrate how flat a sports story is without a people angle. The *News & Observer's* Carr illustrates how the pros can turn *any* story into something readable by accenting the people angle.

WHAT HAPPENED?

Answer that question with only the score and you'll not satisfy serious sports fans — those who want to know what *really* happened.

That is, the basic game story must answer "What happened?" by describing *game strategies* that led to the score, *turning points, individual player efforts* and other influences on the outcome — including *calls by officials, coaching decisions* and *weather.*

Here's a writer who focuses on *individual effort* to illustrate what happened:

If Saturday's victory over the Portland Trail Blazers was a senior moment for the Clippers, then Monday night's victory over the Chicago Bulls at Staples Center was *the young guns' show.*

Two nights after being non-factors on the bench, Quentin Richardson, Keyon Dooling, Corey Maggett and Darius Miles each got a chance to *strut their stuff* in a 102–82 victory before 11,144 as the Clippers sent the Bulls to their franchise-record 15 consecutive loss.

Richardson and Dooling each scored 13 points, Maggette had 11 and Miles had 10 in a reserve role for the Clippers, who have won

three in a row for the first time since
December 1999 . . .

Lonnie White
Los Angeles Times[7]

This writer focuses on a *turning point*:

The Vols *blew a 16-point first-half lead*, allowing Georgia to win on a Chris Daniels layup in the closing seconds of the second overtime. During their second-half collapse, the Vols couldn't stop Georgia guard D.A. Layne, who scored a game-high 24 points.

Andy Staples
Chattanooga Times Free Press[8]

This writer sees *playing strategies* as key:

Andre Hutson had 15 points and Zach Randolph added 14 as the fifth-ranked Spartans (21–3, 10–3) beat Indiana 66–57 Tuesday night, again *featuring their suffocating defense and tenacious rebounding*.

The Associated Press[9]

An AP reporter finds the key in a University of New Hampshire 93–85 victory over Drexel: "*UNH used full-court pressure defense* to jump to a 7–0 lead and Drexel never got closer than 5" . . . . [10]

THE STATISTICAL CONTEXT

Yes, boxes and linescores will accompany your stories.

Yes, your editors will fill *columns* with agate (small type) statistics.

And yes, despite all that, your story must include lots of numbers that put the game in statistical context.

Not to suggest, of course, that you indiscriminately throw statistics into your writing. *Carefully* select only those that illuminate your reporting on a game's key elements.

Below, the statistical context is built around *individual performers*:

Predrag Stojakovic *scored a career-high 39 points and hit a three-pointer with 45 seconds left* in triple overtime as the Sacramento Kings beat Toronto 119–118 on Friday night.

Doug Christie, playing in Toronto for the first time since the Raptors traded him to Sacramento before the season, *added 20 points and seven rebounds*.

Toronto's Vince Carter *had 38 points and 10 assists in 63 minutes*. Antonio Davis *had 20 points, six in*

the final overtime, and added 12 re-
bounds and six blocks.

The Associated Press[11]

A hockey writer uses statistics to illuminate *turning points*:

Jeff Cowan's first goal in 16 games helped lift the Calgary Flames to a 5–3 victory over the Colorado Avalanche on Friday night in Denver . . . .

Mike Vernon, who shut out Colorado in December, *stopped a flurry of shots in the final two minutes* and finished with 34 saves for Calgary. Dave Lowry *got an empty-net goal with eight seconds left.*

The Avalanche outshot Calgary 37–23 *but made costly turnovers that led to two Flames goals.*

The Associated Press[12]

Below, a writer gives over his *entire story* to statistics:

Friday was a record (and near-record) night at the Chiles Center, where the Portland Pilots ended a *six-games losing streak.*

They missed only two of 27 *free throws, blocked 10 shots*, and sophomore center *Tim Frost became Portland's No. 1 career shot-blocker* during an 83–74 victory over the Saint Mary's Gaels.

"We needed this win," said Frost, *who blocked six shots to run his career total to 89.* He also tied his *career high with 22 points.*

The win, *in front of 931,* was the first of four West Coast Conference home games for Portland (*10–2, 3–6*) and extended Saint Mary's losing *streak to 13 . . . .*

John Nolen
Portland (Ore.)
Sunday Oregonian[13]

In any other journalism, including business writing, I would tell you too many figures are jammed into that story above. But for sports fans, the more statistics, the merrier. Just be sure to pace your delivery so numbers don't choke your writing flow.

THE LOOK-AHEAD ANGLE

Your basic game story must *look ahead* to establish the broader meaning of a game.

Here, in its most direct form, is the look-ahead angle:

Candice Adams came off the bench to score seven of her game-high 17 points in the first quarter, leading Gordon Lee to a 54–41 win over Adairsville in Monday's Region 6-

A play-in game. *The Lady Trojans (11–13) will play in the region tournament on Wednesday.*
Chattanooga Times Free Press[14]

Below, a writer leads with the look-ahead angle, *subordinating the game itself:*

Evensville, Tenn. — A lot of basketball will be played on the Rhea County High School gym floor the next two weeks as the District 5-AAA and Region 3-AAA tournaments unfold.

But the host Rhea County girls

won't be joining in the fun.

Tuesday night, the Lady Golden Eagles were eliminated on the first night of district play . . . .

David Jenkins
Chattanooga Times Free Press[15]

And, with a very nice featurish touch, a reporter covers two games, then writes this:

Basketball in Hixson isn't exactly a household word.

The Wildcats had no cheerleaders and only a smattering of fans Tuesday night at the District 6-AAA tournament. but this morning the Wildcats have two region-bound basketball teams . . .

The boys broke from a 26-all

half-time deadlock with East Ridge and pulled out a 56–46 victory over East Ridge. The girls had to go a third game against Red Bank and pulled out their third straight triumph over the Lionettes with a flurry of 3-point shots, 46–35 . . .

Ward Gossett
Chattanooga Times Free Press[16]

BEFORE AND AFTER THE GAME

Games themselves are only part of the sports story for your reader/fans. What happens before and after — year round — is of compelling interest to them, too.

Three areas of reader/fan interest offer you particularly strong story possibilities:

- Player lifestyle.
- The business of sports.
- Health and injuries.

STORIES ON PLAYER LIFESTYLE

Ask your roommate or friend these questions: Who is U.S. secretary of state? Secretary of defense?

Now ask: Who is Michael Jordan? Tiger Woods?

That short quiz will underline the strong, unending interest Americans have in sports stars and their lifestyles.

Off-court and field, as well as on, athletes are among our most visible public figures, and, thus, by custom and law, open to press and public scrutiny.

For principled journalists, that scrutiny does *not* extend to sordid voyeurism, merely poking around in an athlete's dark closet of life in mindless search for scandal.

It *does* include penetrating even the zone of privacy normally surrounding any individual if in search of a larger, meaningful story that the public has a right and need to know.

Thus, it's news — to be covered in detail — when a star football player is arrested in a barroom brawl and suspended from your school's team or when a baseball star's private life is in such disarray that his playing abilities are affected.

For a campus newspaper, either of the above is a front-page story. For a nearby metro, (which may need stringer help in off-season!) it's news, too.

Caution on two points:

- Don't think only *bad* news is news. It's news also when players distinguish themselves academically or do neighborhood volunteering.
- When you do report bad news, be doubly cautious, reporting what authoritative sources say and what the official record reveals. Laws of defamation and privacy may kick in. More to the point, you may be dealing with an athlete's reputation — his or her good name, a priceless asset for anyone. (We'll discuss the ethics of this and law of the press in a subsequent chapter.)

STORIES ON THE BUSINESS OF SPORTS

By any measure, sports is huge business in the United States. And reader/fans — and, thus, sportswriters — have justifiable need to know where the money comes from and where it goes.

Think, for example, of the sports business on your campus, and the legitimate news-needs of your student readers:

- What portion of student fees goes to athletics, and what do students get (or not get) in return?
- What's the spending breakdown on spectator sports involving relatively few student players and intramural programs that might involve thousands?
- What's the ticket allocation (and price) for students, compared to tickets and other courtesies laid on for big-spending alums?
- How do coaches' salaries and the spending on athletic facilities compare to salaries for professors and spending on student-friendly academic facilities?

In pro coverage, money is even a larger factor, of course.

On the surface, contract negotiations and player salaries turn the pro sports world. Cover them closely.

Beneath the surface, even more interesting — and important — stories await you: What's the cost to taxpayers of the new stadium being built for a *privately owned* sports team? How do ticket prices compare historically and to prices for other teams elsewhere?

STORIES ON HEALTH AND INJURIES

Bone scan . . . magnetic resonance imaging test . . . torn rotator cuff . . . "ring fracture of base of skull". . . All are terms that could be lifted from a medical journal but, of course, are from sports pages.

Virtually every day, in very major ways, stories on health and injuries are pivotal in discerning, meaningful sportswriting.

A bone scan is the look-ahead lead element in a story on University of Tennessee basketball:

Knoxville — A sprained right ankle likely will keep University of Tennessee guard Tony Harris out of Wednesday's basketball matchup with Kentucky.

The senior had a bone scan Monday as a precautionary measure, and soreness kept him out of live practice, so Volunteers coach Jerry Green doubts Harris will play Wednesday . . .

Andy Staples
Chattanooga Times Free Press[17]

K. C. Johnson leads his story on the Chicago Bulls with an ankle examination:

Ron Mercer underwent a magnetic . . . .
resonance imaging test on his left
ankle late Friday and his injury may
be more serious than first thought

K. C. Johnson
Chicago Tribune[18]

And, of course, the skull fracture is Dale Earnhardt's, suffered in his fatal crash in the 2001 Daytona 500 and central to widespread discussion about the safety of auto racing.

Lessons:

- The *meaning* of an individual player's injury lies in its impact on performance by the player and team. Focus on that look-ahead angle.
- You must translate medical terms. Explain, for example, that a rotator cuff is in the shoulder joint, and injury to it causes terrible pain and restricts arm motion — thus it can be a career-ending injury.

Now, drugs.

The *bad* kind are present in sports, as, it seems, in most sectors of society. Use *is* news, so cover it diligently (and with all the reporting safeguards you put in place on any story involving illegalities).

The *good* kind also are present, of course, so don't confuse the two types. Be particularly careful in reporting on performance-enhancing drugs and dietary supplements. Many are perfectly legal and widely accepted as proper, when used under the guidance of medical experts.

STARTING ON SCIENCE

Children are taught that Samson was a hero who fought the Philistines and fell victim to Delilah's wily charms.

But writing in a psychiatric journal, four physicians offer slightly different interpretations. They argue that the son of Manoah — who lied to his parents, stole from his neighbors, brawled with regularity and killed with abandon — is a classic example of someone suffering from antisocial personality disorder . . . .

> By accident, scientists peering into icy waters far beneath the North Pole have found a hidden world of fire . . . .

Samson a psychotic? *Fire* beneath the North Pole? What's this?

It's science writing at its best: fascinating research reported accurately and written cleverly to translate the mysteries of science into understandable lay terms.

The writers, Erica Good and William J. Broad, respectively, of the *New York Times*, are leaders in covering this news specialty (to the delight of readers; Gannett Newspapers found 72 percent interested in science and technology).[19]

You can get started, on campus, in covering science news. Even if you don't plan a career in this specialty, it's good to get experience because science, in one form or another, plays a role in virtually all reporting.

You'll not cover local government for long before writing about toxic waste dumps outside town or threats to clean air and the environment. Science and medicine play huge roles in sportswriting. And how can you cover the cops beat without knowing something about alcohol blood tests and DNA evidence?

When a science story comes your way (as it will), keep these points in mind:

- Accuracy is paramount.
- Translate all technical terms.
- Be a conservative, cautious "show-me" reporter.

ACCURACY COMES FRST

Incorrectly reporting a running back's yardage gains is an unfortunate error. Falsely raising hopes for a cancer cure is a journalistic felony.

Even if you must sacrifice clever writing to ensure accuracy, take the path of accuracy every time in science writing. Real people, with real hopes and fears, are reading your stories.

Note how this leading science writer constructs an open and readable but not particularly engaging lead. Her emphasis is upon quoting *authoritative sources* (three times in her first two grafs):

Washington — Taking the prescription flu drug Tamiflu not only treats influenza, but a pill a day during an outbreak can also prevent the misery-inducing illness almost like a vaccine, *the government announced yesterday.*

But don't deliberately skip the flu shot thinking you'll just pop a few Tamiflu pills, *the Food and Drug Administration* stressed. "Our message is still that vaccination is the number one preventive method against influenza," said *Dr. Debra Birnkrant, the FDA's acting antiviral-drug director.*

Lauren Neergaard
The Associated Press[20]

Be careful how you paraphrase what experts say or summarize their finding. *Accuracy lies in precision reporting.*

For example, when Sen. Joseph I. Lieberman ran for vice president, Lawrence K. Altman of the *New York Times* reported that Lieberman and his two doctors said he was in excellent health. Altman added:

Mr. Lieberman's blood tests at his last checkup in March were reported as normal, *the doctors said.* His total cholesterol (188) and other lipids H.D.L. (high density lipoprotein, or good cholesterol — 46), his L.D.L. (low-density lipoprotein, or bad cholesterol — 123), and triglycerides (96) are normal. The prostate specific antigen test for prostate cancer was a normal 0.82. His blood pressure was 112/72.

Lawrence K. Altman
New York Times[21]

TRANSLATE AND PERSONALIZE

John Noble Wilford has the difficult task of explaining to newspaper readers a breakthrough in optical astronomy. He chooses his words *very carefully*:

San Antonio — *As if peeking through a keyhole on the inner sanctum of the universe*, the Hubble Space Telescope focused for 10 consecutive days last month on one especially narrow sector of the sky, taking long-exposure photographs deeper into space than ever before achieved and recording a bewildering number and variety of galaxies stretching back toward the beginning of time.

One thing was stunningly clear: with this achievement, the estimated number of galaxies in the universe had multiplied enormously—to 50 billion, five times as many as previously estimated. The Sun is one of 50 billion to 100 billion stars in the Milky Way, generally considered to be an ordinary galaxy . . .

Astronomers are excited about studying this narrow segment of space, Wilford reports. How narrow?

The observed slice of the heavens . . .
was no wider than one–25th of one
degree, *equivalent to the size of a*
grain of sand held at arm's length

John Noble Wilford
New York Times[22]

If you're like me, the universe is *still* pretty mysterious — but at least Wilford characterizes for us the scope of the study.

Say, on another subject, did you hear that hospitals have a new accreditation test to meet? No, and you don't want to hear, right? Well, how about this:

Washington — When you enter a hospital, you have a right to have your pain properly treated.

That sounds so commonsense, yet millions of Americans suffer every day because pain is routinely ignored or undertreated.

But starting next week, the nation's hospital must make a major change: New standards require that patients' pain be measured regularly from the time they check in — just like other vital signs are measured — and proper pain relief begun or hospitals risk losing their accreditation.

Patients should expect at least to be asked to rate how they're feeling, from zero — no pain — to 10, the worst pain imaginable. (Small children will use pictures to rate pain.) The score determines what steps the hospital must take to help . . . .

Lauren Neergaard
The Associated Press[23]

Doesn't that "you" lead above make all the difference? Of course it does, because it reduces a broad *issue* to *you* and the pain *you* might suffer.

That's how to translate and personalize science news.

BE A CONSERVATIVE REPORTER

Science writing frequently takes you deep into the unknown. *That's* Problem #1.

Problem #2: You can't always trust the experts you ask to explain the unknown.

Dr. Jerome Kassirer, editor in chief of the highly regarded *New England Journal of Medicine*, says, "Investigators sometimes exaggerate the importance of their work, and reporters sometimes don't understand."[24]

The Journal of the American Medical Association says, for example, drug researchers tend to publish misleading finding on drugs' benefits.[25]

Problem #3: Great reporters *lust* for the "big story," for Page-One play. In science writing, don't. Control your lust.

Editor & Publisher magazine suggests precautions:

- Go beyond articles published in science journals and at conferences. Get first-hand interviews with reputable, authoritative sources.
- If quoting a journal, remember that peer-reviewed journals are the safest sources. Their articles are critiqued by objective experts before publication.
- Check researchers' credentials, particularly whether they are publishing in their area of expertise. An expert in one area may be an amateur in another.
- Report research methodology, just as you would in reporting a public opinion poll. How many people (or mice) were studied? For how long?
- Be specific — using *direct quotes* from experts — on the meaning for human treatment.
- Seek opposing comment from scientists who disagree.
- Don't stretch for a colorful or entertaining lead and thus pump your story beyond its hard-news merits. After writing your lead, doublecheck its accuracy and, if necessary, insert reservations or qualifications.[26]

In other words, don't get blinded by the miracle of science. It often turns out less than miraculous.

STORIES TO BEGIN WITH

Four types of stories offer particularly attractive opportunities for beginner science writers on virtually every campus:

- Covering on-campus research for off-campus newspapers and magazines.
- Localizing distant science stories for student-oriented publications on campus.

- Writing health and fitness stories for student readers.
- Reporting environmental news that affects your college community.

COVERING ON-CAMPUS RESEARCH

First, problems you face:

Your campus newspaper, if typical, probably has neglected covering hard-science departments for years, and it will be difficult to find sources.

When you do find them, they'll suspect your ability to cover science accurately. Scientists tend to distrust journalists and prefer talking with scientists only. Breaking into that closed circle is difficult.

Nevertheless, your efforts can pay off in stringer assignments for off-campus newspapers.

For example, most states have large agricultural industries, and universities conduct supportive research. Newspapers serving farm readers are prime targets for you.

Medical and engineering schools regularly yield research meaningful to off-campus newspapers.

As in all reporting, you need sources to alert you when stories develop. All universities have information offices; most colleges or departments within universities do, also. Alert them to your interest in science news. And don't forget to alert deans and department heads. They *want* coverage, whether their scientists do or not.

LOCALIZING DISTANT STORIES

Many science stories that break off campus have great news value for student readers of on-campus publication.

National and regional newspapers, magazines, the Associated Press, network television — all are sources for your first alert on a meaningful story.

That is, the successful journalist is the well-read journalist, who stays atop all the news, all the time.

Spot a distant story, then interview campus experts on its meaning for your readers. For example, a story on eating disorders, by Jane Brody,

The New York Times' famed health writer, should lead you quickly to the student health center for statistics on the problem at your university (and, it *is* a problem at *all* universities).

<h3 style="text-align:center">REPORTING HEALTH AND FITNESS</h3>

The obsessions of students: tick them off — sex, and the dangers therein; drinking and drugs, ditto; exam stress and how to survive it; eating well, feeling good, looking beautiful . . . .

Why, you're *surrounded* by health and fitness stories crucial to your student readers.

Something to avoid, something to do:

Don't take the "gee whiz" approach. ("Gee whiz, there sure is a lot of casual sex on campus; gee whiz, we sure drink a lot.") That's meaningless sensationalism.

Do write with a helpful attitude, a constructive how-to approach. Do three things:

- Define the problem carefully, citing expert sources, for example, on the incidence of binge drinking, the number of bulemics who seek medical center help.
- Describe how student readers can spot the problem, in their own behavior or a friend's. *Precisely what* defines binge drinking? How much do experts say is too much?
- Cite experts on what to do about a drinking or stress problem, complete with details on where to seek help.

<h3 style="text-align:center">COVERING ENVIRONMENTAL STORIES</h3>

Broadly, two opportunities await you:

- Stringing for off-campus newspapers on what campus experts say about pollution, toxic waste and the many other environmental problems affecting our wider world.
- Reporting for your on-campus readers environmental issues that concern the university community, its dorms, its classrooms, its dining halls.

Believe it: If a faculty demographer forecasts a huge increase in commuting by auto in a nearby city — and predicts a commensurate increase in air pollution — that's a story you can offer to that city's newspaper.

If the ag faculty discovers massive leakage of farm fertilizers into a river, that's a story for every newspaper along that river.

Believe this, too: Your student readers are vitally interested in how science departments on campus dispose of toxic waste. They're also interested in asbestos in classrooms, foul air in dorms, unsanitary conditions in dining halls . . . .

Special warning: Environmental disputes are highly inflammatory, and special-interest groups often enter them with hidden agendas.

For example, a dispute over clean air, which everybody favors, may really be a fight over real estate development, which not everybody supports. An argument in the City Council over "noise pollution" may really be aimed at multiple-occupancy of off-campus apartments by students.

As in all technical writing, dig deep into any environmental story — and check for hidden agendas.

STARTING ON BUSINESS

Check the numbers:

The *Washington Post* increased its business news staff to 81 from 18 in the period 1980–2000; the *Los Angeles Times*, to 90 from 20; the *Tampa Tribune*, to 14, from two.

In that same period, the *Post* increased business newshole to a 12-page daily section from two pages; the *Times*, to a 14- to 18-page daily section from six to seven pages; *Tampa*, the number of business news pages to a seven-page section from three pages.

And, the number of business news magazines increased to 694 from 359 in an even shorter period, 1988–1999.[27]

Those numbers add up to huge career potential for aspiring newswriters.

But, you may say, "I *want to write*! And business news? Ugh!"

Well, check out these leads:

For Koren Robinson, a two-time All-America receiver for N. C. State, getting ready for the National Football League draft has meant more than 40-yard wind sprints and grueling, three-hour workouts.

It has meant at least a dozen calls a week from financial advisers — so many, in fact, that Robinson recently switched off his home telephone. "When they see you're gonna leave early, your stock rises," says the sophomore . . . . "Everyone wants a piece of you" . . . .

Chris Serres
Raleigh (N.C.)
News & Observer[28]

Yes, that's a *business news* story, on page one (in a huge, colorful display) of a major business section. The story: College athletes turning pro before their senior year are targets of people who want to manage their money.

Newton, Mass. — A wink, a nod, a grimace — all can turn the meaning of a conversation on its head.

And all could add a lot to an e-mail. Ever wish you could see the sender's face to see what he's really saying? Ever wish you could punctuate your own messages with something more powerful than :)?

Justin Pope
The Associated Press[29]

Yes, that is a *business news* story, about a new image-morphing computer technology that brings faces to life on screen.

This also is *business news*, about people who are shopaholics and cannot budget their money:

A lot of things are going right for (Jane Smith.)

At the age of 23, she's making almost $46,000 a year as a clinical assistant at biotechnology giant Amgen in Thousand Oaks. She's athletic enough to play on two company soccer teams and ambitious enough to want to pursue an MBA in her spare time—with her employer picking up the tab.

She loves to travel — Paris last year — and dreams of buying a condo and giving more money to her church.

But (Smith) has a nasty habit that is threatening her dreams and financial well-being: shopping . . . .

Jeanette Marantos
Los Angeles Times[30]

And you didn't think *business* news (ugh!) is interesting! Or that you can write it creatively!

Truth is, covering business news is a wonderful opportunity to do meaningful journalism on campus *and* get started toward an exciting news career after you leave campus.

Three types of stories offer possibilities:

- Economics, broadly the production, distribution and consumption of wealth.
- Business, the manufacturing, buying and selling of commodities and services.
- Finance, the supply, regulation and management of money, credit and capital.

BRINGING ECONOMICS HOME

A university economist researching, say, a new theory on wealth distribution can offer you a stringer story for an off-campus newspaper.

Mostly, however, beginner stories in economics lie in watching distant economic indicators and translating their meaning for student readers on campus.

Three to watch:

GROSS DOMESTIC PRODUCT

Released in Washington about two weeks after the end of each quarter (and reported immediately by all national media), the GDP measures total output of goods and services within the United States. (Gross *national* product measures all output by all Americans, in or out of the country.)

GDP signals whether the nation's business activity is increasing, holding steady or decreasing — and with expert guidance from faculty economists, you can report on, for example, the local job outlook for spring graduates.

Further, swings in the GDP — up or down — can lead you into stories on part-time jobs available (or unavailable) off campus, and the going wage rate.

CONSUMER PRICE INDEX

Issued monthly by the U.S. Bureau of Labor Statistics, the CPI measures price changes for housing, food, fuel, transportation, clothing and so forth.

Compare *local* price changes over the same period, especially on goods consumed by students (soft drinks, beer, chips) and you have a story — whether local prices have risen more or less than national prices.

UNEMPLOYMENT RATE

Issued by the U.S. Labor Department on the first Friday of each month, the unemployment rate measures the size of the nation's civilian work force and number of people unemployed.

Your local connection is obvious: Interview university placement bureau officials and off-campus employers for the local job picture. Comparing local employment with national figures over a period will enable you to spot *trends* in local employment.

And, remember to personalize your writing.

The cold, stark CPI is, in reality, Jane Smith, a university junior, who finds suddenly the cost of her basic living essentials has risen an unmanageable 20 percent.

The federal unemployment rate wears a local face: John Smith, a senior, not only has lost his part-time job in an off-campus factory but also faces dismal job prospects after graduation in a few months.

WALKING THE BUSINESS BEAT

Although a great assignment on off-campus newspapers, covering *company news* is not a prime assignment in on-campus journalism.

Nevertheless, fascinating story possibilities exist. For example:

- Every business school has its student-entrepreneurs who, between classes, launch computer-service firms or late-night limousine companies. The companies — and owners — often provide wonderful profile material.
- Stories based on restaurant and bar health inspection reports can be fascinating reading.
- Your newspaper's music columnist undoubtedly reviewed the local rock band's music. But you can do the behind-the-scenes business story: What is involved in putting a band together? What's the cost of making a recording? Is the band making it financially?

- Profile stores offering special services and prices to students —
  mod clothing stores, for example, or food markets. (And, no,
  that's not free advertising; rather, it's excellent assistance for your
  student readers.)

COVERING FINANCE

For our purposes, we'll make that, "covering *personal* finance." It's pocketbook journalism that reduces finance, a huge subject (money, credit,
capital), to the daily money problems everybody has and, importantly,
tries to point to solutions.

In few areas of journalism can you provide more important service to
your readers than in reporting how they can make more money, spend
less and get better bargains with what they do spend.

Two story forms are most important in campus journalism:

- *Quick-alert* stories that signal readers of impending changes that
  will cost them money.
- *How-to* stories that walk readers through solutions to money
  problems.

QUICK—ALERT STORIES

Where do your readers face short-term financial vulnerability? On *every*
variable cost — and that's most of them.

That is, a financial journalist should report planned increases in loan
interest, proposed tuition hikes, impending new bank charges on checking accounts — all among significant costs students face.

Characteristics of well-done quick-alert stories:

- They are *authoritative.* Quote expert sources on *anything* concerning your readers' pocketbooks.
- They are *timely.* Rush to your readers with news that helps them
  avoid new costs or prepare for the unavoidable.
- They are *precise,* filled with hard news – dollars and cents to be
  made, saved or spent; percentages up or down; deadlines for
  avoiding new costs.

- They provide *follow-up information:* addresses of offices to visit, telephone numbers to call, Internet Web sites to consult, experts to see.

HOW-TO STORIES

This journalism takes you (and your readers) beyond the definition of a problem and deep into how to solve it.

Most times, you quote experts; sometimes, you relate a personal experience. *Always,* you write to capture reader attention:

> By her own admission (Jane Smith) isn't the kind of person who would change a flat tire. So what was she doing peering into the trunk of a sedan in the driveway of her Boca Raton, Fla., country club? Shopping. When Ms. (Smith's) head popped up from out of the trunk, she was the owner of a $400 fake Chanel bag.

That's Ken Bensinger's lead on a *Wall Street Journal* story on fake luxury goods.

Bensinger identifies the knockoff industry as big business: $99 "Big Bertha" golf clubs, $1,300 fake Rolex watches, and an estimated $2 billion in high-end fakes sold annually. Now, *personalized walk-through writing*:

> To check on the quality, we went look-alikes shopping. Scoping out New York street vendors, Chinatown stalls and the Internet, we amassed a trove of top-end fakes and showed them to a group of retail experts and seasoned shoppers. The results won't exactly thrill those who make the real thing. Four out of five of our testers — including a publicist for the fashion industry — were duped by a faux Prada duffel bag. The same number were fooled by an "Hermés" Birkin handbag with leather so nice that one panelist practically cooed. We had to wrest a fake Bulgari watch off the wrist of one tester and a Burberry scarf from the hands of another . . . .

Now the surprise: This isn't a story on how to *avoid* buying fakes. Rather, it describes how buying fakes is "cool":

> (These fakes) increasingly tempt a wider range of customers to dabble in this shady world. (Although it's illegal to make and sell fakes, in most places, there are no laws against buying them.) For consumers who want to own the fashion of the moment — albeit a fake, at a fraction of the cost — there is little risk. If anything, owning a

fake has become a status symbol, especially in circles where thrifti-ness is considered cool . . . .

"There's something different in the mind-set today," says (a trend analyst) at a Minneapolis ad agency. "It's cool to say you didn't pay re-tail, even if it's a fake . . . ."

Ken Bensinger
Wall Street Journal[31]

Incidentally, note above that Bensinger avoids the perpendicular pro-noun "I" and, instead writes that "we" went shopping. Some newspapers, responding to ancient journalistic custom, forbid reporters from injecting themselves into a story with "I." I disagree. Who is the singular "we," anyway?

It's December, and an AP writer pegs a how-to story to the Christmas spirit:

It's the time of year when a lot of Americans like to play Santa Claus, not only by making sure there are plenty of gifts for friends and fam-ily but also by opening their hearts — and pocketbooks — to those less fortunate.

"Charitable giving is about the love of others," said Eugene R. Tempel, executive director of the Center on Philanthropy at Indiana University . . . .

It's also about saving on taxes, and that's where AP's writer takes readers:

There are thousands of charities in the United States and myriad differ-ent ways to contribute to them. The bonus, aside from making you feel good, can be a nice deduction at tax time . . . .

Eileen Alt Powell
The Associated Press[32]

Now, a step-by-step how-to list: Get receipts for contributions over $250, establish "fair market value" of donated used goods, donate stock and not cash . . . .

A St. Petersburg Times writer puts a human face on a how-to story:

Financial security means a lot to (Jane Smith) who grew up poor in New York City.

"We were always being evicted," she said. "I knew I didn't want to live like that."

(Smith) worked her way up through the city's hospital system from a clerk making $3,250 a year to an administrator earning $106,000. She joined the pension plan and the credit union. She bought a home. She even signed up for payroll deduction for retirement savings. But it wasn't until she was on the brink of retirement that (Smith) considered investing in the stock market . . . .

Now, a bit more about (Smith), then a transition to how-to specifics:

(Smith) is one of many women waking up to the world of investment	Helen Huntley *St. Petersburg Times*[33]

Writer Huntley now details for women how to get started investing, how to seek broker advisers, how to explore women-oriented Web sites (including: go to Women's Financial Network at www.wfn.com).

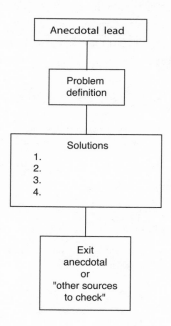

That's helpful how-to writing! A highly readable story structure looks like this:

Try your hand at how-to writing:

- How to get a student loan.
- How to get best terms for a checking account.
- How to handle credit card debt.
- How to catch traps in apartment leases.
- How to get confidential checkups for sexually transmitted diseases.
- How to get counseling for drinking or drug abuse, stress and other personal problems.

The list of how-to possibilities is endless . . . .

NOW, PRESS CONFERENCES AND HANDOUTS

Many basic stories originate in press conferences, public relations handouts, speeches, debates and seminars.

Keep this in mind:

First, what a speaker or PR handout says is news isn't always truly the news. News is what is important to your readers, not the speaker.

Second, successful enterprise reporters glean *ideas* from a press conference or handouts. But they develop meaningful *stories* through probing research that goes far beyond what's said in the press conference or handout.

A few tips:

PRESS CONFERENCES

Lead your story with *news* from the press conference, not the *process* of the press conference itself.

No:

Yes:

Football coach Fred Smith called a press conference today to discuss issues of team discipline.

SPEECH STORIES

Football coach Fred Smith said today he is benching three first-team starters for illegal drug use. Smith told a press conference...

Steel yourself to listening to many speeches in a journalism career — and to listening carefully from start to finish. News can be closer to the end than the start.

Yes, you're responsible for reflecting, even briefly, major points the *speaker* wants to make. But news is what you decide your *readers* want and need, not what the speaker wants to get across.

Keep in mind:

- You can develop news — *possibly exclusively* — with questions asked privately of the speaker before or after the speech.
- If you have an advance copy of a speech, follow the speaker's delivery word-for-word. Omissions or additions during delivery can be news.
- As in all reporting, establish for your readers the speaker's authoritative credentials (or lack thereof.) Answer your reader's question: Why should I pay attention to what this speaker says?

SEMINARS, DEBATES AND MEETINGS

Your responsibility here is to find a commonality or central thrust after listening to two or more speakers.

No:

Three experts on drug addiction told a University audience today that cheap designer drugs are creating thousands of youthful addicts.

Yes:

A panel of experts today discussed drug issues before a student audience in Campbell Hall.

Do all sides and all views in a meeting or debate deserve coverage? Yes, but parcel out wordage in *strict accordance with news value.* Judge — and treat differently — views of compelling importance to your readers and ideas that patently are nonsense.

PR HANDOUTS

Thousands of PR practitioners out there want access to your keyboard.

Some are paid to legitimately gain public hearing for a company, a product, an idea, a cause or political personality.

Others are paid to spin you, push you, prod you into viewing a news development *their employer's way*, not a reporter's way.

Some use above-board techniques: providing background fact sheets, access to officials, tips on forthcoming news breaks. Others are not so principled.

Bottom line: PR practitioners can be enormously helpful. But trust nothing from anyone without checking it out. (Journalism lore has it that an editor in Chicago once snarled to a reporter, "If your mother says she loves you, check it out!")[34]

SUMMARY

- Clips of published stories demonstrate your commitment to journalism and are essential in a job interview, so start — now — reporting on campus.
- Story ideas focused on hard news can win you stringer assignments from off-campus newspapers.
- Volunteering to cover intramural sports or secondary sports can win staff assignments on your college newspaper or magazine.
- Focus story ideas on news as defined *by your target newspaper* and explicitly state what kind of story you will deliver and when.
- Don't promise editors anything you can't deliver; missing deadlines is a journalistic felony and marks you as an unreliable amateur.
- Sports provides marvelous beginner stories *if* you know your game and can write expertly for reader/fans who are experts themselves.
- Basic game stories should focus on key elements: people, what happened, statistics and the look-ahead angle to the next game, the next season.
- The "what happened?" element must cover not just the score but, as well, game strategies, turning points, individual efforts, calls by officials, coaching decisions.
- Important stories off-court and off-field include player lifestyles, the business of sports, health and injuries.
- Principled journalists don't dig in the dark closets of athletes' lives simply for scandal, but readers have a right and need to know about stars' lifestyles if they affect performance.

- Science writing is a news category wide open for beginners, and you need experience, anyway, because science enters virtually all reporting.
- In science writing, accuracy is paramount, and you must translate all technical terms for lay readers.
- Be a cautious "show-me" reporter when covering science because the miracle of science often turns out less than miraculous.
- Accuracy comes from precision reporting and quoting authoritative sources — on *all* sides of an issue.
- Many beginner writers disdain business writing but it opens wonderful story opportunities in economics, finance and business.
- In covering economics, fascinating stories come from watching distant economic indicators and translating their meaning for student readers.
- National figures on gross domestic product, consumer price index, the unemployment rate — all can be translated into meaningful stories on local employment and job prospects for Spring graduates.
- How-to stories are vehicles for great service to readers, informing them how to get student loans, avoid credit card debt, catch traps in apartment leases—how to live better lives.
- In covering press conferences, speeches and meetings, always search through what is said for news important to your readers, not what's important to speakers.

RECOMMENDED READING

Sportswriting is covered in detail in Conrad Fink, "Sportswriting: The Lively Game" (Ames, Iowa: Iowa State University Press, 2001). Also see David Halberstam, editor, "The Best American Sportswriting of the Century" (Boston: Houghton Mifflin Company, 1999).

See additional discussion of science writing in Conrad Fink, "Introduction to Professional Newswriting" (New York: Longman, 1998) and Conrad C. Fink and Donald E. Fink, "Introduction to Magazine Writing" (New York: Macmillan, 1994).

Business writing is covered in Conrad Fink, "Bottom Line Writing: Reporting the Sense of Dollars" (Ames, Iowa: Iowa State University Press, 2000).

EXERCISES

1. Write for your instructor, in no more than 150 words each, four ideas for sports stories. Using guidelines discussed in Chapter Seven, write two for campus stories you will offer to *off*-campus publications. Write two for campus publications.

2. In about 150 words each, write for your instructor four ideas for science stories. Using Chapter Seven's suggested story-idea format, write two ideas you will offer to off-campus newspapers, two for campus publications.

3. In about 150 words each, write four story ideas for how-to articles aimed at campus publication and its student audience. Emphasize how-to guidance on pocketbook issues of real dollars-and-cents concern to students.

4. From this week's *New York Times* (or another newspaper designated by your instructor), select four sports stories that focus on 1) the people angle, 2) the "what happened?" angle, 3) game strategies, or 4) turning points. In about 100 words each, discuss how successfully the writers structured their stories. Was there adequate statistical context for key elements?

5. Select from this week's *Wall Street Journal* an example of how-to writing. Analyze the story structure, using as guidelines the pointers in Chapter Seven on this story form. What are the characteristics of the story? Is there an anecdotal intro? Is the problem well-defined and are how-to solutions outlined adequately? Write this in 250–300 words.

NOTES

1. Simmons Market Research Bureau, quoted in Newspaper Association of America's "Facts About Newspapers 1998," p. 8.

2. "Florida Steals Victory," Feb. 17, 2001, p. G–1.

3. "O'Brien Not Silenced by Sonic Boom," Feb. 17, 2001, p. G–3.

4. Dispatch for morning papers, Feb. 23, 2001.

5. Dispatch for morning papers, Feb. 23, 2001.

6. "Devils, Pack Prepare for Games in Different Ways," Feb. 11, 2001, p. C–1.

7. "Younger Clippers Make a Statement," Feb. 6, 2001, p. D–1.

8. Dispatch for morning papers, Feb. 21, 2001.

9. Dispatch for morning papers, Feb. 16, 2001.

10. Dispatch for morning papers, Feb. 24, 2001.

11. Dispatch for Sunday papers, Feb. 11, 2001.

12. "Pilots End Six-Game Slide on Free Throws, Frost's Blocks," Feb. 11, 2001, p. B–10.

13. "Gordon Lee Wins 6-A Play-in Over Adairsville," Feb. 13, 2001, p. D–5.

14. "Rhea Boys, Cleveland Girls Win, Feb. 21, 2001, p. D–7.

15. "Hixon Boys, Girls Triumph in Playoffs," Feb. 21, 2001, p. D–7.

16. "Vols Search for Answer to Continuing Slump," Feb. 13, 2001, p. D–3.

17. "Bulls Fighting to Stay Motivated," Feb. 24, 2001, Section 3, p. 1.

18. Erica Good, "Samson Diagnosis: Antisocial Personality Disorder, With Muscles," *New York Times*, Feb. 20, 2001, p. D–7; William J. Broad, "Under Icy Arctic Waters, A Firey, Unexpected Find," *New York Times*, Feb. 20, 2001; research is Laura Dalton, "Explaining the Unexplained," *Gannetteer*, July/August 1994, p. 6.

19. Dispatch for morning papers, Nov. 21, 2000.

20. "'Aches and Pains' Aside, Lieberman and His Doctors Say He's Healthy," Oct. 21, 2000, p. A–23.

21. "Suddenly, Universe Gains 40 Billion More Galaxies," Jan. 16, 1996, p. A–1.

22. Dispatch for morning papers, Dec. 26, 2000.

23. Joe Nicholson, "Of Mice & Men," *Editor & Publisher*, Oct. 3, 1998, p. 24.

24. Denise Grady, "Medical Journal Cites Misleading Drug Research," Nov. 10, 1999, p. A–18.

25. Joe Nicholson, "Of Mice & Men," op cit.

26. Diana B. Henriques, "News in The Age of Money," *CJR*, November/December 2000, p. 18.

27. "The Money Men," Feb. 11, 2001, p. E–1.

28. Dispatch for morning papers, Feb. 19, 2001.

29. "Shopaholic Finds Best Bargain in Exercising Control," Feb. 13, 2001, p. C–1.

30. "Can You Spot The Fake?," Feb. 16, 2001, p. W–1.

31. "Can You Spot the Fake?", Feb.16, 2001, p. W-1.

32. Dispatch for morning papers, Dec. 26, 2000.

33. Dispatch for morning papers, Dec. 26, 2000.

34. I discuss public relations operations and ethics in Conrad Fink, "Media Ethics" (Boston: Allyn and Bacon, 1995).

PART FIVE
Features and Profiles

Features and Profiles

Our study of writing so far in this book has focused mostly on spot-news stories — reporting *now* and writing *now* the basic Five-Ws-and-How events of the day.

I emphasized such basic story forms because editors who interview you for your first job likely will be most interested in whether you can handle the two-car wreck story, the speech, the school board meeting — the basic newspaper chronicle of life in a community.

Nevertheless, there is more — much more — to writing for a newspaper.

Yes, newspapers must offer crisp, hard-news dimensions. Yes, deep-dig looks into what happened last night are essential.

But we also must highlight the human element with featurish writing that provides insightful background and, frequently, entertainment, a major offering of any successful newspaper.

So, without neglecting any hard-news writing lessons learned so far, let's now escalate your writing challenge — and fun — by moving into another dimension: features and profiles.

In Chapter Eight, Handling Longer Narratives, we'll study writing that pulls readers into — and through — much more wordage than normally is offered in a spot-news story. Learn to write with color and drama but without getting tangled in blind-alley writing or excess verbiage.

We'll look at these forms:

- *One-shot features*. These one-time offerings to readers may (or may not) be tied to an ongoing news story. They enable you to write about something important, helpful or just plain off-beat and amusing.
- *Feature series*. When a hugely important (and complex) story cannot be handled in a one-shot feature, break the story into logical and manageable components your readers can digest easily one by one.
- *"Come-along" features* are useful for drawing readers into the news and for enabling them to "see" an event you witness.
- *Profiles*. You can profile individuals to give readers behind-the-scene-glimpses of important news stories.
- *Obituaries*. Dull, routine stories assigned new reporters to labor through as a rite of passage? No way. Obits today are written colorfully at many newspapers to celebrate life, not death, to explain and illuminate, not merely bid farewell.

8
Handling Longer Narratives

YOU CANNOT FUNCTION successfully in journalism today without learning to write with a featurish style.

Indeed, because newspapers and magazines long ago conceded spot-news breaks to radio, television and the Internet, strong feature-writing ability can be your ticket to a fine career in print journalism.

Need proof? Well, think of newspapers you might regard as wedded to a hard-news (read that, "dull") format:

The *New York Times*. "The good, dull mother *Times*?" Publishes some of the best, most colorful feature writing in journalism.

The *Washington Post*. Wedded to straightforward, humdrum political reporting? Has marvelous writers who are given plenty of newshole for writing that *dances*, that *sings*.

Wall Street Journal? Ask any editor about the *Journal*'s Page One features. Rare jewels are hidden among those stock market tables and commodity reports.

You get the point: Great *news*papers are repositories of great feature writing that entertains as well as informs. Let's look at examples.

WRITING ONE-SHOT FEATURES

Evan Ramstad and Tina Susman are writers facing huge challenges.

A Journalist's Other Mission

Critics who see journalism as the inverse of entertainment demean both enterprises. They would have us believe that the more we enjoy the news, the less its value. In truth, great journalists, at least since Homer and Plutarch, have always managed to be entertaining.

–Max Frankel, "Macho Man vs. The News,"
New York Times Magazine, Nov. 28, 1998, p. 40.

His is to get *Wall Street Journal* readers into yet another story about high-tech education. Hers is to snare *Newsday* readers into yet another story about misery in Congo.

To reach their goals, both writers lace together enormously interesting one-shot features. Here is the *Journal's* Ramstad at work:

Crookston, Minn. — This is definitely not our father's biology class — nor, in all likelihood, yours.

At the University of Minnesota-Crookston, students in (Fred Smith's) biology class conduct experiments by first attaching probes to their laptop computers. (Smith) projects images of cells from his microscope onto a screen. He then snaps a digital picture of the cell in the microscope and electronically forwards it to each of his students.

Instead of drawing the cell on paper, as they did previously, students store the picture on their laptops, which saves time and yields a more realistic reference aid.

(Smith's) use of computers within the classroom isn't uncommon at UMC . . . . In fact, the school has been providing all of its students, faculty and staff with laptop computers for the past eight years — the first university to do so . . . . UMC has become a laboratory itself — a pioneer in using technology to transform the behavior of students and teachers in and out of the classroom. Administrators from colleges and universities around the world have visited the school to study its technology-based approach to education . . . .

Thus does a superior feature writer open a 1,750-word takeout that easily could drive readers *away*, rather than pull them deeper into the *Journal's* columns, if written in "straight" hard-news style.

Picture this dismal hard-news alternative:

Crookston, Minn. — The University of Minnesota-Crookston has attracted the attention of educators from around the world with its use of computers in classrooms . . . .

Rather than settle for such a dull intro, writer Ramstad uses the neck-of-the-vase structure *and* talks directly to you, the reader, in a friendly, relaxed way (. . ."your father's biology class — nor, in all likelihood, yours")

But, you might ask, isn't there any news? Yes, and Ramstad moves to it quickly, in the next graf:

Although colleges and universities have long been at the forefront of computer use, until recently computers remained a tool used mainly outside the classroom, accessed instead in data centers, libraries, labs, offices and dorm rooms. Several years ago, a few schools began requiring students to bring computers to campus, though not necessarily to classes. About 100 colleges and universities have gone a step further, creating lease and purchase programs to equip everyone with the same type of laptop and making network connections ubiquitous on campuses.

As a result, computers and the Web are altering the boundaries of the classroom . . . .

Those two grafs above widen the Journal's story to the impact *nationally* of computerized classrooms. There is brief reference to their use at Wake Forest University in Winston-Salem, N.C., then, back to Crookston (and note the transition language at start of the graf):

In most UMC classes, students sit down, open up their laptops and plug them in to power and network jacks at each seat. Often, they operate several windows on their computer screens simultaneously, typing notes in a word-processing document, following Powerpoint slides or Web-based material in browsing software and watching electronic chats or instant messages.

Detailed examination of the Crookston experience follows, and there is a strong *informational component* to the story. It's a good read, all right, but you learn a great deal while enjoying your reading.

Finally, a kicker: The university was threatened with closure because of small enrollment *before* computers. Now, writer Ramstad notes, so many students are attracted to the campus that administrators wonder "where to put all the students. For several weeks last fall, about 20 students lived at a motel because of campus-housing crunch."[1]

Picture the *Journal's informational* feature as having this structure:

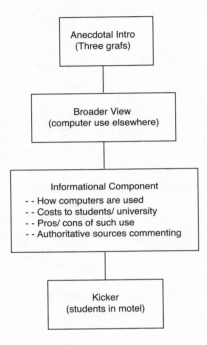

A very different approach is taken by *Newsday's* Tina Susman as she trolls before readers yet another suffering-in-Congo story.

Mugeri, Democratic Republic of Congo — Terror is a way of life here, so common, so routine, that Salfata Nakachate describes the agonizing death of her baby boy casually, as if she were reciting a recipe.

"He died from the rain. He died from the cold. You know, when it rains a lot and you're living in the forest and you have no protection, no blankets," she explains with a slight shrug to a foreign visitor who, in truth, can't imagine such a predicament. The 20 or so people sitting near Nakachate understand, though, and they nod in agreement or cluck sympathetically while rocking slowly back and forth on hard wooden benches as they wait to tell their own tales.

After reading these first two grafs, don't you want more?

In this one-shot feature, Susman writes with enormous drama and pathos to achieve her informational purpose.

And note, in the second graf above, how Susman injects herself into the story, as the "foreign visitor who, in truth, can't imagine such a predicament." The feature story, unlike the hard-news story, sometimes communicates effectively if you step — briefly but only when appropriate — into the action.

After that personalized intro, Susman, in her third graf, widens the view:

> Like Nakachate, most have reached this sparse village by foot after fleeing rebel attacks on their farming hamlets and hiding for weeks or months in the heavily forested mountains surrounding Lake Kivu. They have eaten wild grass, roots and bugs, gnawed on tree bark, given birth on sheets of rain-soaked leaves, watched their newborns shiver to death in the rain and fog, and lived like wild animals . . . .

For more than 1,200 words, Susman sketches horror upon horror: 2.3 million persons dead in two years; measles alone killed 1,400; the war took about 2,600 lives *daily*. And, a telling quote:

> "The loss of life in Congo has been staggering. It's as if the entire population of Houston was wiped off the face of the Earth in a matter of months," Reynold Levy, the International Rescue Committee's president, said.

Then, the kicker: 34 percent of deaths blamed on the war were children under five years of age; 47 percent of all victims of violence were women or children.[2]

These characteristics, then, mark the successful one-shot *informational* feature:

- It is *timely*, achieving greatest effect if you write about an event in the news. But you need not "peg" it to an event last night or last week.
- Whether the informational component dominates your feature or is a relatively minor part of it depends on your news judgment. You can write principally to communicate information or, instead, to catch drama and pathos.

- You can — and sometimes *should* — inject yourself into the story, if that enhances communication.
- Whatever your mission or writing style, strong reporting and authoritative sourcing are required in an informational feature.

With less informational thrust but great imagery, the *Washington Post*'s Emily Wax sets out to report how schools mark Ramadan, the Muslim holy month:

Squeezing through a thick swarm of his giggling and gregarious sixth-grade classmates, Luis Macias, 12, stood on tiptoe to get a peep at a table crammed with clothing from the Middle East, sesame candies and leather-bound books with curly swirls of Arabic writing.

Within seconds, he spotted what he wanted: a black, green and velvet Kufi hat, with round mirrors and glitter dotting the sides. He placed the hat from Afghanistan atop his mop of black hair and quickly scrambled to his seat.

"Now that you are all wearing clothes from the Middle East, we can talk about them and what the upcoming special month for Muslims is," said Samir Hussein, a guest speaker at E. Brooke Lee Middle School in Silver Spring. "Does anyone know what is coming up?"

Blank faces. Embarrassed shrugs. Even though Luis was smiling in his Kufi, the boy from Ecuador had never heard of Muslims, let alone what their holy month was . . . .

Note the leisurely writing pace in that intro, the *impact on your senses* of giggling children, sesame candies, leather-bound books. You're more than 100 words into the story before getting to what it's all about — Ramadan. Still, the "color" writing continues:

"It's Ramadan, my holiday," answered Daad Mohamed, 12, a Sudanese American student. "We fast and get gifts at the end."

Eyes grew wide. Hands starting shooting into the air with questions as Hussein . . . explained the 30-day period of fasting and reflection that started this week.

Now, the informational component:

As the Muslim population in schools soars, lessons like this . . . have become more common in classrooms across the Washington region. It's part of a growing effort in public schools to increase understanding and decrease stereotypes of Muslim students and their traditions . . . .

Emily Wax
Washington Post[3]

Note the feature above *is* timely; Ramadan is approaching. However, the story essentially is a *mood piece*, a writing effort (successful, I think) to let readers "see" and "hear" giggling students.

This type feature is perfect for story ideas we all see — and often ignore — each day.

Take, for example, those harried hostesses at busy restaurants who try to remain calm and cheerful while telling impatient and sometimes angry diners they must wait for tables. Ever wonder how they manage? Judy Hevrdejs of the *Chicago Tribune* did, and that led her into a highly readable stand-alone feature:

It is 4:30 p.m. on a recent Saturday, with only a handful of shopping days left before Christmas. The 38 tables inside Maggiano's eatery in the Oakbrook Center are full.

There are about 100 people on the waiting list for a table. Estimated wait: 45 minutes.

Ground zero is the hostess stand, where the crowds huddle hoping to get seated, as soon as possible, please. It's a scene that is played out at popular . . . restaurants throughout the year, but it intensifies during the holidays when getting a table without a reservation — or with a reservation, for that matter — can be a challenge.

"Debbie F. party of four," a voice booms from the intercom.

While some of the waiting customers have gone off to browse nearby stores, others insist on waiting at the host stand, persistently checking on the status of their reservations and regularly scooping up handfuls of the multi-colored candies sitting in a small bowl.

"We have to feed you as soon as you get here. We're Italians," laughs Christi Granato, as she refills the bowl.

Granato is indeed Italian. She is also the restaurant's hostess, the first person people approach when they work their way to the hostess stand . . . .

Judy Hevrdejs
Chicago Tribune[4]

That story above is just a light-hearted feature that began with a reporter *seeing a story in the obvious*, then answering a question lots of people ask but never trouble themselves to answer: How *do* hostesses manage?

I always wondered about this: How do professional wine tasters stay sober? So I read with great interest (as I am sure *thousands* of readers did) a feature by two wine critics for the *Wall Street Journal*, Dorothy J. Gaiter and John Brecher:

Week after week, (Fred Smith) of Windermere, Fla., read our wine

column, wondering. Finally, he had to ask. "OK, I'll just blurt this out," he wrote. "How do you drink so frequently without getting completely blotto?"

In the three years we've been writing "Tastings," we've fielded more than 8,000 questions and comments . . . from how to make the best wine and food pairings to why wine distribution is so screwy (it's a hangover from Prohibition). But the most common queries are often ones that we'd never expect.

Start with Mr. (Smith's) — that's our 10th most-asked question. Rarely do people ask about the winemaking process itself. We haven't received a single question, for instance, about the different qualities of French and American oak barrels . . . .

We also get a lot of queries that would make a good trivia game. Why do raisins float in Champagne? Who planted the first grape in Australia? . . .

That wine feature *led* the *Journal*'s prestigious weekend feature section, and the writers cleverly teased readers deeper into the story, answering the lead's question only several hundred words later:

We taste six or eight wines every night, about 50 for each column, but the operative word here is "taste." We sniff, we swirl, we talk a lot and we spit a lot. In fact, we drink less now than we did before we became wine writers. We used to split a bottle every night, sometimes two when we were much younger . . . .

Now we just taste. We're evaluating wines, not having a party. In any case, the sight of six or eight bottles of wine in front of us is pretty sobering.

For 25 years, we never wasted a drop of wine. Now, at the end of the night, John pours it all down the kitchen sink after Dottie leaves the room. She can't stand to watch. And, no, our neighbors don't get leftovers . . . .

Dorothy J. Gaiter,
John Brecher
Wall Street Journal[5]

Ever wonder who makes fruit cakes? A *Los Angeles Times* writer did — and readers benefited. Note:

Ava, Mo. — On this autumn morning, when the chapel bell tolls, a moonlit mist shrouds the monks' cloister in the thick woods of the Ozarks. Just before the "Great Silence" ends, at 3:15 a.m., Brother Gabriel Friend slips on a white habit and heads to prayer services in a chapel that hints of incense. A few hours later, in a bakery smelling of rum and sweet pineapple, Brother Friend and his monastery brethren throw aprons over their everyday robes.

They are working against a pressing deadline now, these fruitcake bakers . . . . At Assumption Abbey, one of the most secluded Trappist monasteries in the world, the 20 monks cannot afford to shut out entirely the intrusions of society. Not with 28,000 two-pound fruitcakes to sell by Christmas and no other major means of support.

Renee Tawa
Los Angeles Times[6]

Chapel bells tolling . . . moonlit mists shrouding a monk's cloister. It's 3:15 a.m., and the monks — and the *Times'* Tawa — are on the job.

Fruitcakes may have triggered this story, but the writer goes far beyond them, into life in Assumption Abbey (the monks range in age from 21 to 76, they eat simple vegetarian meals in silence, rarely leave the grounds . . .).

Lessons: Sometimes, the most mundane events — seeing a harried hostess, tasting a fruitcake — can trigger ideas for highly readable features. *Watch. Listen.* Ideas await you out there.

Occasionally what *you* do — writing a wine column, for example — makes a good feature, too.

And make it a rule: *Never* pass up a humorous feature. Editors and readers alike will thank you for anything funny.

Sportswriter Allen Barra of, yes, the sober, stolid *Wall Street Journal* understands that. With "March Madness" approaching in basketball, he uses a *question-and-answer format*:

The NCAA Men's basketball tournament may not be the nation's premier sporting event — the first few rounds seem to spark mostly local interest — but March Madness is likely the most popular in America's office pools. In making your own picks, you may want to know what the recent past indicates about the present, so we sifted through the 945 games played since the tournament expanded to 63 games from 31 in 1985, in order to make this clip 'n' save Q & A guide. Here are some of our most frequently asked questions.

Q. Realistically, what chance does a 16th seed have for that big first-round upset?

A. About the same chance Custer had when he rode into the valley. Since 1985, No. 1s have been a perfect 64–0 against 16th seeds, and that's probably not going to change this year. Our computer, Mad Max, puts the odds at about 250 to 1. Worse, these 16s don't seem to have much of a chance to make a game of it: The average margin of victory has been 24.8 points (up from 23.8 in 1995, which was up from 22.7 in 1990, so it actually appears to be getting worse). Come to think of it, Custer had a better chance: The odds against him were just 15 to 1 . . . .

Allen Barra
Wall Street Journal[7]

Onward rolls writer Barra, trailed, I am sure, by many readers out to have a good time — but learning something, too. Behind the humor, Barra supplies bountiful statistics for hard-core basketball fans.

THE FEATURE SERIES: A CASE STUDY

For the *Charlotte (N.C.) Observer*, the journalistic challenge is clear:

Something is wrong with the city's 911 emergency response services. People are dying while awaiting help. And the public has both a right and need to know why.

The *Observer*'s response is a detailed, highly readable three-part series titled, "Race Against Death." It's a case study of how outstanding newspapers (of which the *Observer* is one) marshal huge resources for significant stories.

Involved in reporting and presenting the story are six reporters, two editors, one artist, one photographer and two page editors.

Computer-assisted analysis is done on *24,000* emergency runs by ambulance crews, and reporters interview dozens of medics, patients, experts and officials.

The three-part result:

PART ONE

The first story in the series is about 1,900 words, headlined, "Heart Attack. You Call 911. Help Is on The Way, They Say. But It May Come Too Late."

The writer, Ames Alexander, opens this way:

A firefighter blistered his knees trying to revive a heart-attack victim as he waited for an ambulance. It took 20 minutes.

An ambulance crew fought miles of city traffic to reach a retiree who heart had stopped. The response time: 21 minutes.

A 12-year-old girl gravely injured in a car wreck awaited paramedics–for 23 minutes.

Dennis Goodman, Julian Cook and Angel Baker–they all died. Now their relatives wonder if quicker ambulance service could have saved them.

Virtually all the Charlotte region's ambulance squads provide good care, experts say. But swamped with calls and short of dollars, many respond too slowly.

The result: saveable patients die.

Lesson: No matter how detailed your research, how clinical or statistical your findings, you must *write the human element* to pull readers into your series. Otherwise, your message is lost.

Alexander reveals to readers in his next graf that the *Observer* indeed engaged in a massive computer-assisted analysis of more than 24,000 emergency calls. But this series is about *people*, not computer analysis, and that's the thrust of Alexander's writing.

He now quickly moves to highlighting precise details of the problem, with a series of "dash-matter" paragraphs:

- Long waits for ambulances are commonplace. . .
- The implications are sometimes deadly. . .
- On average . . . ambulances take more than eight minutes to respond to emergencies. . .
- National comparisons show some (local) counties lag. . .
- Most first responders in the Carolinas — unlike most nationwide — can't do advanced life-saving techniques like defibrillation. . .

Now, Alexander *swings back to detailed examination of the examples he used to open his story*, and each is written in such dramatic human terms that the underlying message about ambulance service is made graphically clear. For example, deep in his story, this:

On the night of July 1, 1994, a drunken driver plowed into a '64 Chevy pickup in southern Cabarrus County, hurling 12-year-old Angel Baker from the truck's bed. The north Charlotte girl suffered massive injuries to her head and chest. But she had to wait 23 minutes for paramedics.

The ambulance had come from Central Cabarrus High School, some 10 miles away, and had to battle thick holiday weekend traffic. Despite the efforts of paramedics and first responders, Angel didn't make it . . . .

Lesson: Even when deep in a technical story (*24,000* emergency calls are being analyzed!) you must "juice" your writing with dramatic vignettes to maintain reader momentum.

In Part One, Alexander defines who, what, where, when. Still unanswered: why?

PART TWO

This second story in the series answers why. It runs about 2,000 words, under the headline, "Overworked Personnel and Overloaded System Can Spell Disaster."

Alexander's intro goes directly to the question readers must be asking:

Why are so many ambulances in the Charlotte region running late?

Though the reasons are numerous and complex, the answer often boils down to four words: more calls, limited dollars.

"The problem that creates is increased response time, burnout of personnel, people having to make decisions when they're too tired to make decisions, equipment breaking down," says Bob Bailey, director of the N.C. Office of Emergency Medical Services . . . .

Now Alexander refreshes readers on the basic problem described in Part One: "In a computer-aided study of recent ambulance runs, The Observer found that the region's paramedics took more than 15 minutes to respond to about one in eight medical emergencies."

Lesson: As you move through thousands of words in a multi-part series return occasionally to the series' underpinnings. Readers otherwise can lose track of your principal message.

Alexander continues:

Some of the reasons:

• Medicare reimbursement for ambulance rides is (too low) . . . .

• Some counties fail to collect from people who use ambulances . . . .
• The volume of emergency calls is surging . . . .

Lesson: Dash matter, though not beautiful writing, is helpful in breaking out discrete points that need individual emphasis.

Even in this dollars-and-cents portion of his series, Alexander strives for readability by inserting interesting anecdotes along the way. To illustrate his point that many 911 calls are not true emergencies, this:

York County medic (Fred Smith) remembers the late-night emergency run to the home of a 911-caller who looked perfectly healthy. Dressed in coat and hat, the man was holding a beer, flicking a cigarette and walking toward the ambulance.

This, it turned out, was the "patient." He merely wanted a ride to the hospital so he could get his stitches out.

Now, reflect on the *Observer* series so far:

Part One defines the problem in dramatic detail.

Part Two reports why the problem exists.

What now? *Solutions*. In this type of reporting, *if you don't offer solutions you become part of the problem.*

PART THREE

This is 1,700 words under the headline, "The Quick and The Living: Here's How to Cure Ambulance Woes."

But, as he does several times in Part Two, Alexander revisits the principal thrust of the series: People die or live because of what we're talking about. Alexander's intro:

(Fred Smith) was watching television one summer night when, suddenly, he couldn't breathe. Within seconds, he passed out.

Summoned by a 911 call, highly trained paramedics arrived at (Smith's) Norfolk, Va., home in 3 1/2 minutes. They found trouble:

The retired naval officer had no pulse. His face was ashen. His heart was literally quivering.

But with repeated electrical shocks and powerful medication, paramedics restored (Smith's) heartbeat — and his life . . . .

That opening anecdote from *Norfolk, Va.* — which "once had one of the nation's slowest urban ambulance systems" — sets up Alexander's readers for this comparison:

In interviews with the *Observer*, experts said public officials in the Charlotte region can also improve ambulance service. Here's how:

• Set response time requirements – and take steps to ensure ambulances meet them . . . .

• Consider sweeping changes, such as merging fire and ambulance departments . . . .

• Train first responders to perform advanced life support techniques . . . .

• Switch paramedics in busy systems from 24-hour shifts to considerably shorter ones . . . .

Ames Alexander
Charlotte Observer[8]

The successful multi-part series, then, has these characteristics:

- It's used primarily on large, complex issues that don't fit neatly into a single stand-alone feature.
- You must break your series into logical components for detailed examination, as the *Observer* broke its series into 1) defining the problem, 2) examining the "why?", and 3) offering solutions.
- Strong reporting is a must (recall the *Observer*'s computer-assisted analysis of 24,000 ambulance calls.)
- *But write the people angle*, and don't let your detailed reporting turn your writing into a dry statistical report.

THE "COME-ALONG" FEATURE

A successful feature writer says to readers, in effect, "Come along with me . . . see, as I see; hear what I hear; touch, feel and sniff with me."

Thus my choice of title for the "come-along" feature, your vehicle for carrying readers to places they otherwise never would go, to meet people they never would meet, to see sights they never would see.

Shortly after Vincente Fox is elected president of Mexico, two *New York Times* reporters travel with him — and take us along:

Mexico City — It happened fast, out of the spotlight, on a roadside in southern Mexico: President Vicente Fox used the power of his office to try to change a life.

As his motorcade headed to a rally honoring the national oil company last weekend, a girl in a wheelchair caught Mr. Fox's eye. He ordered his driver to stop, and then got out of his dark Suburban to meet the girl. Her parents froze in disbelief at the sight of the 6-foot–5-inch president towering above them in a blinding white guayabera and his signature cowboy boots. Then, seizing the moment of their lives, they breathlessly explained that they were too poor to afford therapy for their girl . . . .

Now, with all of us standing on that roadside in Mexico, the *Times* writers show us contrasts in how Fox and his predecessors approach politics:

That detour, his supporters say, shows how Mr. Fox is trying to transform this country, starting with the regal culture of the presidency. While most of his predecessors were generals and lawyers and masters of economics, President Fox was a businessman who sold Coca-Cola, and a rancher who sold cows and cauliflower.

When past presidents mixed with the public, they were aloof, their handshakes were polite; their language, flowery and highfalutin. Mr. Fox pulls people toward him, kissing women on the cheek, and his speech is as earthy as a barnyard.

The old presidential style was often akin to the pope's: cloaked in power, granting indulgences, rarely visible. Mr. Fox is making four to five speeches a day. For the first time, he has opened the presidential manor, Los Pinos, to limited public tours . . . .

Note, we're not talking here about breathless, uncritical adulation. Indeed, the *Times* writers report Fox tells the girl's parents, "We are going to help you" and that an official tells the president he will tend to the matter "the next morning." Then: "(Two days later, officials . . . said nothing had been done.)"[9]

Michael Tackett, *Chicago Tribune* political editor, takes you along on a visit to a politician (and can't you just *feel* the melancholy?):

Washington — The office is spare, but the view is spectacular. There is a temporary look and feel to the room—veneer furniture, bare off-white walls. The bookshelf is empty; the desk has some scattered papers and no inbox. But when William Daley looks out of the eighth-floor window from the Watergate complex, he has a commanding view of the Potomac River and the official Washington he is leaving behind.

The man who bears a name syn-

onymous with urban politics admits he is smitten by the nation's capital. "I've been around the White House and the presidency," said Daley, who was chairman of Vice President Al Gore's presidential campaign. "There is tremendous allure to it all. Potomac Fever is pretty strong.

"But it is also very transitory" . . . .

Michael Tackett
Chicago Tribune[10]

Look, as a *Los Angeles Times* writer looks, at an "architectural nirvana":

Palm Springs — The gasps were audible as 50 pairs of eyes settled on the scene: a circular living room covered by an enormous, weighty cement dome, floor-to-ceiling glass walls revealing a stunning panoramic view of the city. If there is such a thing as an architectural

nirvana, this may have been it.

The setting was the Elrod house, designed by John Lautner and now used primarily for entertaining by its current owner . . . .

Jeannie Stein
Los Angeles Times[11]

The "come-along" structure is perfect for those feature-writing assignments that propel *you* into the story. Here's Rowan Philp of the *Washington Post*:

Woodstock, Va. — The chatter is of beef and baseball as our school bus jounces across a bridge over the Shenandoah River. The meadows in the valley are so thick that each cow seems dug-in for the day, bereft of any good excuse to move.

We 13, all journalists, have been promised coffee, cake and a cozy log cabin for our early-morning briefing in the woods . . . .

No one notices the military truck on our tail.

Bang! A large explosion in front of the bus forces our driver to brake hard . . . .

What's this? An explosion? In Woodstock, Va.? Want to read more? Of course you do:

New bangs now — it's hard to tell the gunshots outside from fists pummeling the sides of the bus. It's hard to tell anything.

There is a louder bang from the front, and the bus driver slumps over in his seat.

Three people holding .45 pistols and wearing camouflage shirts and black balaclavas charge into the bus

. . . .

"Get off the (expletive) bus!" is the shrieked command—a woman's voice.

It's echoed by two male voices and repeated relentlessly as we are yanked powerfully by the shoulders, one-handed, up the aisle and down the stairs . . . .

Philp is thrown face down in roadside grass, and, "I feel a cold muzzle pressed against my neck" . . . A kidnapping? No. Well, not a real one, anyway:

Our kidnappers are ex-British Royal Marines from a training outfit called Centurion Risk Assessment Services, and the abduction is an unexpected . . . part of a five-day course titled Hostile Environments Training.

It's the first war correspondent training held in the United States, and the pilot for monthly courses at the Massanutten Military Academy next year, reflecting a growing concern among journalism institutions about the increasing dangers reporters face in the world's hot spots . . . .

Rowan Philp
The Washington Post[12]

Talk about "come-along-with-me"!

Here's a similarly personalized feature that so impressed editors of the *Philadelphia Inquirer* that they gave it major front-page play in a Sunday edition, then jumped the story inside to a full page, with photos.

For more than 20 years, since suffering a heart attack in 1980, I have lived with the dark thought that this disease was slowly getting worse and would eventually kill me.

So it was with a lot of skepticism and a little hope that I arrived at Chestnut Hill Hospital in September to start a rigorous 10-week program of exercise, diet and meditation that promised to reverse the disease.

That's *Inquirer* staff writer Donald Drake taking readers along *as he strives to stay alive.*

For thousands of words — *gripping* words — Drake describes the 10-week program and even compares what he "once ate" with what he "now eats" (for example, then, "English muffin, two pats of margarine" and now, "oat bran.")

For *thousands* of readers conscious of health and diet, Drake shares intimate moments with readers, such as:

. . . the moment of truth was last month, one month after completing the program, when I was weighed and given blood tests.

I was surprised and overjoyed by the results.

I'd lost 14 pounds and was now close to my ideal weight. My total cholesterol count had been slashed by 27 percent, from 183 to 134. My triglycerides were reduced by 68 percent, from 274 to 87 . . .

Finally, and with a touch of humor, a kicker:

The need to exercise constantly nags at me, and I've settled into a routine of planning my exercise each day.

I've even come to look forward to snacks of tiny carrots and grape tomatoes.

And I'm beginning to forget what chocolate-chip cookies taste like, though I do have a vague recollection that they taste wonderful.

Donald C. Drake
Philadelphia Inquirer[13]

The "come-along" features has these characteristics:

- It takes readers *behind the news but is best when close to it* (thus the exciting off-beat look at Mexico's new president; the mood-catching look at a politician about to leave Washington's power center.)

- It requires strong powers of observation *and* the ability to catch telling details in colorful language ("parents froze in disbelief" . . . at sight of the president in his "signature cowboy boots").
- As in all journalistic writing, you must be balanced and fair in "come-along" features and avoid uncritical adulation (as in revealing President Fox's promise to the parents wasn't kept immediately).
- *Mood* writing is crucial (as in noting that "gasps were audible" as visitors saw for the first time "an architectural nirvana," in the *Los Angeles Times* piece.)
- "Come-alongs" are perfect for highly personalized writing, in which you take readers, one by one, along on your dramatic trip (as the *Inquirer's* Drake takes us along as he tries to save his own life.)
- To be effective, the "come-along" must be tightly written — woven, really — into an entire fabric, complete with kicker (how Drake loved chocolate-chip cookies!)

THE PROFILE

Ever "people watch" at an airport or mall, noting the tall ones and the short ones, the young and old, wondering who they are and where they're going?

It's a gentle form of voyeurism stirring in many of us and, particularly, in newspaper readers.

Readers are attracted to the people element in news. So, as noted throughout this book, good journalists whenever possible write that element as part of a story.

In profiles, the human element *is* the story, not merely part of it. And if you're a true student of the human condition (as are all good journalists) the profile is enormous fun to write.

For one thing, the profile puts you in touch with both the famous and the *in*famous.

First, the famous:

Pretoria, South Africa — The pink light of dawn was on the runway at Waterkloof Air Force Base near here when Nelson Mandela settled into a specially padded seat aboard his presidential jet. The flight attendant knelt to remove his shoes and, in what seemed like a well-worn routine, helped him lift his swollen legs high onto two pillows.

It was the start of a working day for the 80-year-old President, one that would include a visit deep into a rural backwater, moving from the luxurious jet to an army helicopter for a hot, bumpy, hourlong ride there and another back.

That's Suzanne Daley of the *New York Times* profiling a famous African leader whose photograph is known to tens of millions.

But do those millions know of his swollen legs and the effort he must make at 80 to discharge his official duties? That behind-the-scenes detail is what Daley is out to reveal.

First, for an American audience perhaps unaware of Mandela's current status, this:

After nearly five years in office, Mr. Mandela is still beloved, a leader who can scold an audience for two hours and still get a standing ovation . . . .

His popularity crosses all racial lines and is such an absolute here that even opposition leaders attacking his party, the African National Congress, pause to make it clear that they don't mean him, too. In a recent national survey, 43 percent of those asked to rate his performance gave him a perfect 10.

Now, back to Mandela, *the man*:

In stark contrast to the leaders of many African countries who use imperiousness to make themselves seem imperial, he always strives to charm. He works crowds instead of stalking past them. He tells white-haired women how attractive they still look. He waits for the answer when he asks, "How are you?"

He makes rueful, tongue-in-cheek comments about becoming old and unemployed . . . . When choruses sing to him, he dances his trademark jig.

But he can be cranky, too. The charm comes on at the stops. In between, he hardly speaks . . . .

And onward swings the *Times*' Daley, weaving together 2,100 words of the good and bad about Mandela (including that he didn't like her first question in an interview and "snapped" at her.)

Of course, Mandela is news for *what* he is – a famous leader — as well as *who* he is. So Daley laces together subtle political insights and personal details.

And, Daley carries readers toward a "kicker" ending. Mandela, it seems, once described opposition political parties as "Mickey Mouse parties." Tony Leon, an opposition leader, retorted that Mandela was running a "Goofy government."

Now the kicker:

A few weeks later, Mr. Mandela was visiting a friend in the hospital when he heard that Mr. Leon was also there, recovering from heart bypass surgery.

He approached Mr. Leon's bed from behind the curtains. "Mickey Mouse," he called out in a deep voice, "this is Goofy come to see you."

Suzanne Daley
New York Times[14]

Thus is deeper political understanding communicated through the profile of a famous man.

*In*famous personalities, with their own deep and dark messages, can be great fodder for profiles, too. Keith L. Thomas of the *Atlanta Journal-Constitution:*

Lewisburg, Pa. — He went by many names, this cocky, scrawny young man who stands beside a window overlooking the unfamiliar territory of central Pennsylvania.

"Little Ricky," his friends called him back home on the streets of Savannah, Or "Yellowboy," for his light complexion. Or "Fly."

There were other names as well. Police compared him to men who led the same kind of life: Dillinger, Capone, Manson.

Now he goes by a number — 07–649–021 — and many in Savannah hope Ricky Maurice Jivens wears it all his life.

"For a while there, I was on top of the world," says Jivens, sitting quietly in a small room at the aging federal penitentiary at Lewisburg, where he is serving a sentence of life without parole.

His world, officials allege, was a world of drugs, money, terror and death . . . .

Details of gang life are fascinating: Police say Jivens led a gang of 30 heavily armed men, dealt crack cocaine and "raked in at least $1 million a year."

But it's details about "Little Ricky" that build this profile:

Jivens cruised Savannah in a red Mercedes convertible, always protected by menacing bodyguards, and controlled the city's most formidable drug empire with a beeper and a head for business that belied his lack of education.

He's built a cultlike loyalty out

of raw fear, yet dispensed clothing and champagne with the elan of an inner-city Robin Hood.

At 21, Jivens is boyish, bumpy-faced and slight; with 138 pounds on his 5-foot–10-inch frame. He wears a drab blue prison jumpsuit and white Chuck Taylor Converse All-Stars . . . .

Note the writer's splendid eye for detail: Jivens cruised Savannah not in a Mercedes convertible, but in a *red* Mercedes convertible; he wears a *drab blue* prison jumpsuit; he's not in white jogging shoes, but, rather, in white *Chuck Taylor Converse All-Stars*.

It bears repeating: In jumping from the Five Ws and How of spot news to in-depth feature writing, you must develop powers of observation that are *strong*!

In profiling any infamous hoodlum, as in sketching a famous politi-cian, your writing must take readers to a deeper understanding, into meaning not easily captured in daily spot-news reporting. For writer Thomas, that deeper story is why and how Jivens became a convicted nar-cotics-dealing killer despite a loving family ("I got a lot of love and atten-tion growing up," he says).

So, the profile widens to a family, to a culture, really, and Thomas travels to Savannah to interview father, mother and friends. Thomas even goes out on the street to talk to a drug-selling teenager who now stands where convict Jivens once stood:

"Man, you can't ever stop drugs—not in Savannah, not in Atlanta, not even in Washington, D.C., where George Bush lives," says a 16-year-old who sells a "little rock" now and then. "If people want to buy, some-body has got to sell it."

Like all strong writers, Thomas doesn't let his profile merely trail off. He sets up a kicker by revealing the convict has three children, including Little Ricky Jr., who constantly asks when his daddy is coming home. Back to that prison interview with Jivens:

"Do I want my son to grow up to be like me?" he asks. "I don't think so. I mean, I do want him to be suc-cessful, and be his own boss, his own man. I definitely don't want him to have to kiss anybody's butt.

"But no," says Jivens, as the guard comes to take him back to his windowless cell, "I don't want him to end up *like* me. Look at me."

Keith L. Thomas
Atlanta Journal-Constitution[15]

Reflect on characteristics of successful profiles:

- Virtually anyone — the unknown and infamous, as well as the famous — can be profiled as a means of carrying your readers into a deeper, important story (politics in South Africa, drugs in Savannah).
- You must build a recognizable portrait of your subject, including physical appearance (swollen legs, white Chuck Taylor Converse All-Stars), and speech mannerisms (Mandela "snapped" at the *New York Times* reporter).
- Establish the physical surroundings of your subject to support the thrust of your profile (the profile of hard-working Mandela opens in the "pink light of dawn" at Waterkloof Air Force Base; the ex-drug lord is interviewed "sitting quietly in a small room at the aging federal penitentiary at Lewisburg").
- Communicate the uniqueness of your subject, the weaknesses and strengths of personality; get as deeply as possible into the inner person — hopes, goals, dreams, disappointments, accomplishments.

WRITING OBITUARIES

Col. Donald Conroy, a storied Marine fighter pilot with such a courtly domestic code that it was said he never struck his daughters and did not begin beating his sons until after they had learned to walk, died on Saturday at a hospital in Beaufort, S.C. He was 77 and best known as the model for the tyrannical title character in the book and movie "The Great Santini."

That reads like something out of the police blotter, doesn't it? But it's actually an obituary in the *New York Times*, and a perfect example of how "obit" writing has changed.

Not long ago, you would have studied a rigid writing format for obits that included telephoning the funeral home for details, then carefully listing survivors and pallbearers, but never, never writing anything "not nice" about the dear departed.

Today, obits in many newspapers are unblinkered looks at life as the deceased truly lived it, written in engaging, featurish style. Top writers are assigned to obits.

Robert McG. Thomas Jr., one of the *Times'* best, wrote the Conroy obit, and in addition to breaking the "not-nice" rule, he immediately broke another. His second graf:

His family said the cause was colon cancer.

"Cancer" once was a forbidden word in obit writing at many newspapers. Not today. Cause of death — including suicide — is reported routinely. Neither is it forbidden to really zero in on the deceased's ugliness. Thomas continues:

It is surely a tribute to the resilience of the human spirit, the enduring quality of family love and the capacity for personal redemption that in the last months of his life a man who had terrorized his wife and seven children, administering torrents of verbal abuse and beatings with savage and inexplicable regularity, was accompanied lovingly on his medical rounds by his oldest and most beaten son, the author Pat Conroy, the very one who had exposed his father as a paternal brute in the autobiographical novel "The Great Santini."

Until the book was published in 1976, the fear and loathing at the core of the Conroy household had been a family secret so carefully guarded that on the way to the emergency room after an especially vicious beating, a bleeding Conroy son would be instructed by his mother on what lie to tell to portray the injury as the result of an innocent mishap . . . .

Robert McG. Thomas Jr.
New York Times[16]

For 1,100 words, Thomas continues with the "Great Santini," creating a highly readable piece virtually unrecognizable as an "obit" — except that it *does* list survivors at the end.

The *Times* isn't alone in creating feature obits. Here's Robin Hinch in the *Orange County (Calif.) Register*:

Mariann wanted to live. And Mariann wanted to die. As she cruised the dark, deserted streets of Huntington Beach, her husband, Brett, said she repeatedly called him. The couple had recently separated, he said. She was so very sorry, she said. She wished she could make it all go away. She loved him and the kids, she said, more than anything . . .

Mariann was found at 1 p.m. on Dec. 9 in the back parking lot of a Huntington Beach industrial park. Her seat was reclined and she appeared to be sleeping, with photos of her children — Dylan, 7, and Brandon, 5 — spread across her lap. She was dead of an overdose at age 28.

Robin Hinch
Orange County Register[17]

The *Register*'s Hinch told *American Journalism Review* how she approaches obits:

"I don't write about people's deaths. I write about their lives . . . . I try to avoid people of notoriety. I try to just choose people who lived. And I write about the whole person — their foibles and their downfalls. It's no fun if you can't tell about the temper tantrum they had standing in line once . . . and even when I've written these (unflattering anecdotes), people will call and say, 'Yep, that's Dad, all right.'"[18]

Now, reality: Many newspapers, especially smaller community newspapers (where most journalism careers start), have firm policies *against* such featurish writing in obits. Community convention, particularly in small-town America, still strongly opposes judgmental writing, particularly of any dark side of the life just lived.

But, whatever your writing thrust — featurish or traditional — your obit must include basic information:

- The deceased's full name, age, address, occupation, achievements.
- Survivors, birthplace and (if your newspaper's policy permits) cause of death.
- Clubs, organizations.
- Time and place for public viewing.
- Time and place for funeral service and burial.

SUMMARY

- Learning to write features is essential even though your first job probably will be in spot news, the newspaper's chronicle of life in a community.
- One-shot features enable you to inform in an entertaining fashion, using colorful language to entice readers into subjects they might otherwise evade.
- There must be a strong *informational component* if one-shot features treat serious subjects.
- Informational features should be timely because you achieve greatest effect if you write about an event in the news.

- Strive for impact on reader senses by drawing word pictures of sights, sounds, smells.
- Successful feature writers have a knack for seeing story ideas in the obvious — a story about harried hostesses in restaurants comes from waiting in line for a table; a feature on monks who make fruitcake comes from eating a piece of cake.
- Write a feature series on an issue so important and large that it defies successful treatment in a single story, breaking your series into logical components for detailed examination.
- Do strong reporting for a series but write the people angle; don't let massive research turn your writing into dull statistical analysis.
- Successful feature writers say to readers, in effect, "Come along with me . . . see as I see; hear what I hear."
- The "come-along" feature enables you to take readers places they never go, to see people they don't know, to see sights they otherwise never see.
- Strong powers of observation are necessary in feature writing to catch telling detail.
- Many people share a gentle form of voyeurism — an interest in other people — so the personality profile is perfect for reaching many readers.
- Write profiles on the unknown and infamous, as well as the famous, as a means of telling a deeper, meaningful story.
- In profiles you must build recognizable word portraits of your subject, including physical appearance and speech mannerisms.
- Many newspapers treat obituaries as feature stories celebrating a life, not a mark of death, that frequently include reporting the dark side of the deceased as well as nice things.
- Particularly in smaller communities, however, obituaries still are written in traditionally flattering — or at least neutral — language without any attempt to report the person's life as it truly was lived.

RECOMMENDED READING

The *Philadelphia Inquirer* regularly produces fine long-form stories of the type discussed in this chapter, and has won many Pulitzer Prizes for them. Watch also the *New York Times* for examples of outstanding one-shot features and multi-part series.

A fine single source is Roy Peter Clark and Christopher Scanlan, "America's Best Newspaper Writing" (Boston: Bedford/St. Martin's, 2001). This book is a collection of award-winning stories over a 20-year period. Also see David Halberstam, editor, "The Best American Sportswriting of the Century" (Boston: Houghton Mifflin Company, 1999).

EXERCISES

1. Study a one-shot feature in today's *New York Times* (or another newspaper designated by your instructor) and, in about 300 words, discuss the following: Is the feature timely? Does it concern a subject currently in the news? What do you believe to be the writer's objective? Is the feature designed to explore a deeper, more meaningful issue? If so, what is that issue? In your opinion, does the writer succeed?

2. Analyze an issue currently in the news that is so complex and important that reporting on it would require a series of at least two articles. This might be a complex administrative or financial issue confronting your university, or an issue of national or state importance. Outline, in the wordage required, a plan for 1) separating that issue into two or more logical components and 2) conducting the research and interviews necessary to properly report this multi-article series. You must write, in effect, an "attack plan" you would follow in reporting and writing on the issue.

3. Outline, in about 200 words, a plan for a "come-along" feature in which you would chronicle a personal experience. For example, this could be reporting on your efforts to find a new apartment (including costs, leases and other considerations you would encounter) or going through class registration and reporting on ways to ease the bureaucratic difficulties encountered.

4. Profile a well-known person on your campus. Your subject can be a student leader, teacher, administrator or coach, for example. In

colorful language, sketch the person's appearance, mannerisms and speech habits. Draw a recognizable word picture of the person. The deeper meaning of your profile must be revelation of that person's role in life or some equally probing look at more than superficial appearances. To be effective, a profile such as this must be done in no fewer than 350 words.

5. Interview a classmate and write an obituary. Your obit should reveal the bad, as well as the good. Get as close as you can to how that person lives life and report as objectively as you can. Use as a model the Conroy and Mariann obits discussed in this chapter.

NOTES

1. "The Classroom," March 12, 2001, p. R–25.
2. Dispatch for morning papers of Nov. 23, 2000.
3. "Lessons of Inclusion," Nov. 28, 2000, p. B–1.
4. "Barbarians at The Gate," Dec. 21, 2000, Section 2, p. 1.
5. "Don't They Ever Get Drunk?" March 16, 2001, p. W–1.
6. Dispatch for morning papers, Nov. 23, 2000.
7. "By The Numbers," March 16, 2001, p. W–9.
8. My thanks to Ames Alexander for submitting to a telephone interview on 27 March 2001. His series started in the *Observer* on Sunday, 25 March 1996, under the headline, "Race Against Death," p. A–1.
9. Ginger Thompson and Tim Weiner, "President of Mexico Does Not Stand on Ceremony," *The New York Times*, March 21, 2001, p. A–3.
10. "After Bitter Fight, Daley Looks Ahead," Dec. 21, 2000, p. A–1.
11. "Destination: Modernism," March 1, 2001, p. E–1.
12. Dispatch for morning papers, Nov. 20, 2000.
13. "Combating a Killer With Diet, Exercise," Feb. 18, 2001, p. A–1.
14. "Beloved Country Repays Mandela in Kind," March 23, 1999, p. A–1.
15. "Cracking Little Ricky's World," May 3, 1999, p. M–1.
16. "Donald Conroy, 77, Model for 'The Great Santini,' Dies," May 14, 1998, p. A–19.
17. Judith Sheppard, "A Stylish Send-off For Regular Joes,*" American Journalism Review,* April 1999, p. 49.
18. Ibid.

PART SIX
Writing That Explains and Advocates

Writing That Explains and Advocates

There was a time (trust me) when writing for newspapers and magazines was much simpler.

That, of course, was before electronic media began reaching our audiences faster than we did. Until then, *we* broke news.

That also was before live television began reporting more colorfully than we did. (How *do* you *write* color on a fire story to match a TV reporter *showing* the audience the burning building?)

And, those bygone days were before the world got so complex — or, perhaps, before we realized our readers were so deeply affected by so many of its complexities. Until then, straightforward reporting of the good old Five Ws seemed enough.

So, here we are, in a world of new journalistic realities, still writing for "snail" media, still putting black ink on white paper, but now wrestling with ever-more complicated stories we must write.

How can we compete? More importantly, how can we serve our readers properly?

By analyzing and interpreting the news.

Of all media, newspapers and magazines are best at plowing deeply into complex issues and forcing true meaning to surface. From that flows unique journalistic strength and validation for print.

This book already has touched on interpretive writing *as part of* straightforward, objective reporting — finding the "real what" and "real why," comparing and characterizing to illustrate deeper meaning.

Now, in Part VI, we move significantly beyond that and study writing whose *central thrust is analytical* — writing that offers interpretation as a starting point, then weaves in supporting facts.

In Chapter Nine, Explanatory Writing in News, we'll look at story structures ideally suited for writing complex news stories that beg for interpretation. You will learn how to step into the spot-news flow and serve readers with in-depth reporting and explanatory writing.

In Chapter Ten, Writing Editorials, we'll move even deeper into persuasive writing with study of editorial writing that expresses the institutional position of a newspaper or magazine on issues of compelling importance.

We'll get very personal in Chapter Eleven, Writing Personal Commen-

9

Explanatory Writing in News

IT'S A BIG step for a writer that you're taking in moving from straightforward, objective reporting into explanatory writing.

Luckily, you can edge gradually — carefully—into this new world of writing with a variety of approaches and story structures.

In the chapter ahead, we'll look at these:

- *Internal balancing* is the first effort you must make as a newswriter, to go beyond Five Ws reporting to gather facts and background that will ensure clarity and fairness in a story.
- The *Explanatory Follow* enables you to come in behind a news break with interpretation that takes readers beyond the obvious meaning.
- The *Explanatory Precede* is of great use in helping your readers get set to understand the deeper meaning of an event ahead.
- The *Newsfeature* is a story structure you can use to intervene arbitrarily in the news flow, stop the action, and put together bits and pieces that summarize for readers just what is going on.
- *News Analysis* is a story form differing so much from objective newswriting that it must carry the description "news analysis" (or, in newsroom parlance, be *slugged* "news analysis").

INTERNAL BALANCING

Your basic responsibility is to depict for readers, as honestly as possible, the wider context of every story.

That requires more than merely reporting who said what to whom, more than simply awaiting a spot-news break — an announcement, a speech, an arrest — and much more than limiting your writing to only those facts that automatically float to the surface.

Honest writing requires you to probe deeper than the obvious, to seek additional facts and balancing material beyond the news break at hand. It also requires ensuring basic elements of a story are not lost as the story evolves over days and weeks.

For example, a 14-year-old boy is convicted of first-degree murder for killing, when he was 11, a 6-year-old neighbor girl. During weeks of coverage, initial horror over the *girl*'s death turns into a pathetic story of a mere *boy* convicted of murder. The boy claims he was only practicing wrestling holds on the girl and reporting skews heavily toward sympathy for *him*. Not at AP.

In its continuing coverage, The Associated Press doesn't lose sight of a basic element — an innocent girl suffered a horrible death. An AP writer inserts one graf that achieves internal balancing in a story about the boy's trial:

An autopsy showed (the girl) suffered a fractured skull, lacerated liver, broken ribs, internal hemorraging and cuts and bruises.

Terry Spencer
The Associated Press[1]

A *New York Times* reporter shows keen reportorial instincts in ensuring internal balance in a behind-the-scenes story in Washington. The context is former President Clinton's Monica Lewinsky sex scandal, at the time preoccupying many politicians and reporters.

First, the setup:

Washington — Congress savored the sheer comfort of asexual political skirmishing this weekend as lawmakers struggled with lost legislative causes and artificial doomsday deadlines in their attempt to quit and go home . . . .

"I wasn't sent here to talk about Monica Lewinsky," said Representative Dennis J. Kucinich, hurrying from committee room to House floor as the leadership pushed, then failed, with a plan to finish by Sunday. He darted about as the nation's lawmakers tried to disentangle themselves from a harrowing closing week that was dominated by the House's impeachment challenge to President Clinton even as other issues wilted on the agenda.

"I'm going home to talk health care, Social Security, jobs and education," Mr. Kucinich, Democrat of Ohio, insisted, radiating delight at the hometown prospect of Monica-free vox pop, far from the maddening Beltway.

Now, starting in the fourth graf, marvelous insights that balance the reader's view of what's happening in the halls of Congress:

For anyone numbed by the White House scandal, the last-minute hagglings between and within the two houses in the Capitol is a tonic .... Public debate can once more romp far from the body politic's erogenous zones to topics like the usual last-minute repriming of the Federal budget, the length of the duck season in Mississippi, and the Sense of Congress Resolution Concerning the Inadequacy of Sewage Infrastructure Facilities in Tijuana, Mexico.

The simple sight was bracing when two gangs of rival politicians crossed each others' paths in the Capitol press gallery to fence and parry over the patients health care bill, which was failing on Friday even as the impeachment inquiry took off. They verbally charged and countercharged beyond all grand-jury risk of perjury.

The partisan scrum featured lighthearted exchanges of greetings at the door then hard stares of umbrage before the cameras ....

Francis X. Clines
New York Times[2]

Note above the *impressionistic* reporting, the effort by Clines to capture mood and then depict it, as in his fifth graf ("The simple sight was bracing").

Edge cautiously into such impressionistic reporting. It's a radical departure from traditional efforts to be objective and dispassionate through standardized recital of the Five Ws.

Note also the revealing honesty of the last graf above. Clines watches the pols greet each other warmly, then put on hard (and false) stares for the camera. Clines witnesses — and captures for readers — the phony posturing of Washington politicians. That goes far beyond reporting "objectively" what politicians say. It also demonstrates that what is presented by the camera — false hard stares, in this case — can be a lie.

Now, let's move beyond such careful inclusion of balancing facts in straightforward reporting and, instead, discuss story forms devoted primarily to analysis and interpretation.

THE EXPLANATORY FOLLOW

Get the picture and (especially) the timing:

On *Friday*, President Bush issues an executive order blocking a strike by Northwest Airlines employees, and that, of course, is flash news.

Saturday morning, all across America, newspapers publish *hard-news* stories tightly pegged to the President's official act. Something like this:

> Washington — President Bush signed on Friday an executive order blocking . . . .

But, beyond the obvious, what does that mean?

For *Sunday* papers, Leigh Strope of The Associated Press structures a story of *analysis and interpretation*:

> Washington — President Bush's intervention in the Northwest Airlines labor dispute and his threat to avert other potential airline strikes *seems to signal an end to a hands-off policy largely followed since the Nixon administration.*
>
> Bush's move *creates uncertainty in the industry* for bargainers *and has union officials questioning his motives.*
>
> "Everyone is going to watch this particular negotiation because they're trying to figure out if there's a different set of rules in place or not," said Purdue University professor Frank J. Dooley, author of two books on the Railway Labor Act, which gives the president authority to intervene in transportation labor disputes.
>
> Leigh Strope
> The Associated Press[3]

Note these characteristics of the *explanatory follow*:

- It enables you to come into the news stream *after* an event to explain what it means to your readers, who sometimes are desperate to measure the impact of distant events on their own lives.
- Even AP, a hard-core, straight-news outfit if there ever was one, frees reporters — nay, *requires* reporters — to do analytical writing. It's widely accepted in journalism that mere (and somewhat old-fashioned) recital of facts — the Five Ws — is inadequate in today's complex world.
- Infrequently, if ever, do we reporters get the full truth of any complex story, and the explanatory writing we're discussing doesn't

compel you to pretend you do. Note AP's Strope reserves wiggle room with "seems" in the first graf.

- Note the story moves quickly, in the third graf, to an authoritative source. You cannot be an expert on all subjects. But in explanatory writing you must be expert at finding and quoting sources who are.
- Note AP's story was published on Sunday. Much hard news breaks Monday-Friday, when the world is at work. Relatively little government or business news breaks on Saturdays for Sundays, or on Sundays for Mondays. So, you have better chance of obtaining major display if you can schedule your analytical "work-ups" for the larger newshole available on Sundays and Mondays.

Below is an explanatory follow that led the *Los Angeles Times*, taking the upper-right position on page one normally reserved for the day's top hard-news break. Note the explanatory dimension — the deeper meaning — gets first-graf emphasis.

Southern California Edison edged closer to insolvency Tuesday by declaring that it would not make nearly $600 million in electricity and bond payments, the legacy of months in which it has paid far more for energy than it was allowed to collect from customers . . . .

Nancy Rivera Brooks, Miguel Bustillo, James F. Peltz
Los Angeles Times[4]

Not too long ago, newswriting students like you would have been told to go out and *find someone* to say the utility "edged closer to insolvency." Today, *if the facts warrant such interpretation*, newswriters say it — and that, perhaps, is the basic distinction between objective newswriting discussed in Chapters One to Seven and the explanatory writing under study here in Chapter Eight.

Note above, also, the writers tie together, *in the same graf*, the spot news development (won't make payments) and meaning (edged closer to insolvency.)

Below, a writer does that *to bring to readers immediately the meaning of a distant event*:

Jerusalem — Egypt announced yesterday that it was recalling its ambassador to Israel *in a further unraveling of the fragile peace in* *the Middle East.*

Barbara Demick
Philadelphia Inquirer[5]

It's difficult enough to interpret for readers what happened yesterday. It's much more difficult to shed light on tomorrow. But try we must.

THE EXPLANATORY PRECEDE

How do you explain what's likely to happen tomorrow? *Very carefully.*

Note this careful look-ahead intro, published on Tuesday, one day before the event:

Washington — When a congressional committee grills the heads of the five largest television networks Wednesday about their error-plagued coverage of presidential election results, this much will not be in dispute: The networks screwed up.

Just about everything else about election night will be in dispute.

Now two grafs of background:

Although committee Republicans have billed their inquiry as bipartisan, emotions still run deep along party lines.

Whose candidate did the premature calls of victory in Florida — first for Democrat Al Gore and later for Republican George W. Bush — damage more?

Now back to the look-ahead, *which is limited to straightforward statement of the Republican's and Democrat's positions*:

Republicans argue that the networks' early call for Gore reflected a built-in statistical bias in the exit polls shared by the networks to project the winner. And making that call 10 minutes before polls closed in the Florida Panhandle, they maintain, discouraged Republicans from voting there and in other states where the polls were still open.

Democrats will focus on the networks' later, but still premature, decision to give the state to Bush. That put Gore on the brink of publicly conceding the election — he already had made a concession call to Bush — and contributed to a widespread perception that the subsequent recount was an effort to snatch the election from Bush.

Then, after making clear that a partisan political fight is ahead, the story presents the official view:

The hearing's stated purpose is narrow: to ask top news officials and the director of Voter News Service, the organization that provided exit polling data and election projections to the networks, what went wrong . . . .

Megan Garvey,
Elizabeth Jensen
Los Angeles Times

A couple points about the example above of the explanatory precede:

- It is tentative in its assumptions of what's likely to happen. This deserves emphasis: You're not expected to predict the future; but do sketch lines along which it might develop.
- No matter what *your* interpretation may be, include the views of participants (in this case, the "stated purpose") and other experts.

This explanatory writing first looks *backward*, although it's clearly pegged to a *look-ahead angle*:

Baseball is just now recovering from the strike that canceled the 1994 World Series and part of the 1995 campaign. Yet in recent months there's been a buzz in the media about how the same thing could happen next season.

Why? Along with baseball Commissioner Alan (Bud) Selig, many owners believe the large revenue disparity between some teams threatens the sport's competitive balance . . . . Their solution? Have richer teams like the New York Yankees . . . give a lot more of their revenues to poorer teams like the Montreal Expos . . . . Proponents of more generous revenue sharing say their system would be good for baseball because it would allow poorer teams to sign more star players.

Those two grafs "set up" readers for what's to come. Note the author is tentative (which is smart in look-ahead writing) on just what that will be:

But don't look for the big boys to open their wallets just yet. As it is, Yankee boss George Steinbrenner already forks over $20 million a year to his poorer rivals, more than any other team pays. Steinbrenner has said there's no way he'll pay out more un-less the players agree to a salary cap.

The current collective bargaining agreement between the owners and players is set to expire after this season . . . .

Michael K. Ozanian
Forbes[7]

Below, a writer looks back (at an arrest) and sees a look-ahead element (effect on U.S.-Russian relations.) Note the writer is *very* tentative (using "awkward") in explaining precisely how relations will be affected. The story, published on Thursday, looks ahead to a meeting on Saturday:

Moscow — *In an awkward bit of diplomatic timing*, the arrest of FBI agent Robert Philip Hanssen on charges of being a Russian spy came just days before U.S. Secretary of State Colin L. Powell and the Russian foreign minister were to meet in an effort to defuse increasing tension between the two countries.

The accusations against Hanssen are a potent reminder that the two former superpower rivals still have an often-adversarial relationship years after the Cold War ended.

Russia's government had no comment on the arrest of the agent, who is accused of passing damaging U.S. secrets to the Russians for 15 years.

U.S.-Russia relations have soured in recent weeks . . . . Powell and Russian Foreign Minister Igor Ivanov had been expected to soften some of their differences in a meeting Saturday in Cairo, Egypt.

Then came Hanssen's arrest.

"This case can increase the tension," said Yevgeny Volk, a Moscow analyst . . . .

Dave Montgomery
Knight Ridder News Service[8]

Note the story above is another example of explanatory writing that very quickly swings into quoting an expert (analyst Volk.)

Lesson: Much of your explanatory writing, *particularly if you're looking ahead*, should communicate analysis and interpretation through careful arrangement of facts *and opinion from expert sources*.

That is, don't look into *your* crystal ball and deliver *your* opinion. Rather, create factual substance that communicates meaning. Let's look more closely at that technique.

THE NEWSFEATURE

Note *news*feature.

We're not departing from hard news in turning to this story form. Rather, we're looking at a wonderful vehicle for arranging facts and background in featurish but nonetheless *analytical hard-news writing*.

Newsfeatures have these characteristics:

- They're usually major reporting and writing projects that go considerably beyond the 250–300 word range of many straight news stories.

- You can use innovative writing approaches, such as the neck-of-vase intro or personalized lead, to focus on the human element — the who — of stories.
- Newsfeatures enable you to intervene in a continuing story at any point and time of your choosing — to halt the action for special examination, then summarize past developments and project into the future.
- Newsfeatures are highly useful for dipping into complex multi-dimensional events and focusing on especially interesting highlights of meaningful dimensions.
- Because they are part breaking news and part analysis, newsfeatures are highly useful in localizing for your readers the meaning of a distant event.

Let's look:

LOCALIZING DISTANT EVENTS

In Washington, the Justice Department releases new data on child sexual abuse nationwide.

In Philadelphia, an alert editor at the *Inquirer* assigns Jane Eisner to write a newsfeature localizing the story.

After deep-dig reporting and many interviews, Eisner produces — 25 days after the news broke in Washington — a 1,100- word story that opens this way:

A youth minister in Perkasie is charged with videotaping four boys simulating sex acts.

A Darby Borough child molester documents his sexual involvement in a journal containing the names of hundreds of children, some of them as young as 3 years old.

A Solebury man accused of sexually abusing two children commits suicide.

Three Montgomery county men are charged with luring boys to an Abington apartment for sexual and pornographic acts.

These headlines from the last month are enough to suggest . . . that an epidemic of child sexual abuse is afflicting our mixed-up, immoral nation . . . .

Now, Eisner moves to *interpretive* writing that focuses on official analysis of the data (and localizes it for Pennsylvania and nearby New Jersey):

The stories are true. The conclusion is less so.

In fact, a study just released by the U.S. Department of Justice shows a dramatic decline in reported and substantiated cases of child sexual abuse from 1992 to 1998. The word *dramatic* is not used lightly. Nationwide, the drop in substantiated cases was 31 percent. In Pennsylvania, 42 percent. In New Jersey, 66 percent . . . .

Now, the *look-ahead* element:

These data have enormous implications for policymakers, advocates, physicians, educators, the judicial system, and for families and communities trying to keep children safe from physical and emotional harm . . . .

For several hundred words, Eisner recounts interviews with Philadelphia-area experts in child abuse, noting some fear the nationwide drop in incidents might lead to premature declaration of victory. Eisner uses *judgmental language* that would be unacceptable in an objectively written news story (emphasis added):

How true. Politicians have eagerly claimed credit for the reduction in violence, poverty and teen pregnancy in the 1990s (which *obviously* is connected to the trend in child sexual abuse cases).

Deeper into her story, Eisner analyzes, in her own words, the meaning of some data.

There are grounds here for those who contend it's the economy, stupid. "All the social services we throw at crime are secondary to economic conditions," (one source) said.

And there's the real possibility that this decline isn't real. The data on child sexual abuse are famously untrustworthy. Children often give inconsistent testimony, particularly if the alleged perpetrator is someone familiar, as it is in most cases . . . .

Quoting experts as she goes, Eisner moves toward concluding that "education, intervention, incarceration, treatment and public awareness can combat this unpalatable crime."[9]

Reflect on these characteristics of Eisner's newsfeature:

- It *localizes* a distant news break and uses a featurish neck-of-vase writing structure to draw readers deep into the story.
- It *summarizes* recent local cases of sexual abuse and puts them into perspective within the context of nationwide data.

- It is based on *weeks* of reporting and interviewing of local authoritative sources.
- It is *judgmental*, with Eisner stating "how true" that politicians eagerly claim credit, and the *facts indicate* poverty and child abuse are linked.

INTERVENING IN A CONTINUING STORY

Major news stories often bubble along over lengthy periods without any single news development warranting significant coverage.

Yet, journalists must keep track of such stories, updating them and placing them before the public on occasion.

The newsfeature is perfect for the task.

For example, Jamil Abdullah Al-Amin, once known as H. Rap Brown, is arrested on a charge of murdering a police officer. It's a major story for Atlanta, and Mae Gentry of the *Atlanta Journal-Constitution* publishes a 2,100-word updater. The timing is an anniversary — one year after the officer was shot:

As Jamil Abdullah Al-Amin awaits trial in the Fulton County Jail, filmmakers as far away as Germany are clamoring for the rights to his life story. The images are compelling: student activist, black radical, devout Muslim, husband and father, accused cop killer.

Al-Amin, known as H. Rap Brown when he was a member of the Student Nonviolent Coordinating Committee and later the Black Panther Party, took a different tack following the turbulent 1960s.

While in prison on a robbery conviction, he embraced Islam, then moved to Atlanta in 1976 and became the leader of a small mosque . . . . For the past 25 years, Al-Amin has maintained a low profile, trying to rid the neighborhood of drugs, helping to broker peace between rival gangs and addressing the United Nations about the slaughter in Bosnia.

That quiet existence ended one year ago today, when two . . . sheriff's deputies trying to serve a warrant on him were shot, one fatally. Al-Amin, who denies being the shooter, has been charged with murder and 12 other offenses by a prosecutor seeking the death penalty . . . .

Note the intro above has only the slimmest spot-news peg (filmmakers are clamoring.) In writing this type of newsfeature, *you* choose the precise time to intervene for a major takeout, rather than wait for a news break. For reasons lost in journalism's distant past, anniversaries often are used as pegs for updaters, although of course you can do updaters any time.

Now, writer Gentry summarizes the past year:

In the year since the shooting, the surviving deputy has returned to work. His dead partner's family continues to grapple with the loss.

And defense attorneys and prosecutors are busy preparing for an October trial . . . .

And, that is followed by a look-ahead angle:

The case pits an icon of black America against the city's African-American power structure — Fulton County Sheriff Jackie Barrett and District Attorney Paul Howard — and involves the shooting of two black cops.

"For a large part of his life, he worked for the uplift of black peo-

ple, for them to be able to assume positions of responsibility and hold public office," said Al-Amin's brother, Ed Brown. "The irony is, those people have become his tormentors and persecutors" . . . .

Mae Gentry
Atlanta Journal-Constitution[10]

FOCUSING ON A HIGHLIGHT

Some truly major stories break like star bursts in a fireworks display. Many colorful, fascinating fragments soar briefly into view, then disappear.

The newsfeature is perfect for pulling some of those fragments back into view for the in-depth examination they merit.

For example, an FBI agent is arrested on charges of spying for Russia. For the following Sunday (a day when most newspapers have relatively large newsholes), three analytical writers swing into action:

Washington — Perhaps the most startling aspect of the espionage firestorm that broke over Washington last week was that for many years neither the KGB nor the FBI knew the identity of the spy.

Senior officials of the KGB and its successor, Russia's SVR, were doubtless ecstatic to have another incredibly valuable mole planted some-

where inside the U.S. intelligence establishment. But the spy had refused to reveal his name, to meet face to face with the Russians or even to say where he worked. He was known to them only as "Ramon."

The Federal Bureau of Investigation, in turn, had for several years suspected that a mole was burrowing away inside its ranks, but only within the past few months was it able to narrow the search to Robert Philip Hanssen . . . .

David Wise
Los Angeles Times[11]

The Cold War may be over, but the spies haven't come in from the cold.

The arrest last week of veteran FBI agent Robert Hanssen on charges of spying for the Russians for the last 15 years in return for $1.4 million underscored a hard reality the U.S. intelligence community has been living with for a decade.

They may no longer be Reds. They may no longer be Soviets . . . .

Russian agents are keeping up their espionage efforts with as much vigor as in the bad old days when the Berlin Wall was the front line of cloak-and-dagger superpower combat.

"They never stopped," said a senior U.S. intelligence official last week. "We see it now more than ever" . . . .

Michael Kilian
Chicago Tribune[12]

Throughout American history, from the time Nathan Hale's only regret was that he had but one life to lose for his country, the people who have spied against their homeland have done so typically because they believed in some mighty cause. For much of the last century, that generally meant they either embraced the socialist world vision of Karl Marx or wanted to

prevent it from becoming reality.

The common denominator today among people who export their nations' secrets, however, can be better described with a line from a Hollywood screenwriter than from a German philosopher: "Show me the money" . . . .

Adam Pertman
Boston Globe[13]

Lesson: After a major story bursts on front pages (as the spy story certainly did), search through what was written for story angles that deserve in-depth examination, even if they were touched upon in initial coverage.

But don't merely re-hash earlier coverage. Each spy story above contained new *added-value reporting.*

Kilian of the *Chicago Tribune* sought out an authoritative source, a U.S. intelligence official, on his angle, that the Russians never stopped spying. Wise, a frequent writer on espionage, drew from his own background on other spy cases. For *Sunday Globe* readers, Pertman interviewed psychiatrists on psychological dimensions of spying.

Andrew Cassel of the *Philadelphia Inquirer* sorts through a week or so of bad news on the U.S. economy and focuses on what he says is a key factor: faltering consumer confidence. Cassel is blunt:

I'm not indulging in the usual cheap journalistic populism here. What the average household thinks about the economy right now may really be more important than the experts' prognostications, for a reason that the experts themselves acknowledge: Confidence is crucial.

Even under the best of circumstances, the pace of economic growth inevitably rises and falls over time.

A big demand for cars, for instance, causes automakers to ramp up production, which puts more cars on dealer lots than the dealers can move, which leads to cutbacks and plant layoffs, and so on, around the circle.

If confidence weren't a factor —

that is, in the unlikely event that all of this could happen without affecting anybody's attitude — the consequences of such cycles would be minor and short: Some temporary production slowdowns, some extra price-cutting by retailers — no sweat.

But mess with confidence, and you're asking for trouble. If consumers begin to believe that tougher times are here to stay, they'll postpone purchases and hunker down. Businesses will do the same, delaying expansion or cutting back. Eventually, prophecies of gloom become self-fulfilling, as happened during the 1930s and (somewhat less dramatically) in the 1970s . . . .

Andre Cassel
Philadelphia Inquirer[14]

Cassel's writing is notable, I think, for several reasons:

- He personalizes it with the pronoun "I" and translates a rather esoteric economic concept into something all readers can understand — car production and sales.
- He bluntly poses a worst-case scenario — self-fulfilling prophecies of gloom that could lead to deeper economic difficulties, as in the 1930s and 1970s.
- Cassel's writing is strong and exudes authority. *He knows his game.*

ROUNDING UP BITS AND PIECES

Writing news to make sense sometimes is like putting together a jigsaw puzzle — you fit bits and pieces together to create a recognizable picture.

In newsfeature writing, the *roundup story* is a vehicle for seeking and then presenting facts arranged appropriately to reveal deeper meaning, as you see it.

Note this involves much more than quoting a Democrat, then running around to find a Republican for balancing comment.

The roundup places extraordinary responsibility on you to be fair and balanced as you reach out in different directions for sources and facts.

In keeping with the interpretive mission of newsfeature writing, *your* analysis and *your* thinking may belong in the story. How much of yourself to insert in the story depends primarily on the nature of the news and how experienced you are (and, thus, how much your editors trust you.)

For example, on a hugely important story — talk of malfeasance at high levels — *New York Times* reporters write a roundup that pulls together isolated facts from disparate sources. The result is presented *without* first-person interpretation by the writers themselves. The intro:

Washington — The furor over President Bill Clinton's pardons intensified today as Congressional investigators focused on Roger Clinton and his efforts to win pardons for friends and associates from his brother, government officials said.

In discussions with the former president, Roger Clinton sought clemency for about 10 people, although he was not paid for his efforts, said Julia Payne, an aide to the former president. She added that all of the requests were denied. Congressional officials said they are investigating Roger Clinton's assertions that he pressed for the pardons without pay.

Note above that already, in just two grafs, the writers have rounded up input from Congressional investigators, government officials and Julia Payne. Now, in quick succession, the writers reach out:

- To New York City, and a U.S. attorney there.
- To Sen. Hillary Rodham Clinton, in Washington.
- To President Bush, at a news conference.
- To an interview with Harold Ickes, adviser to the Clintons.
- To even more sources in government, politics and law enforcement.

The final result: A tightly woven roundup with a panoramic and overarching view of a complex story pulled together from far-flung sources.[15]

Quite another type of roundup is written by the *New York Times'* Mike Freeman, a highly experienced (and highly regarded) sportswriter. He pulls together facts on the playing capabilities of football quarterbacks.

We're dealing here with news less important than what happens in the Oval Office. And Freeman's relaxed style signals that. His intro:

The place to be for two days this summer was Hawaii, not because of the sandy beaches and the sunsets, but because some of the best young quarterbacks in the National Football League were competing in the Quarterback Challenge, a sort of "Survivor" for passers. The sexiest event, by far, was the long-distance throw.

One by one, the throwers lined up like gunslingers readying for a shootout. Peyton Manning of Indianapolis and Jake Plummer, the scrambler from Arizona, each threw his pass 69 yards. Cade McNown, the Chicago Bears' quarterback, and Donovan McNabb of Philadelphia did even better, each tossing for 72 yards. Eventually, McNown and McNabb faced off in the finals. That's when the Eagles quarterback with the big arm blew away his competition.

McNown's throw went a healthy 69 yards. Then came McNabb's pass, and it sailed, and sailed and sailed, landing 76 yards downfield. The other quarterbacks, who are accustomed to making fans gawk at their plays, were themselves taken aback at McNabb's raw power . . . .

Now, however, Freeman's roundup turns harshly subjective as he personally evaluates quarterbacks:

- Charlie Batch, Detroit. Hits deep throws, but is injury prone.
- Brian Griese, Denver. Good touch on passes, but is arrogant.
- Ryan Leaf, San Diego. Unlimited potential, but is a knucklehead . . .[16]

THE NEWS ANALYSIS

All your newswriting is designed to persuade, if only with the limited goal of persuading readers to see the facts as you see them, to understand them as you do.

Now, however, in the news analysis, we turn for the first time to writing aimed at persuading readers to *accept your opinion* of the facts, to agree with meaning *as you define it.*

The news analysis ventures so far beyond objective and dispassionate newswriting that most newspapers and magazines assign it to only those expert writers with demonstrated grasp of a subject.

And you are such an expert.

Who, after all, is a greater authority than you on student life on your campus? Who has greater expertise than you in student thinking? Who knows more precisely than you how the day's news affects students on your campus?

That is, the news analysis is a writing tool you can use, right now, with huge effect *if* you handle with great care the responsibility of laying *your* opinions and *your* analysis before readers who just might believe you and who might reorder their lives, even if only in small ways, because of what you write.

Characteristics of the news analysis:

- Though carrying *opinion*, it is published on *news* pages and, thus, must carry the slug, "News Analysis," to differentiate it from objective newswriting.
- The news analysis is used sparingly because it tends to blur, in readers' minds, barriers between objective newswriting and opinion. Thus, principled newspapers use news-page news analysis only on stories of compelling importance so complex that analysis is required.
- The news analysis is timely and close to the news event it is designed to illuminate. Mostly it is published as a sidebar, placed next to the hard-news story it analyzes.
- The news analysis is used to display deeper meaning as seen by the writer, to put a news event into wider context, to show potentially greater impact — all difficult to do within the constraints of a traditional Five-Ws news story objectively written.
- Despite being a vehicle of opinion, the well-done news analysis, like *all* sound journalism, is strongly based on detailed reporting and interviewing of authoritative sources.

An example:

The *Los Angeles Times* leads its front page with this hard-news story:

Washington — The controversy over President Clinton's eleventh-hour pardons escalated Thursday as Sen. Hillary Rodham Clinton (D-N.Y.) denied knowing that her brother had received a large sum of money to push two clemency requests and a spokesman for former President Clinton acknowledged that the president's brother personally lobbied for clemency for several of his "friends and acquaintances."

Sen. Clinton was asked by reporters at a Capitol Hill news conference about the activities of her
brother Hugh Rodham as well as
revelations that her campaign treasurer had handled the pardon appli-
cations of two Arkansas men convicted of tax evasion . . . .

Richard A. Serrano,
Stephen Braun
Los Angeles Times[17]

That spot-news story above quickly broadens to developments in
Florida and California, and beyond President Clinton and his senator wife
to include relatives and other politicians. And all are involved in a hugely
complicated story.

Of compelling interest, of course, are the implications for Hillary
Rodham Clinton, newly seated in the U.S. Senate and just launched on
her own political career.

Who can sort it all out? Two *Times* writers ride to the rescue with an
adjacent news analysis headlined, "News Analysis: Sen. Clinton Is Where
She Didn't Want to Be." Their intro (opinion emphasized):

Washington — She came to Capitol
Hill amid lofty expectations, the
first presidential spouse ever elected
to public office and one of a pha-
lanx of Democrats who gave the
party new life in a Senate evenly
split with Republicans.

But the debut of Sen. Hillary Rodham Clinton, *while promising initially, has become a disaster.*

For the new senator from New
York, mounting questions about what
she and her husband did and didn't
know when he issued last-minute
pardons to felons and a fugitive are *a
monumental embarrassment.*

This new episode and other ethical questions that have shadowed
Sen. Clinton during her transition
from the White House to the Capitol — a mega-deal for her memoirs,
the acceptance of a shower of gifts
from wealthy friends — have come
at the *worst possible time* for her
and her party . . . .

Now, the analysts broaden their interpretation:

Controversies that dog the Clintons are overshadowing the Democratic party's strategy for opposing President Bush, and Sen. Clinton's
greater political ambitions are jeopardized:

. . . a coherent (Democratic) strategy, if it yet exists, has been eclipsed
by the seemingly never-ending
string of Clinton controversies . . . .

"It is certainly not how I would
have preferred or planned to start
my Senate career," Sen. Clinton acknowledged Thursday in a news
conference, "and I regret deeply
that there has been these kinds of
matters occurring" . . . .

"Clinton fatigue has reached its

climax," said one senior Senate Democratic strategist, who, like several others, declined to be quoted by name. "They have virtually no defenders in any of this" . . . .

"Not only can she forget about running for president," said University of Virginia political analyst Larry Sabato, "she isn't going to be on anyone's credible list for [vice president]. To do so would produce two months of scandal stories — just regurgitating what's happened" . . . .

Nick Anderson,
Janet Hook
Los Angeles Times[18]

Note these characteristics of the *Times'* news analysis:

- It is strongly judgmental and uses subjective language to express opinion (Mrs. Clinton's debut is a "disaster"; she suffers "monumental embarrassment.")
- It gives Sen. Clinton her say (her news conference statement).
- It is strongly reported (sources quoted in the excerpts are only a few of the many quoted in the story, which we don't have room here to examine in full).
- It relies, in part, on anonymous sources, which you should use sparingly and *only* when you have no other way of getting crucial information your readers need.

To be effective, a news analysis need not be as strongly judgmental as the *Los Angeles Times* example above. You can focus on *un*answerable questions, as well.

For example, the *New York Times'* front page is dominated by this hard-news story:

Jerusalem — Prime Minister Ehud Barak of Israel said today that peace talks were not "on the shelf" and Yasir Arafat called for an emergency Arab summit meeting as violence tore through Israel and the Palestinian territories for the fifth straight day.

William A. Orme Jr.
New York Times[19]

In adjacent columns, the *Times'* Deborah Sontag presents this news analysis:

Jerusalem — Last week, Prime Minister Ehud Barak and Yasir Arafat, the Palestinian leader, were having a garden party, breaking pita bread and trading jokes in the yard of Mr. Barak's private suburban home in Israel.

This week, their people are

killing each other. Palestinian rocks are flying, Israeli tanks are charging, and bodies are piling up at the morgue. With every day of violence, each leader is expressing greater distrust of the other side, and both sides are reverting to the negative dynamic of their old, familiar roles as enemies . . . .

Now, Sontag describes how actions of Ariel Sharon, an Israeli opposition leader, were seen by Palestinians as provocation, and adds, "there are bound to be bitter debates" about what motivated him. Then:

But whatever the answers, the explosion showed how quickly everything can turn upside down here. How quickly, too, the language of force can take over, pushing aside the careful legalese of the many peace agreements, with all their prefaces, appendixes and coda. How quickly the peacemaking relationship can give way to the basest, barest ethnic religious animosities, jeopardizing so much of what has been established during the last seven years.

For the moment, five days and 48 deaths into the worst violence since 1996, everything is unclear: how long the conflict will last and what will be its toll on a human level, politically and diplomatically . . . .

Deborah Sontag
New York Times[20]

Lessons:

- Writing news analysis doesn't compel you to answer all questions, explain all mysteries. On events as complicated as Middle East violence, don't try.
- However, focusing on future dangers and developments (as Sontag does with, "But whatever the answers") can be enormously helpful to readers.

One form of news analysis to approach with great caution is the "instant" or "snap" analysis — an interpretation of an event just hours (or minutes) old. Nevertheless, if written carefully *and with restraint*, quick-reaction analysis can aid readers greatly.

For example, the *New York Times* leads its front page with this:

Washington — President Bush turned full force to the difficult task of selling the Congress and the country on his legislative agenda tonight, using a nationally televised address from the House chamber to cast his proposed $1.6 trillion tax cut as reasonable and responsible.

In the most formal and comprehensive speech of his nascent presidency, Mr. Bush said a blessed era of robust surpluses would enable the federal government to reduce taxes by that amount over 10 years and still spend all that it needed to on education, prescription drugs and social programs . . . .[21]

In adjacent columns, Adam Clymer, a veteran Washington correspondent, analyzes the speech. Clymer's intro:

Washington — President Bush's budget speech, with its emphasis on his tax cut, education proposals and debt reduction plan, reflected both his campaign and his record as governor of Texas, but it was more narrowly focused than most presidents have chosen to be in their first nationally televised address to Congress.

While Mr. Bush in his speech tonight talked about issues like rebuilding the military, encouraging charitable contributions and fighting rising energy prices and racial profiling, he stopped short of offering an array of new programs and mini-initiatives. He talked of a government that was "active but limited."

Much the same could have been said of his speech.

Mr. Bush did not go quite as far as Gerald R. Ford, who said, "I have no legislative shopping list here this evening," when he addressed Congress just three days after Richard Nixon resigned. Yet neither did he offer the sort of vast legislative agendas that Jimmy Carter, Ronald Reagan, George Bush and Bill Clinton all presented to the Congress and the nation in their first speeches . . . .

Adam Clymer
New York Times[22]

The Clymer analysis was written minutes after Bush spoke, otherwise Clymer would not have met his deadline for the next morning's paper. Note Clymer therefore *writes with restraint*, limiting his focus to 1) how the speech reflected Bush's campaign promises and his record as governor, and 2) how the speech compared with those of previous presidents.

Lesson: When pushed by your deadline, don't stretch your analysis too far. Collect background early, as Clymer undoubtedly did before Bush spoke, then focus your analysis on what you know. Don't speculate.

One writing structure lends itself to, shall we say, *gentle* analysis plus the roundup function of a newsfeature. This is the "letter from . . ." structure.

When your news beat yields tidbits that individually don't justify hard-news treatment but that nevertheless are fascinating, write a letter home. That's what Richard Chacon, *Boston Globe* correspondent in Colombia, does:

Letter from Bogota

Bogota — The U.S. Congress is back in session this week in Washington, and no one could be more relieved than the staff at the U.S. Embassy in Colombia.

Congressional recesses, like the one last week, have become prime time for visits from US senators and representatives to this conflict-torn country, which is home to a 40-year civil war and the world's largest cocaine-making industry — and a government that, despite its best intentions, seems unable to eliminate either.

It's as if the country, with its internal strife, jungles, helicopters, and more recently, millions in U.S. taxpayer money, has become the Beltway's version of "Survivor," a distant tropical setting where wing-tipped pols can rough it, and brag about it.

Last week, during the brief Presidents' Day recess, the U.S. Embassy in Bogota hosted six congressional delegations . . . .

Richard Chacon
Boston Globe[23]

Note above that the "letter from" is just that — a chatty letter that enables you to round up bits and pieces for the folks back home.

If you're a football beat writer, how about, "Letter from the Locker Room"? If you're covering cops, how about, "Notes from the Police Beat?" Covering, say, the Student Affairs Office? How about, "Letter from Student Affairs"?

SUMMARY

- Competitive pressure from electronic media and the complexity of news stories often force newspaper and magazine writers to focus on analysis and interpretation.
- Of all media, newspapers and magazines are best at plowing deeply into complex issues, and from that flows unique journalistic strength and validation for print.
- *Internal balancing* is the first effort you must make to go beyond the Five Ws of objective reporting and to gather facts that ensure clarity and fairness in your story.

- The *Explanatory Follow* enables you to come in behind a news break with interpretation that takes readers beyond the obvious meaning.
- The *Explanatory Precede* is of great use in helping your readers get set to understand the deeper meaning of an event still ahead.
- The *Newsfeature* is a story structure you can use to intervene arbitrarily in the news flow, stop the action and put together bits and pieces that summarize what is happening.
- The *News Analysis* includes your opinion and differs so much from objective newswriting that it must be slugged "news analysis."
- Honest writing requires you to probe deeper than the obvious, to seek additional facts and balancing material beyond the news break at hand.
- Impressionistic reporting — catching the mood and tone of an event — is a radical departure from traditionally objective newswriting and can be very helpful to readers.
- Reporters seldom get all the facts or the entire meaning of a complex story, and analytical writing shouldn't lead you to pretend you do.
- Strong analytical writing, like all journalism, is soundly based in reporting and interviewing of authoritative sources.
- Reporters are obliged to keep track of significant stories that bubble along beneath the surface and bring them into public view even though no major news development provides a "news peg."
- *Roundups* are vehicles for fitting bits and pieces together to create for readers a recognizable picture of a significant story.
- Much analytical writing is strongly judgmental, but be sure to tell readers when you don't know and when some questions are unanswerable.

RECOMMENDED READING

Any student of analytical writing will benefit from close study of *New York Times* news analyses. *The Times* is adept particularly at same-day analysis of an event in the news. Note also how the *Los Angeles Times* and *Chicago Tribune* use staff and syndicated columnists with a high degree of expertise for analytical writing.

EXERCISES

1. Search today's *New York Times* (or another newspaper designated by your instructor) for examples of *internal balancing*, as discussed in this chapter. Did writers search beyond the obvious for balancing facts and quotes? Do you think readers were substantially advantaged by the writers' efforts? Did you see examples of stories that *lacked* internal balance? Write your report in about 300 words.

2. Search today's *New York Times* (or another newspaper designated by your instructor) for an example of *explanatory follows* — analytical stories that come in behind an event with background and interpretation designed to explain the event. What reporting and writing techniques does the writer use? Does the explanatory follow explain thoroughly a complex event? If not, why not? Write your report in 250–300 words.

3. Search today's *New York Times* (or another newspaper designated by your instructor) for an example of an *explanatory precede* — a story that alerts readers to the possible meaning of a news event scheduled to develop in days ahead. Is the story well backgrounded? Does it include helpful interpretation or analysis? If not, what are the story's weaknesses? Write your report in about 300 words.

4. With your instructor's approval, write a *newsfeature* on a story of compelling interest on your campus. This should be a story you put together of bits and pieces pulled from a variety of sources. If possible, select a story that is ongoing — bubbling beneath the surface — and write it to "stop the action" and bring your readers up to date on the story's status and meaning. Use wordage warranted by your story.

5. Try your hand at a news analysis, as defined in this chapter — authoritative reporting and interviewing with an overlay of your opinion and interpretation. Select a major news event that developed *this week* on your campus. Slug your story "news analysis" and make every effort to bring to the attention of your readers the true meaning of the event. Write to the wordage warranted by the event's importance.

NOTES

1. Dispatch for morning papers, Jan. 26, 2001.
2. "In Congress, a Break in a Season of Scandal," Oct. 11, 1998, p. A–1.
3. Dispatch for Sunday papers, March 11, 2001.
4. "Edison in Default; Assembly Passes Plan to Buy Power," Jan. 17, 2001, p. A–1.
5. "Egypt Recalls Ambassador, Citing Israel's Use of Force," Nov. 22, 2000, p. A–1.
6. "TV's Election Night Errors Still Ignite Partisan Rancor," Feb. 13, 2001, p. A–5.
7. "Too Much to Lose," June 12, 2000, p. 94.
8. Dispatch for morning papers, Feb. 22, 2001.
9. "American Rhythms," Feb. 18, 2001, p. E–1.
10. "Al-Amin Awaits Trial for Murder," March 16, 2001, p. E–1.
11. "Diamonds Are a Spy's Best Friend," Feb. 25, 2001, p. M–1.
12. "The Spying Never Stopped," Feb. 25, 2001, Section 2, p. 1.
13. "Why They Spy," Feb. 25, 2001, p. E–1.
14. "Recovery? Recession? Answer Lies with Consumers," Feb. 21, 2001, p. A–1.
15. "Clinton's Brother Requested Clemency for Some Friends," Feb. 23, 2001, p. A–1.
16. New Wave of Quarterbacks, New Pressures," Sept. 3, 2000, Sports Section, p. 34.
17. "Family Ties to Clemency Cases Dog Clintons," Feb. 23, 2001, p. A–1.
18. "Sen. Clinton is Where She Didn't Want to Be," Feb. 23, 2001, p. A–1.
19. "As Arabs and Israelis Fight On, Albright Seeks Talks," Oct. 3, 2000, p. A–1.
20. "At Arms Again, Suddenly," Oct. 3, 2000, p. A–1.
21. "Bush, Spelling Out Agenda to Congress, Makes Tax Cut Centerpiece of the Budget," Feb. 28, 2001, p. A-1.
22. "A Short Shopping List," Feb. 28, 2001, p. A-1.
23. "Observers Crowd US Embassy in Bogota," Feb. 26, 2001, p. A–10.

10

Writing Editorials

YOU HAVE STUDIED how to report the views of *others* in spot-news reporting.

You have learned to write analysis to interpret what *they* are saying.

Now, let's turn to *you*, to your thinking and how you can write persuasively to advocate the institutional viewpoint of your newspaper or magazine.

Whether newspapers and magazines *should* publish editorials is a matter of some debate in journalism.

Critics say we are presumptuous to editorialize on issues of public policy and to thus tell readers what they should think. Give us news, these critics say, and we readers will decide what to think about it.

Nevertheless, almost without exception, publications of significance regard editorials as an important public service. Journalists reason that they have the time, resources and reportorial expertise required to analyze public policy, and most readers don't. And, this reasoning goes, presenting a publication's viewpoint as *one* contribution to public dialogue can aid readers who, of course, are free to make up their own minds.

Consequently, writing editorials could be part of your early career in journalism.

On smaller papers and magazines, reporters, copy editors and everyone else in the newsroom do many things, and editorial writing frequently is among shared tasks.

On larger publications, experienced reporters with demonstrable expertise in analytical writing get editorial assignments. Many metropolitan papers promote reporters to editorial writing after they have developed strong background in certain subjects — education, for example, or city government or the environment.

So, if advocacy writing — sooner or later — appeals to you, now is the time to begin preparing.

In Chapter Ten, Writing Editorials, we'll look first at the special responsibilities of editorial writers and how issues are selected for examination by their newspapers or magazines. Then, we'll turn to the advocacy writing that gives editorial writers such loud voices in the marketplace of ideas.

YOUR NEW RESPONSIBILITIES

As you shift from *objective* news reporting and analysis to *subjective* advocacy writing, you escalate dramatically your journalistic responsibilities.

Before, news broke spontaneously out of what someone else said or did. Now, *you* are singling out issues for public discussion and stamping them with *your* definition of importance.

Before, you reported the views of authoritative sources. Now, you are thrusting forward your newspaper's corporate view as authoritative.

Before, you and your newspaper were sideline observers. Now, you're both marching onto the playing field as players — and important players, indeed.

In hundreds of communities across America, the newspaper is one of a handful of local power centers. With perhaps the business community, the churches and the schools, your newspaper will help decide *how things work*, how local government functions, what gets done and what doesn't.

At the very least, your advocacy writing will help shape the public dialogue and sketch out the priorities of that dialogue.

The heavy responsibility inherent in that leads to much sober discussion among editorial writers.

FOUR GUIDING PRINCIPLES

Codes of ethics in journalism single out four broad areas of responsibility for editorial writers:

- Serve the public in all that you do.
- Create a forum within the marketplace of ideas where readers, community and nation can conduct the public dialogue.
- Be society's watchdog and walk patrol on behalf of your public.
- Write to inform readers and guide them *in causing change.*

SERVE THE PUBLIC

The Basic Statement of Principles of the National Conference of Editorial Writers is unmistakably clear:

Editorial writing is more than another way of making money. It is a profession devoted to public welfare and to public service. *(Adopted Oct. 10, 1975)*

Use your advocacy power "in the public interest," counsels the ethics code of Associated Press Managing Editors Association, a nationwide group of newspaper members in AP.

The Society of Professional Journalists says in its code, "The purpose of distributing news and enlightened opinion is to serve the general welfare."

That echoes in the American Society of Newspaper Editors' code: "The primary purpose of gathering and distributing news and opinion is to serve the general welfare by informing the people and enabling them to make judgments on the issues of the time."[1]

In editorial writing, you'll be *advocating*. In their ethics codes, your editorial-writing colleagues are telling you to always use your power of advocacy for the *public good*, not your newspaper's, not yours, certainly, and not for the good of the many special-interest groups that will be clamoring for your support.

CREATE A FORUM FOR IDEAS

Advocacy writing is *not* a license to propound your views to the exclusion of others. All ethics codes of professional journalism organizations agree, as do codes of individual newspapers.

"Listen to the voiceless," admonishes the *Washington Post's* Code of Standards and Ethics.

"Voice should be given to diverse opinions," says the editorial writers' statement of principles, adding that the opinions of others must be "edited faithfully to reflect stated views."

The American Society of Newspaper Editors lays on heavy responsibility: "Newspaper men and women who abuse the power of their professional role for selfish motives or unworthy purpose are faithless to (the) public trust."

The call, then, is to open each of your editorials to the views of others and, also, ensure your editorial *pages* create an open forum for your entire community.

BE A WATCHDOG

Being a watchdog — monitoring the powerful — is ingrained in the journalistic ethic. The American Society of Newspaper Editors' Statement of Principles states:

The American press was made free not just to inform or just to serve as a forum for debate but also to bring *independent scrutiny* (emphasis added) to bear on the forces of power in society, including the conduct of official power at all levels of government.

(Adopted Oct. 23, 1975)

From this concept flows the sense among editorial writers that they must raise their voices in critical, not to say *adversarial*, examination on behalf of the public, of all power centers in our society.

Implicit in that sense of mission is the need to stay independent of those power centers and to exercise the power of the editorial page solely as a public trust.

Two compellingly important attitudes arise from all this:

First, the media hold that they serve as the "Fourth Estate," a balancing mechanism serving to prevent abuse of power by the three other "estates" — the executive, legislative and judicial branches of government.

Second, *critics* of the media frequently assert that journalists are arrogant in assuming such an important voice in our nation's affairs and that we exceed the free-press guarantees of the U.S. Constitution. "Who elected you?" is a question often asked of journalists.

CAUSE CHANGE

Now comes a fundamental difference between news writing and advocacy writing:

In news writing, you learned to *inform* readers.

In editorial writing, you must learn to stir them to action, *to guide them in forcing change.*

Your chief duty, says the National Conference of Editorial Writers, "is to provide the information and guidance toward sound judgments that are essential to the healthy functioning of a democracy."

Let that sink in for a moment. That statement presumes you, as an editorial writer, can show readers the path toward what is true and right.

So, write editorials only after careful research and reflection. Write only with due regard for conflicting and opposing views. Write only with a sense of fairness and balance.

PICKING YOUR TOPICS

As an editorial writer you cannot move away from the news and into an ivory tower of grandiose ideas disassociated from life in your town.

To the contrary, you must stay close to the news to succeed in editorial writing, close to your readers' lives.

So, the news value and judgments that guide you in spot news must guide you also in editorial writing. That means paying detailed attention to crime, taxes, education, government, the environment — all the hot-button topics that drive journalism generally.

Depending on the size of your newspaper, its geographic market and the demographics of its audience, issues selected for editorial treatment can be "big picture" (United Nations, nuclear disarmament) or intensely local (whether lovely old oaks lining Main Street should be chopped down and whether dog-leash laws should be enforced).

On smaller papers, topic selection and editorial angle may be decided by you alone or perhaps in a brief chat with the publisher. On larger papers, editorial boards deliberate over topics and decide the institutional position. (The *Atlanta Journal-Constitution*, for example, has an editorial board of seven.)[2]

Many editorial writers cite news stories in their own newspapers as a principal source of ideas. A front-page story on, say, property tax assessments can inspire thoughtful comment on the editorial page.

National magazines and newspapers — particularly the *New York Times* and *Wall Street Journal* — are cited frequently as providing inspiration for editorials. A *Journal* news story on, say, air pollution nationwide can lead to editorial comment that addresses local concerns.

In selecting topics for comment, it's easy to fall into a "bad-news syndrome" — writing day after day only about doom and gloom.

Well, there *is* a great deal of doom and gloom in the world and it *does* require considered commentary. But lighten up once in a while! Walk your readers through an essay on spring time, butterflies and green grass; use humor now and then for a bit of relief from the "serious" issues of the day.

RESEARCHING YOUR EDITORIALS

Bring *added value reporting* to your editorial writing if you want to be read and, more importantly, if you truly want to cause change.

You cannot write merely, "This newspaper believes" and convince anyone of anything.

Rather, successful editorials — those that inspire public debate and cause change — must be reported and researched as carefully as any major spot-news story.

Indeed, it's not too much to say that a strong editorial should be 80–90 percent original reporting and reasoned consideration of alternative viewpoints, with 10–20 percent devoted to stating your newspaper's position.

As in all news writing, careful reporting also lends authority and strength to editorials. Writing with obvious balance and fairness — presenting all sides — lends credibility and believability.

And, without well-rounded reporting, an editorial inevitably will lack fundamental honesty. For example, it's *dis*honest to write about the positive impact of business expansion in town (new jobs, new payrolls) without commenting on the negatives (increased traffic congestion, air pollution).

However, an agonizing reality: In editorial writing, as in most journalism, you face unyielding deadline pressure. One researcher quotes 58 percent of editorial writers in a national survey as saying they don't have enough time to research editorials; 44 percent complain they don't have enough time to write them.[3]

A few hints:

- Focus your reporting on essentials. Don't spend precious time investigating facts of secondary importance. This will help you focus your *writing* on factual substance of true added value. Remember: readers devote about 30 minutes to the *entire newspaper*. You'll lose readers quickly if your editorials don't focus sharply on substantive matters.

- Report to translate and characterize meaning. We report news breaks on page one; on editorial pages, we must translate "issues" into terms meaningful for readers. Characterize facts and figures to translate the incomprehensible into everyday language all readers understand.

- Beware of two dangers in computer-assisted reporting: a) The enormous quantity of available information, some erroneous and much misleading, can overwhelm you, and b) the ease of surfing cyberspace can lure you into thinking that stroking a keyboard hour after hour is a satisfactory substitute for first-hand interviewing and street-smart reporting. It isn't.

- And, as in all reporting, ask yourself: Is this the investigative path *my readers* want — and need — me to follow? Yes, editorial writers comment on what readers *want*, just as we write news stories and features they want. But editorial writers also must pursue topics that they, as trained journalists, think readers *need* to know.

EDITORIAL WRITER'S MANTRA: SEA

Strong editorials don't emerge from a rigid writing formula as a delicious apple pie emerges from strict adherence to a recipe.

Nevertheless, strong editorials *do* contain basic ingredients, just as effective spot-news stories contain the Five Ws and How.

In writing editorials, mutter this mantra to yourself: SEA—Stimulate, Explain, Advocate.

STIMULATE

Press beyond the news story's mission of informing. Write editorials to stimulate thoughtful discussion. Write to start debates, over breakfast, in the business office and during lunch on important issues. Poke, prod, urge readers to think in new ways, to see new viewpoints, to see new solutions.

EXPLAIN

Use added-value reporting to focus new light on old issues. Go beyond what is reported on the front page. Take readers into new dimensions of understanding.

ADVOCATE

Don't be wishy-washy: "On the one hand, but on the other." Use persuasive and logical reporting plus convincing writing to lead readers to new conclusions, *new determination to act.*

HOW TO STIMULATE DEBATE

The *Boston Globe* clearly intended to *stimulate* discussion with this provocative intro:

There is stark contrast this fall between the beauty of Vermont's foliage and the ugliness of some of its political rhetoric. A state that in the past has kept its balance while wrestling with land-use controls or fair education financing is having a more difficult time with Vermont's pioneering law giving gay and lesbian couples an alternative to marriage that provides many of its benefits.

And, in the second graf, no punches are pulled:

A low point was reached last week when a state representative from Barre City, Oreste Valsangiacomo, suggested that Governor Howard Dean had appointed Jeffrey Amestoy as chief justice of the state Supreme Court in 1997 with the specific purpose of legalizing gay couples' relationships. In December of last year, Amestoy wrote the court's opinion that the Legislature had to find some way of granting gay couples access to rights that married heterosexuals enjoy. The Legislature responded by passing the state's civil union law . . . .

Now, the views of Valsangiacomo — the subject of the *Globe*'s attack — are explained. To be taken seriously, *your editorials must give a fair shake to the opposing viewpoints.*

Explaining the controversy, the *Globe* notes:

The civil union dispute has cut through both parties in Vermont. Dean, a Democrat, defends the civil union law while his Republican opponent, Ruth Dwyer, is a harsh critic of it. But Valsangiacomo is a Democrat who made his accusation about Dean and Amestoy while endorsing Dwyer. Amestoy, as it happens, is a Republican, as were several legislators who had voted for the civil unions law and then were upended in GOP primaries this fall by opponents of the law.

Opinion polls have consistently shown that the state is deeply and roughly evenly split on this issue. The law was passed last April after four months of spirited but respectful debate.

Finally, the *Globe* turns to advocacy (emphasis added):

Now we hope that supporters of civil unions will use this election to persuade more of their fellow Vermonters why it is fair and neighborly to offer committed same-sex couples the rights of the married.

Critics of the law could spell out whatever dangers they see in it and why those are important enough to justify removing civil-union backers from office. But political dialogue only suffers when it is clouded with baseless accusations. *Ruth Dwyer should disavow the one that her supporter has thrown at Governor Dean and Chief Justice Amestoy.*

Boston Globe[4]

Characteristics of the *Globe* editorial:

- Though dealing with a hot-button issue, its tone is moderate. Mindless ranting and raving won't stimulate rational discussion. Yes, push hard — but in moderate language — on your point; no, don't prompt pitchfork revolutionaries to run amok in the streets.

- The editorial is balanced carefully. Opposing views are examined. But the editorial concludes with strong advocacy of the *Globe*'s position.
- The editorial is sharply focused on the central issue *and* is held to about 260 words. Short, punchy editorials can be much more effective than long, windy meanderings.
- No doubt is left about whose views are being expressed. It's "we" — the *Globe*. (Some papers prefer, "this newspaper," "this page" or, even, "this space.")

Below, the *Chicago Tribune*, in enormously provocative writing, stimulates thinking about Chicago politics:

Not three months after Mayor Richard Daley's top political operative leaves his government job, he helps close a *$1 billion* deal with the city to build a new airport terminal. (Fred Smith) left his position as the city's chief lobbyist in December. On Thursday the city announced that a firm (Smith) now represents won the most lucrative contract in Chicago history.

Now, with all the audacity of a mathematician who asserts that 2 x 2 = 10, city officials stand before news cameras and the public, insisting nothing's odd here.

As if they had instruction from the master of disingenuousness himself, Bill "Depends on what the definition of 'is' is" Clinton, the mayor's minions are twisting themselves into knots to explain how the city ethics ordinance was not violated.

Now, a single — but essential — graf that explains the law involved:

That ordinance states no former city official or employee who was "substantially involved" in a project may lobby for parties interested in that project for a year after leaving his job.

Clever writing maintains reader momentum:

For all the good he's done for Chicago, it's a shame the mayor routinely allows himself to get tarred by deals like this. We've seen the City Hall dance about ethics so many times over the last few years Daley's beginning to look like Bill Murray in "Groundhog Day."

And this:

... city aldermen are fuming about all the Daley lectures they've had to endure about clean government. They mind themselves by writing out $75 reimbursement checks when a lobbyist takes them to a Bulls game, and look like chumps while the mayor's guy hauls in a $1 billion contract.

Finally, the *Tribune* advocates that Chicago voters "keep in mind" who is involved in this City Hall deal.[5]

Note this about the Tribune editorial:

- It hits hard — by name — at principals in the event, putting personal reputations and political futures at stake. When writing in similar vein, examine carefully the laws of defamation (not violated in this editorial) and your personal code of ethics and sense of fairness.
- Mayor Daley, a principal target of the editorial, is given credit — though briefly and in passing — for "all the good he's done Chicago." Remember to be *balanced and fair*.
- The editorial gives readers essential background — a standard of comparison — by citing, in the fourth graf, the pertinent city ordinance. Don't merely state somebody acted "wrong." Wrong by what standard? Measured by what yardstick?
- Zesty writing makes the editorial (and its issues) open and inviting, a reader delight. But did you catch the meaning in the reference to Bill Murray in "Groundhog Day"? And if *you* did, can you be certain *all Chicago readers did*? Beware of writing pegs you pull from your writer's closet of dim memories. Though they make sense to you, they might not to readers.

EXPLAIN BACKGROUND CLEARLY

If you're pegging an editorial to a spot-news event but are uncertain readers are following the news, give them background facts early in your editorial. An editorial is opened by a writer who does that (emphasis added):

The tragic death of nine Japanese seamen and students when a rapidly surfacing American nuclear submarine off Hawaii over-turned their fishing boat has once again brought into question practices too long taken for granted. President Bush and other high officials have properly expressed deep regret to their counterparts in Japan, but the

United States will still be perceived as callous *unless the investigation ordered yesterday by Bush* is thorough, its results announced with complete candor, and procedures swiftly improved.'

Boston Globe[6]

Sometimes you achieve special impact with reference to a specific spot-news event that triggered your editorial (and will trigger memories of many readers):

The tragic death of an innocent civilian during a high-speed chase through the streets of Berkeley this week should spur a rethinking of a police practice that sometimes causes more harm than good.

Theodore Abraham Resnick was killed when his car was wrecked by a suspected drunken motorist who was being hotly pursued by California Highway Patrol officers, presumably hoping to apprehend the erratic driver to prevent him from hurting someone.

But a single vignette should serve only to open wider discussion. The writer broadens the editorial:

That's the problem. The National Highway Safety Administration found that 40 percent of police chases result in accidents — 20 percent with injuries. In 1998, the most recent year available for study, 314 people were killed during police pursuits. Two were police officers, 198 were people being pursued — but 114 were civilians with no connection to the chase.

Note above the factual substance — facts and figures that underscore the writer's admonition that a problem exists. "Problem," like "issue," is vague, almost meaningless. But 314 people killed reduces the "problem" to real-life understanding.

Now, the call for change:

Like shooting into a crowd, the benefits of police pursuits are often overwhelmed by the risk to bystanders.

Though understandably reluctant to let suspects — particularly violent ones — get away, police should reassess the merits of high-speed chases that can cause the very catastrophes they are supposed to prevent.

San Francisco Chronicle[7]

Incidentally, that *Chronicle* editorial above is written in a punchy 176 words. *Long* editorials aren't necessarily *good* editorials.

In the interest of brevity, a *Los Angeles Times* writer searches (successfully, I think) for a brief "nut" graf of background.

First, the intro:

It's disturbing, and it smacks of racial profiling, that some police departments in Orange county are still detaining and taking steps to deport people they suspect of being illegal residents. This is a practice that enlightened police agencies dropped long ago.

Now, the writer explains the history of U.S. Border Patrol policy and local police forces trying in the past to control the flow of illegal immigrants.

Then, in just 52 words, the nut graf explains the current problem:

The nut of the current problem is that local police are trying to determine who is or isn't a legal resident. In an increasingly urbanized area like Orange County, where about three out of every 10 residents is Latino, stopping residents who "look" illegal opens the door to all kinds of abuses.

Then the kicker, an admonition to local police:

Controlling illegal immigration is a federal function. When local police cross that line, they put a barrier between themselves and minority residents.

Los Angeles Times[8]

Some subjects are so complicated, of course, that your readers need more than a single introductory graf of background or a "nut" graf buried deeper in your editorial. A *Chicago Tribune* writer faces that on a hugely complicated topic — welfare reform.

First, a quick opening look at positive outcomes:

When it comes to monolithic government programs, it's always a little strange when things go better than expected. To the surprise of everyone, that is exactly what has happened so far with Illinois' efforts to reform its welfare system.

Caseloads cut in half.

More than 45 percent of those remaining on welfare working at least part-time.

Doubled state spending for child-care supports . . . .

However, huge problems remain. To explain, in acceptable wordage, the editorial writer resorts to a device much used in spot-news and feature writing — dash matter. Examples:

- A mere 14 percent of welfare recipients get jobs through government agencies . . .
- An overwhelming majority (88 percent) of recipients agree that

working should be a condition of receiving welfare . . .
- Child care in low-income neighborhoods isn't working . . .

The *Tribune* writer clearly is working on an 80–20 formula — 80 percent strong reporting, 20 percent informed opinion — because the story is too complicated to explain in a "nut" graf.

Now, a kicker ending that is non-judgmental and very tentative in proposing future action:

Welfare reform is far from over. Lawmakers and advocates will be forced to visit it over the next two years as welfare reform comes up for reauthorization. They should do so with the attitude that welfare policies are sculptures in need of constant reshaping. And taxpayers should pay attention to whether their dollars are being used productively.

Welfare as we knew it indeed has changed. Now it's time for our attitudes about those who need assistance to change, too. These findings lend credence to the idea of welfare being a *temporary* support when the bottom falls out, and that everyone — recipients included — prefers it that way.

Chicago Tribune[9]

Note the two editorials quoted above — the *Chicago Tribune* on welfare, the *Los Angeles Times* on immigration — stop well short of *demanding* specific action. The editorials are aimed, rather, at airing out problems and exposing them to public debate. They present informed background but don't present infallible solutions and demand they be adopted.

It's worth emphasis: It's a complicated world out there, and you're not required to solve all mysteries and answer all questions just because you're an editorial writer.

Indeed, some problems are so complicated that an editorial writer would be *foolish* to suggest a solution. A *Los Angeles Times* writer clearly recognizes that in an editorial on age-old violence between Israelis and Palestinians. The *Times* proposes limited action — and limited expectations of success:

Nevertheless, there *is* a time to speak strongly.

The best the United States can do is encourage both sides to behave re-

sponsibly, in their actions and their rhetoric, and to keep them focused on the future. The status quo may be widely seen as unacceptable. But in the absence of peace, the alternative — unremitting conflict and destruction — would be unbearable.

Los Angeles Times[10]

TAKE PRINCIPLED STANDS

When personal conscience and your newspaper's policy dictate, take strong editorial stands on matters of principle.

An editorial page should present positions well thought out on matters of compelling economic, political and social importance. *And*, that page should be consistent in presenting its views.

Strong ideas that are consistently advocated mark the *Los Angeles Times'* editorial page scrutiny of scandals in the city's police department.

For years, the page demands clean up, and now is on a new development:

This week, the city attorney's office told the city's civilian Police Commission that the Police Department does a poor job of passing on to prosecutors relevant information about officer integrity, creating "a crisis" that could undermine successful prosecution of criminal defendants.

Now added-value reporting:

Taxpayers are feeling the brunt of these and other police conduct-related failures. The Los Angeles City Council on Tuesday approved a $900,000 settlement for a man who spent 7 1/2 years in prison because of what he claims was a false drug charge concocted by (a police officer). This raises the total spending in such negotiated settlements to $2.18 million since April. The City Council will also be asked to ratify payment of $10.9 million to settle 29 federal civil rights lawsuits arising from the scandal. That package is expected to go to the council next week.

And, finally, a clear-cut suggestion for clean up:

The Police Commission should start addressing the problem by instructing the LAPD to create a clearinghouse for officer information and to adopt uniform policies on notifying prosecutors and defense lawyers of situations in which an officer's credibility is in question. This would go far toward preventing costly tainted prosecutions.

Los Angeles Times[11]

Standing on principle can be unpopular, as in taking a contrary view when millions of Americans say harsh punishment is due a convicted terrorist. An example:

The *New York Times* long has opposed capital punishment, and that principle drives an editorial on Timothy McVeigh, as he awaits execution. The *Times'* opener:

> No one expects moral subtlety from Timothy McVeigh, who is awaiting execution on May 16 for the 1995 Oklahoma City bombing that killed 168 people. The enormity of that act was so great that it is hard to believe anything Mr. McVeigh has to say could actually increase public outrage. But he has found the words to do just that. In interviews that form the basis of a new book by two journalists from The Buffalo News, Mr. McVeigh alludes to the 19 children who died in that blast as "collateral damage" and says of the victims and their families, "I have no sympathy for them." He regrets that he "didn't knock the building down."

The editorial continues: McVeigh's comments reveal "a mind warped by self-induced militancy" . . . his comments "are an extension of his terrorism." Now the stand on principle:

> But it is important not to overreact to Mr. McVeigh. He has been convicted by evidence, by common sense, by his own admissions, by a jury of his peers. His words now are harmless. This page opposes capital punishment, and believes the surest way to punish Mr. McVeigh would have been life imprisonment without parole. That would have robbed him of the deluded martyrdom he seeks with execution.
>
> *New York Times*[12]

Obviously, something is drastically wrong if an editorial page consistently is at odds with the views of its readers and communities or the standards society sets in general on social, political and economic matters.

But, courageous leadership on points of principle is a mark of first-rate editorial writing. Winning a popularity contest is not what editorial writing is about; rather, it's about journalism based on careful research and reasoned reflection that says to readers, "Follow us; this is the way."

SELECTING WRITING STRUCTURES

You're probably already picking up on writing structures used in editorials. Examples in this chapter follow structures discussed earlier for news analysis and features.

As you have noted, editorial writers frequently use this structure:

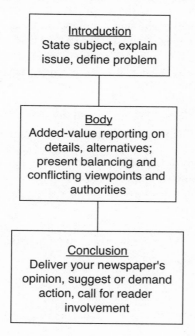

However, the familiar neck-of-vase structure is used, too. Here's a *Boston Globe* example:

Yesterday a woman joined some of the loftiest ranks of the old boys' club: Ruth Simmons was named president of Brown University.

Simmons, currently president of Smith College, will become the first black person ever to lead an Ivy League University, carrying with her a heritage that goes deep into American history. She is the daughter of a black Texas sharecropper, the great-great-granddaughter of slaves.

The youngest of 12 children, Simmons attended Dillard University in new Orleans. She earned a PhD . . . from Harvard.

Previous to Smith, she held administrative positions at the University of Southern California, Spelman College, and Princeton. She serves on the boards of . . .

That opening vignette — or "neck" — leads to fourth-graf widening of the editorial and addressing broader societal implications:

This near-mythic story of possibility in America will no doubt be praised as an inspiring example of how far the nation has come. But once the celebration ends and Simmons gets down to work, she will have to spend some time on just how far we haven't come.

At a time of severe backlash, Simmons has said that while affirmative action is not a panacea, it does promote progress. She'll have to defend this argument while reaching out to students who resent the policy. Simmons should also continue her work of guiding women into mostly male careers such as science and engineering . . . .

After fuller discussion, including background on responsibilities ahead for Simmons at Brown, the editorial ends with a kicker:

It will be a huge load for Simmons, but she is credited as being a fighter with a sense of humor. And given how far she has come, it's wise to gamble that she and any school she leads has great progress ahead.

Boston Globe[13]

Look again at the *Globe* editorial above and you'll see this structure for neck-of-vase writing:

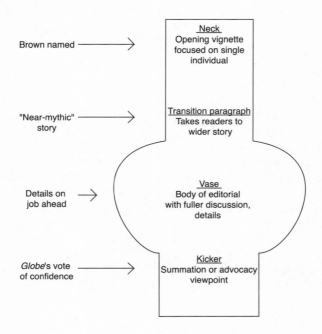

Brown named → **Neck** Opening vignette focused on single individual

"Near-mythic" story → **Transition paragraph** Takes readers to wider story

Details on job ahead → **Vase** Body of editorial with fuller discussion, details

Globe's vote of confidence → **Kicker** Summation or advocacy viewpoint

The two structures sketched above are popular with editorial writers for good reason:

- The introduction-body-conclusion structure enables you to lay out even hugely complicated issues for orderly, logical discussion.
- The neck-of-vase structure invites readers into your editorial by opening with focus not on an "issue" but, rather, on a real, live human being. People are more interested in people than in issues, and writing the "people factor" is a reader-friendly way to open discussion of underlying issues.

However, avoid writing by formula in editorials, as in any newswriting. Don't get in rut. Pick writing structures logical for the issue you are discussing and, importantly, that you can handle well at your current level of writing ability and skill.

SELECTING WRITING PEGS

When and how to write an editorial are dictated principally by three factors:

- A predictable news event in the offing requires analysis to alert readers to what's ahead. Call this the "precede editorial."
- A news event that broke yesterday or very recently requires quick, timely reaction to interpret and analyze — and suggest action. This is the "follow."
- *You* decide an ongoing news story or controversy bubbling just beneath the surface requires comment *even if no single news break occurs*. Because you're pulling together bits and pieces, call this the "sum-up."

WRITING THE "PRECEDE"

The Alabama legislature is headed into an important debate. *In time to influence that debate*, the *Columbus (Ga.) Ledger-Enquirer*, which has large readership in Alabama, comments:

The Alabama Legislature appears ready at last to retire "Yellow Mama," the state's electric chair. According to a survey conducted by the Associated Press, a majority of members of both the House and Senate favor switching from electrocution to lethal injection as the state's method of putting the condemned to death.

Now comes discussion of conflicting attitudes in the Legislature and motives on both sides of the issue.

Next, the *Ledger-Enquirer* — speaking to legislators and voters alike — expresses its view:

Regardless of motivation, we hope lawmakers . . . end electrocution.

Regardless of how you feel about capital punishment, it's hard to imagine supporting this method when more humane ways are already in use in most states . . . .

This has little, if anything, to do with the feelings or rights of the condemned. It has to do with the level of civility on which a state conducts itself. We may all feel on some visceral level that someone who wantonly takes another life may deserve the same kind of treatment he gave his victim. But we do not want to conduct or govern ourselves on that same level.

That said, does it really matter how a person is put to death? If the sentence is death, and the person is put to death . . . exactly how dead does the person have to be?

Michael Owen, editorial board, *Columbus Ledger-Enquirer*[14]

The *Ledger-Enquirer*'s intent is to stir voters to pressure legislators to retire "Yellow Mama." The editorial, without saying so, is a *call to action*.

On a Friday, the *Los Angeles Times* publishes a "precede editorial" alerting readers to a development in the *next two days*:

Mexico's Zapatista rebels are marching north out of their redoubts in southern Chiapas state *this weekend* with the aim of making peace in the capital. The walk, which will cover hundreds of miles and is scheduled to end in Mexico City March 11, is full of risks for both the Zapatistas and the administration of President Vicente Fox, but it also holds the best chance for a new Mexico to gather all its myriad sectors together for the first time in five centuries . . . .

Now, the *Times*' position:

When the Zapatistas meet with Mexico's democratically elected Congress they should not expect an automatic approval of past agreements. Real peace in Chiapas won't come until the ethnic inequality that has characterized Mexico for centuries is ended. That will require congressional courage and Zapatista patience.

Los Angeles Times[15]

With that precede, the *Times* speaks to three constituencies: readers, who are being alerted to the underlying dynamics of a news story they'll see on front pages in days ahead; the U.S. government, which will be formulating attitudes on the rebel march; the Mexican government itself.

Looking a *full month* ahead — and obviously opening what will be a continuing editorial campaign — the *Chicago Tribune* on Feb. 19 alerts readers:

John McCain's crusade to overhaul the nation's campaign finance laws is closer now than it has ever been to becoming law. The House of Representatives has twice approved it, but only this year has the Mc-Cain-Feingold bill gotten enough senators on board to block a filibuster and win passage.

Senate Republican Leader Trent Lott *has scheduled two weeks of floor debate beginning March 19, and a vote could take place by mid-April . . . .*

Now, the *Tribune* explains its position on the pros and cons of the proposed legislation that will be debated. Then, the *Tribune's* suggestion:
Lesson:

McCain-Feingold is just the latest effort to clean up politics by trying to shackle it with rules and prohibitions, which has created more problems than it has solved. It's time to try a different approach.

Chicago Tribune[16]

Though it's impossible to measure the precise impact of editorials, newspapers *can* bring enormous persuasive powers to bear on events *in time to influence outcomes*. The "precede editorial" is a vehicle for influencing *your* newspaper's constituencies. Don't waste that power.

WRITING THE "FOLLOW"

The strength and influence of an editorial page are measured in great part by how quickly it reacts to news breaks.

The *Wall Street Journal* editorial page, regarded by many journalists as one of the strongest in the world, is fast off the mark:

The front pages were filled *yesterday* with headlines about how the U.S. Attorney for the federal district in Manhattan, Mary Jo White, was going to take control of the inquiry into Bill Clinton's pardon of Marc Rich. The import of all this coverage was that now, with a federal attorney taking over the case from two congressional committees, we were really going to get to the bottom of this bizarre pardon.

Could be that's true. Could also be we'll get to the bottom of it the way bodies dumped from the boats off the Jersey shore get to the bottom of the Atlantic Ocean.

Now for the sake of argument and good manners, let us concede the possibility that the U.S. Attorney for the Southern District really will, in short order, unravel whatever paper trail and money trail may exist between Marc and Denise Rich and the former President of the United States. But before everyone else shuts up shop on the Rich pardon and awaits the results from U.S. Attorney White, let us just say for the record: Been there, done that.

The results of conceding jurisdiction over a Clinton-related investigation to Ms. White's shop in the past haven't been particularly revealing or productive . . . .

Now the thrust of the *Journal*'s editorial becomes clear: Beware, dear reader, or another scandal will be swept beneath the rug.

Widening its scope, the *Journal* refers to the then new administration of President George W. Bush and his new attorney general, John Ashcroft:

It certainly will be an inauspicious start if the Bush-Ashcroft Department of Justice allows suspicions of an ongoing coverup to fester.
Wall Street Journal[17]

For Mary Jo White, President Bush and Ashcroft, the warning is clear. The *Wall Street Journal* has alerted the public but it doesn't end there: the *Wall Street Journal* will be watching.

The *Journal* routinely gets into print today with reasoned, well-researched commentary on news that broke *yesterday*. The *Chattanooga Free Press*, which circulates near Atlanta, does also:

The Atlanta community learned to its surprise yesterday that A. W. "Bill" Dahlberg would be stepping down from his role as chief executive of the Southern Co. His career at the regional utility holding company says several good things about how to succeed in business while really trying . . . .

There follows a detailed review of Dahlberg's business and civic achievements. Then a *look-ahead element*:

The values that propelled Mr. Dahlberg through his 41 years won't go out the door with his de-

parture . . . .

Chattanooga Free Press[18]

Lessons:

- Let what happened *yesterday* be your writing peg, but try to explain its meaning for *tomorrow*. (Will Dahlberg's retirement change the corporate values of Southern Co.? No, says the Free Press.)
- However, no one — *no one* — knows what will happen tomorrow. The Free Press doesn't *really* know how Southern Co. will evolve. "Experts" don't *really* know whether the stock market will rise or fall. Neither players nor coaches *really* know who will win tomorrow. In writing look-ahead editorials, take the conservative approach of weather forecasters. They make *educated guesses* based on *painstaking research*.

WRITING "SUM-UP" EDITORIALS

When and how to strike in an editorial is decided relatively easily if you're responding to yesterday's news break or anticipating tomorrow's developments.

More difficult is deciding when and how to intervene in a *continuing story*, one that runs days, weeks or months. Then, you must ask yourself:

- What is my readers' interest in this ongoing story? What is their level of understanding? Are they current on recent developments?
- With causing change as my goal, at what point should I intervene to create maximum impact on government or public opinion?

The *New York Times*, whose editorial board contains subject and area experts, watches Zimbabwe closely and sees developments in "recent days" requiring comment (emphasis added on time elements):

298 / WRITING TO INFORM AND ENGAGE

Zimbabwe's spiral into lawlessness has taken a turn for the worse *in recent days*. President Robert Mugabe, who is struggling for political survival after two decades in power, seems to be shedding whatever pretense of democratic legitimacy he once maintained, cracking down on three vital checks on his otherwise autocratic power — the press, the courts and the political opposition.

Two weeks ago, the printing press of Zimbabwe's only independent daily newspaper, The Daily News, was bombed . . . .

Then last Friday, officials forced the chief justice of Zimbabwe's Supreme Court to resign . . . .

This week the police arrested two leading opposition figures on dubious charges of inciting violence . . . .

Now, the look-ahead element — and a *call to action* from neighboring nations and Washington:

A year from now, Mr. Mugabe will seek a fifth term as president. He is clearly prepared to use violent means to secure victory. His opponents will need the support of their regional neighbors and friends abroad, including Washington, if they are to stick to their course of peaceful change.

The New York Times[19]

Below, the *Chattanooga Times* chooses the halfway mark of a legislative session as time to sum up what Tennessee politicians are accomplishing. Note the halfway mark gives the paper time to judge accurately what the legislature is accomplishing — and still have time to marshal political and public opinion *to force action* in the second half.

Tennessee's legislators are halfway through their legislative session, and they have accomplished virtually nothing in the public interest to show for it. On the contrary, they have passed two bills that let rich special interests — first the check advance industry, and this week the long-distance telephone companies — grab more money from pressed customers. Oh. They've also passed a bill to ban hunting of albino deer.

But for the most part, it's still party time. It's apparently way too early for legislators actually to begin work on the state's troubling budget crisis—now 3 years old and deeper than ever . . . .

Now follows detailed examination of what the Legislature is (and isn't) doing. *Then a call to action*:

Tennessee has begun lagging behind other Southeastern states in investments in education, economic development and public services.

Lawmakers have a serious budget problem to address. They should quit partying, and get down to work.

Chattanooga Times[20]

FINALLY . . .

USE INCLUSIVE LANGUAGE

The *Portland Sunday Oregonian* on a proposed tram (emphasis added):

So much is riding on the Oregon Health Sciences University tram idea that *we all ought to feel nervous about it*. In effect, *we're all up there swaying*.

We all have a stake.

Not just OHSU. Not just residents of some of the neighborhoods surrounding the campus. The research university with its 10,100 jobs is an economic giant in the region, poised to wrest a multi-million-dollar windfall from gene research. That could seed Portland's economy with new businesses, now jobs and other economic payoffs for decades to come.

That's what's been missing in the public discussion so far—the link between OHSU and Portland's economic vitality . . .

Sunday Oregonian[21]

BE CHATTY:

President Bush is off to an inauspicious start in his dealings with North and South Korea. *You'd al-* *most think he longs for the Cold War.*

Chicago Tribune[22]

MAINTAIN HISTORICAL PERSPECTIVE:

For a single editorial on spy trials in Russia, the *Washington Post* examines Moscow's spy paranoia back years, even into old Soviet days, and concludes that "What is really scary" is that distinguished academics, journalists and diplomats are being tried on charges that are "transparently trumped up." In many communities across America, the newspaper — you and your files — are the only historical memory. Write to remind of the past, as well as warn of the future.[23]

RECOMMEND SPECIFIC ACTION.

Don't merely urge readers to "act." Recommend specific action, as does the *Los Angeles Times* in a sum-up editorial on city planning. A lengthy *Times* editorial concludes:

> To Take Action: For a schedule of the public hearings, call DONE at (213) 485–1360 or go to http:// www.lacityneighborhoods.com.
>
> *Los Angeles Times*[24]

WRITE TO ENGAGE READERS

Want your readers to read *all* the way through your editorials and *absorb* your views? Write as a *Wall Street Journal* editorialist writes:

> Senate Minority Leader Tom Daschle yesterday officially kicked off the Beltway campaign to retain most of the surplus in Washington. Sen. Daschle, with Dick Gephardt riding shotgun, denounced the Bush tax cut as a "risky gamble" that would give an "unfair share" to the rich, blah, blah, blah. This tiresome formula is being trundled out again because it has worked in the past. The Democrats would dribble out $900 billion of tax cuts over 10 years, *which is a little like medieval lords tossing coins from horseback* . . . .
>
> *Wall Street Journal*[25]

Magazine Editorials — The Difference

Editorial writing for magazines differs from newspaper writing in four principal ways:

AUDIENCE

As a group, *magazine readers are upscale demographically*, especially in education and income. Forbes, for example, boasts an audience of millionaires. Editorials written for such audiences must be "pegged" appropriately high, in subject matter, tone and language.

TAILORED CONTENT

Most successful magazines focus narrowly on highly specialized content tailored for readers with common interests. Examples are *Aviation Week &*

(CONTINUED)

(CONTINUES)

Space Technology, with engineers and technically skilled readers for an audience, and *Folio*, written for magazine industry insiders. Magazine editorials thus are written for *experts in the subject matter*, which requires writers to have highly specialized background and reporting skills.

FREQUENCY OF PUBLICATION

Magazines published weekly or monthly can't maintain constant links to readers, as do daily newspapers. Magazine writers, therefore, cannot count on readers being current, and must include *more detailed background in an editorial to bring them up to date.*

DELIVERY DELAY

Whereas newspaper editorials are written for delivery to readers within hours, magazine editorials frequently take days to reach readers via the U.S. Postal Service. *Magazine editorials therefore must be written in relatively timeless terms* so they will "stand" — be journalistically valid — days after the writing. The quick day-after editorial follow so popular with newspaper editorial writers isn't part of a magazine editorialist's writing arsenal.

SUMMARY

- Newspapers and magazines generally regard editorials as an important public service, despite some criticism that readers should be left to decide for themselves how to interpret the news.
- Particularly on smaller publications, where journalists perform many tasks, editorial writing might be part of your early career.
- You escalate dramatically your journalistic responsibilities when you shift from *objective* news reporting and analysis to *subjective* editorial writing.
- In advocacy writing, *you* single out issues for public discussion and stamp them with *your* definition of importance.
- In editorial writing, you and your newspaper move from being sideline observers to being players on the field and, with other power centers in your community, help decide how local government functions.

- Codes of ethics outline editorial writers' responsibilities as serving the public, creating a forum for community dialogue, being society's watchdog and guiding readers to cause change.
- The fundamental difference between newswriting and advocacy writing is that in editorials you must learn to *stir readers to action*, not only inform them.
- On smaller papers, editorial writers themselves sometimes pick topics for examination; on larger papers, editorial boards normally decide the institutional position.
- If you truly want to cause change, bring *added value reporting* — new facts, new figures—to your editorial writing.
- A strong editorial might be 80–90 percent original reporting and reasoned consideration of alternative viewpoints, with 10–20 percent on your newspaper's position.
- An editorial writer's mantra: SEA — stimulate, explain, advocate.
- Especially when analyzing hot-button topics, write in moderate tones and avoid mindless ranting and raving, which seldom stimulates rational discussion.
- Stay close to the breaking news and give readers analytical alerts on forthcoming events and quick reaction to those that broke recently.
- Don't equate writing long with success; brief, punchy editorials are among the best being published today.
- The world is complicated, and you're not expected to have definitive answers for all problems—even if you are an editorial writer.
- You'll write much about doom and gloom, but lighten up once in a while — and never pass up a chance for a lighthearted editorial that delivers welcomed change of pace to readers.

RECOMMENDED READING

I discuss advocacy writing more fully in Conrad Fink, "Writing Opinion for Impact" (Ames, Iowa: Iowa State University Press, 1999). Institutional considerations are discussed in my "Strategic Newspaper Management" (Boston: Allyn and Bacon, 1996) and ethical factors in my "Media Ethics" (Boston: Allyn and Bacon, 1995).

No aspiring editorial writer should miss the extremely strong, well-written editorials of the *Wall Street Journal*, which publishes one of the best editorial and op-ed sections in journalism. An education in editorial writing can be obtained by regularly reading editorials in the *New York Times, Boston Globe, Chicago Tribune, Los Angeles Times* and other leading metropolitan papers.

EXERCISES

1. For one week, read editorials in the *New York Times* (or another newspaper designated by your instructor.) In about 350–400 words, comment on the newspaper's apparent institutional position in its editorials. Is the newspaper preoccupied with national and international topics? Are local events treated? Does the newspaper editorialize essentially to air issues and open debate, or does it write to cause change? If change is the mission, how does the newspaper suggest that be initiated?

2. Outline, in about 150 words each, three proposals for editorials you would write for your college newspaper (or another newspaper designated by your instructor.) Why do you think each editorial is timely and required? What should be the newspaper's institutional viewpoint in each? Importantly, what added-value reporting would you do for each?

3. With your instructor's approval, write an editorial for your campus newspaper on a local (campus) event. Select an event/news story that's timely and, in your opinion, warrants an editorial. Do careful added-value reporting; give conflicting attitudes/viewpoints full airing, then advocate a position.

4. With your instructor's approval, write an editorial on an off-campus development (state or nation) that you believe should be brought to the attention of your fellow students. Strive to "translate" the meaning of that distant story into terms meaningful to your campus audience. Localize the story in that manner, then inform readers where and how to take action to cause change.

5. Select a forthcoming news event of some importance on your campus, then write a "precede" that a) informs readers what will

occur, and b) gives them guidance on what the event likely will mean and how the should interpret it. Write an editorial designed to alert readers to cause change by taking action before the event. Write the wordage required to fully describe the event and outlined your proposed course of action by student readers.

NOTES

1. These codes are reproduced in full in my "Media Ethics" (Boston: Allyn and Bacon, 1995) and my "Writing Opinion for Impact" (Ames, Iowa: Iowa State University Press, 1999).

2. Operations of these editorial boards are discussed in my "Writing Opinion for Impact," op cit.

3. This research, by Dr. Ernest C. Hynds, of the University of Georgia, is discussed in my "Writing Opinion for Impact," op cit.

4. "Green Mountain Spite," Oct. 18, 2000, p. A–22.

5. "Fast Times at City Hall," March 4, 2001, Section 1, p. 18.

6. "The Navy's Deep Trouble," Feb. 16, 2001, p. A–18.

7. "The Danger of Police Chases," March 16, 2001, p. A–22.

8. "A Federal Responsibility—Period," Feb. 13, 2001, p. B–8.

9. "Time to Clue in to Needs of the Poor," Nov. 27, 2001, Section 1, p. 12.

10. "Status Quo a Bearable Outcome," Oct. 18, 2000, p. B–8.

11. "Assure Police Credibility," Nov. 10, 2000, p. B–8.

12. "The Bomber Speaks," March 30, 2001, p. A–22.

13. "Brown's Pioneer Leader," Nov. 10, 2000, p. A–26.

14. "Unplug the Chair, Alabama," Feb. 2, 2001, p. A–8.

15. "A 'New' Mexico on the March," Feb. 23, 2001, p. B–8.

16. "The Wrong Kind of Campaign Reform," Feb. 19, 2001, Section 1, p. 10.

17. "That's Rich," Feb. 16, 2001, p. A–10.

18. "Southern-Style CEO," Feb. 21, 2001, p. B–9.

19. "Cracking Down in Zimbabwe," Feb. 9, 2001, p. A–26.

20. "Legislators Missing in Action," March 21, 2001, p. B–10.

21. "The Escalator up The Hill," March 11, 2001, p. G–4.

22. "How to Revive the Cold War," March 17, 2001, Section 1, p. 10.

23. "Russia's Spy Trials," March 14, 2001, p. A–24.

24. "Let's Get Specific," Sept. 16, 2000, p. B–9.

25. "Asides," Feb. 16, 2001, p. A–10.

11

Writing Personal Commentary

No JOURNALIST HAS ABSOLUTE freedom in any newsroom. But being a columnist writing personal commentary comes close to it.

You'll notice the ground rules change the moment you move from writing news or editorials to writing your own column.

In newswriting, editors insist you keep your opinions out of your writing and that your stories be objective and dispassionate.

In column writing, you're turned loose (and paid!) to put your opinions *into* your writing and to infuse it with subjective and, often, personal passion.

In editorial writing, you communicate an institutional view dictated by an editorial board or publisher.

In personal commentary, it's *your* thinking that counts, your selection of topic, your writing angle, your conclusion.

Another characteristic sets off you, the columnist, from you, the newswriter or editorial writer: As a columnist you have high personal visibility in your community, and your byline can be followed by thousands of readers — sometimes hundreds of thousands or even *millions*, if you're syndicated.

Indeed, strong columns are regarded by editors and circulation strategists as among any newspaper's principal reader attractions. Editors put considerable effort (and money) into building a "stable" of byline writers whose columns will pull readers deep into their pages day after day.

The high visibility, relative freedom (and the pay) make writing a column a highly coveted assignment. Competition to get a column is fierce in any newsroom.

To all this we turn in Chapter Eleven, Writing Personal Commentary. We'll break our study into three parts:

- Hard-news columnists who follow breaking news closely, offering added-value reporting and analysis on topical issues. This includes sports.
- Feature columnists who follow where the muse leads, writing in a personal, sometimes chatty tone about the unusual, offbeat and humorous.
- Critics and reviewers whose columns focus on specialties in the arts — films, dance, books — and produce for virtually every major newspaper a reader-friendly corner off the hard-news path.

SO, WANT TO BE A COLUMNIST?

If you want your own column one day, start preparing now — even though you may put in years as a reporter before getting one.

Columns are so important to newspapers that writing one is an assignment normally given only well-rounded journalists skilled in what you are now studying, the basics of our trade.

BUILD YOUR REPORTING SKILLS

No surprise here, of course.

All sound journalism is based in strong reporting, and columns — even the light, fluffy kind — must be founded in accurate, detailed factual substance.

However, the very best columnists are more than strong reporters. They're "scoop artists" who regularly break important news or exclusively reveal important angles missed in daily coverage.

To really succeed as a columnist you must *beat the front-page reporters* on occasion with important stories.

KNOW YOUR GAME

Most columnists focus on specialized subjects — national politics, for example, or college football or business.

That focus, in turn, draws readers who obviously are deeply interested in the subject and likely well versed, if not expert in it.

Your readers probably will spot factual errors immediately and desert you unhappy unless your writing moves their understanding to the next higher level. A columnist's shallow or uncertain grasp of a subject is highlighted for all to see.

DEVELOP SPECIALLY STRONG NEWS INSTINCTS

Specially strong? Here's why:

As a reporter, you can do a spot-news piece, sidebars, features — all on the same story. And, you can repeat that tomorrow, the next day, and the day after that . . .

As a columnist, you get *one* crack at a news development, and you probably write no more than three days or so each week.

If your column is off the mark — too far behind the news, for example — you'll not collect a regular following of readers. If the front pages, magazine cover stories and television newscasts are preoccupied with a single story, beware taking your column in a completely different direction.

Look at it this way: If you're, say, a sports columnist, and the entire sports world is focused on a particularly tight World Series, now is *not* the time for a cute column on badminton. Save that one for an off-season news drought.

DEVELOP STRONG SOURCES

Columnists occasionally propel themselves suddenly into view on the single ability to use the language in interesting ways, chewing over somebody else's news break but in wry, facile writing.

Just as suddenly, these columnists tend to disappear from view *unless* they shift into high gear and travel and talk with people, developing sources who can feed freshness and vitality into their columns.

Little in journalism gets stale more quickly than a columnist who never leaves the newsroom or who depends on mere word play to cover lack of reporting and substance. Constant interviews are necessary — even if each doesn't yield a column.

OFFER BALANCED, INFORMED OPINION

Other columnists who tend to disappear quickly are those whose writing is based solely on mindless ranting of, "I believe . . . I believe . . . ."

First, writing at least a couple times weekly, you may soon run short of subjects in which you strongly, viscerally "believe."

Second, unless you are very clever, you'll not be able to hold readers for long with nothing deeper than off-the-top-of-your-head writing.

Our best columnists trade in *informed* opinion based on strong reporting and research that is presented logically, calmly and with due respect for opposing viewpoints.

SHARPEN YOUR WRITING

As in all journalism, whether you have a good job or great career as a columnist depends in large measure on your writing ability.

Good jobs can be built on writing that is no more than clear, open and engaging *if* there is strong reporting behind it. Some of our most famous columnists succeed with writing that is, well, pedestrian. But what reporters they are! What insights flow from their analysis and interpretation!

Great careers are built on strong reporting *and* true wordsmithing, the delightful ability to weave even highly complex material into a smoothly flowing and logical narrative.

WRITING HARD-NEWS COLUMNS

To win a near-fanatical reader following, write a sports column.

To amuse and entertain, write a humor column.

To influence readers on important issues — *to cause change* — write a hard-news column.

Throughout print journalism, hard-news columnists speak loudly on the day's important social, political and economic issues. And their voices are magnified through prominent display in the pages of important newspapers and magazines.

The *Wall Street Journal*, for example, hands columnist Paul A. Gigot a huge megaphone — top-of-page display on its editorial page, one of the nation's strongest.

The *New York Times*, inventor of the modern op-ed page, and a true opinion leader in government circles and journalism, gives global voice to its William Safire, Thomas L. Friedman, Bob Herbert and other columnists.

Syndication carries outstanding hard-news commentary into hundreds of even small papers, where Clarence Page of the *Chicago Tribune*, David S. Broder of the *Washington Post*, Cal Thomas, Molly Ivins and others are published beside local columnists.

HIT HARD BUT FAIRLY

To attain such national prominence, columnists of course must possess qualities we've discussed — strength in reporting and writing, cutting-edge news instincts, informed and authoritative sources.

Another commonality links them: As a group they write some of the hardest-hitting commentary in all of journalism.

Here's the *Wall Street Journal's* Gigot:

Japan's a mess, the Nasdaq looks like London after the blitz and his boss's tax cut hangs in the balance. So what did Treasury Secretary Paul O'Neill do on Feb. 27?

He personally wrote a three-page memo urging President Bush to act quickly on "global climate change." Among other things, Mr. O'Neill vouchsafed that, "As you know, I think this could be a very big problem." The memo recommended that Mr. Bush establish a panel of "experts" on the issue, mentioning two men by name who'd be just as comfortable in an Al Gore White House.

Does anyone think this is why Mr. O'Neill was named America's financial chief?

Gigot continues: O'Neill has a "political tin ear" . . . he invites (and receives) "liberal criticism" . . . he isn't properly supporting his boss, President Bush. The kicker (which kicks *hard*):

The big political story of the moment is that Democrats are trying to pin the current recession, if that's what it is, on Mr. Bush. This is preposterous, since Japan has been rotting for years, the stock-market started going south last April, and Mr. Bush has been in office all of 55 days. But unless someone offers a different economic history, and sells a strategy for recovery, the point will sink in with voters.

Maybe Mr. O'Neill should warm to that job.

Paul A. Gigot
Wall Street Journal[1]

Cal Thomas, a syndicated writer who represents a conservative viewpoint (as does Gigot), sees the same Democratic machinations:

Chicken Little Democrats are clucking that the financial sky is falling and it's all President Bush's fault . . . .

To mix metaphorical stories, pay no attention to these chickens . . . The sky is not falling and the Democrats, who haven't had a new idea, much less a good idea, in many decades, are wrong about the economy . . . .

Cal Thomas[2]

A far cry, indeed, from the examples of objective and dispassionate reporting that opened this book!

Not to say, however, that *every* hard-news column must skewer some wrongdoer. To the contrary, the best commentators build reputations for balanced clear-headed thinking that readers will find realistic and fair.

For example, columnists Jack W. Germond and Jules Witcover view the "staggering dimensions" of a Middle East crisis and, rather than blame President Bush or any other American politician, fairly state: "There is no blame to be placed here." How could any reader disagree if aware of decades of trouble in that region?[3]

It's worth emphasis: Although paid to lead readers toward solutions, a columnist is unwise to attempt to answer all questions, solve all problems. And, when you don't have the answer, *say so.*

Claude Lewis of the *Philadelphia Inquirer* reports on a controversial corporate strategy of grading employee efficiency — and companies getting slapped with discrimination lawsuits as a result. Lewis sorts through the complexities, all right, but is forced to acknowledge he doesn't have the answer. He is revealingly fair with readers:

It'll be interesting to see how the whole thing shakes out over the next few years. Maybe a more rigorous system of school-type "grading" is at least a little better than the old casual evaluations — but judging by the number of lawsuits pending, we'll have to wait and see.

Claude Lewis
Philadelphia Inquirer[4]

HELP READERS UNDERSTAND NEWS

We, again, are writing for *news*papers, and our readers look to columnists for help on complex news that's in the headlines.

As in any analytical writing, the *precede* — alerting readers to forthcoming events—is important in commentary. In columns, of course, commentators go beyond analytically *explaining* probabilities and, in often heavy measure, add their personal interpretations.

Writing in the *Los Angeles Times* on a Friday, Robert E. Hunter sets the scene by warning of what a misstep in diplomacy could mean:

At the end of this week, Secretary of State Colin L. Powell makes his first foreign trip, notably to the Middle East. But he should understand clearly what is expected of him in the region. Eight years ago, President Clinton's new secretary of state, Warren Christopher, went to Europe to discuss with the allies the war then raging in Bosnia. Perhaps unfairly, the views he presented were widely characterized by Europeans looking for clarity in U.S. policy as lacking a sense of strategy, purpose and commitment, and U.S. leadership was faulted for many months thereafter.

That lesson from Europe applies to the Middle East today . . . .

There follows detailed discussion of Middle East affairs, then pointed personal advice:

Perhaps . . . Powell would have been better advised to delay his first visit to the Middle East until the Bush foreign policy team is fully in place, there is a new Israeli government to deal with and the complexities of the choices facing the U.S. are carefully sorted out. But once in, Powell has no choice but to persevere. He will need a few good ideas, a demonstration of leadership, strong follow-through when he gets back home and a bit of luck to turn this trip to positive account.

Robert E. Hunter[5]

Now, readers, watch next week's headlines to see how it all turns out!

On a Monday, columnist Bob Herbert is in the *New York Times* with commentary looking ahead two days to an event on Wednesday — and obviously trying to prevent it:

This is not about Antonio Richardson, a convicted murderer who is scheduled to be executed by the State of Missouri early Wednesday morning. I've seen no evidence to indicate that Mr. Richardson was innocent, and he seems to have fully exercised his rights of appeal. So it's not about him.

This is about us.

Antonio Richardson was part of a group of two boys and two young men who raped and murdered two young women in St. Louis in 1991. The women were sisters — Robin Kerry, 19, and Julie Kerry, 20. After being sexually attacked, they were pushed off the Chain of Rocks Bridge and into the Mississippi River, where they drowned . . . .

Now, Herbert explains the mother of the victims wants the execution halted because Richardson . . .

. . . was 16 at the time of the attack. He was not a ringleader of the group. And he is so mentally handicapped he is unable to say in which state he lives.

We can rid ourselves of Mr.

Richardson by sticking a needle into him, as planned, at 12:01 a.m. Wednesday. But I would argue with Ginny Kerry that by killing him we'll succeed only in diminishing ourselves.

Herbert strongly asserts his personal belief that execution is wrong, and kicks off with the following (do you infer from it a suggestion that readers contact the governor?)

Governor Holden has until tomorrow night to decide whether to intervene in the execution of

Antonio Richardson.

Bob Herbert
New York Times[6]

So, in writing a *precede*, this columnist goes far beyond merely explaining a forthcoming event and, instead, alerts readers in an effort to cause change, *to prevent the event itself.*

Coming in behind the news, in a *follow*, a columnist below uses a personalized and very angry and hard-hitting approach to a political scandal involving former President Bill Clinton. As you read, reflect on the confessional tone of the columnist's writing. Does it suggest he is "coming clean" on his own journalistic errors of the past, and does your regard for the writer improve as a result?

Dear Bill:

I have been in Europe . . . and I

returned to find a firestorm over your pardon of Marc Rich. And so I read up — many, many articles — and I now have this to say: You let me down.

Yes "me" — me and everyone else who has ever defended you. Me and everyone else who thought that while you might be blemished (and who among us is not, we would quickly add), when it came right down to it, we hated your enemies much more than we could ever hate you. They, those prudes with subpoenas, were dangerous. You were merely sometimes tacky.

Almost always I could come to your defense. Whitewater? A real estate deal in Dogpatch. A nothing.

Filegate? Nothing there. Travelgate? No crime . . . but you shouldn't have lied under oath. You shouldn't have lied.

But I understood. Over and over I wrote that this was a perjury trap. I'm not sure what I would have done under similar circumstances. I bet much of America ran that dilemma through its head and came out with no clear answer. I felt sorry for you. That videotape of you when you testified. You looked drained of color. I could sense your fear. You had the look of what you, in fact, were: a condemned man. . . .

Now, the columnist establishes when his personal support of the President vanished:

With the Marc Rich pardon, though, I have looked and looked for extenuating circumstances, for justifications, and I can find none . . . .

Finally, after extended lamenting over what he clearly considers betrayal by the President, the columnists concludes:

. . . this Marc Rich episode . . . a pie in the face of anyone who ever defended you. You may look bad, Bill, but we look just plain stupid.

Richard Cohen
Washington Post[7]

In his personalized follow, the *Post's* Cohen casts in emotional terms his analysis of his own feelings — and by extension, those of many Americans. Again, note the huge difference between the personal latitude granted columnists and the strictures and conditions placed on newswriters.

Sometimes, great service to readers comes from stepping back from the daily news flow and holding up for examination an overlooked item. Larry Eichel does that in the *Philadelphia Inquirer* on a story that popped all too briefly into view, then disappeared.

One day last June, the *Philadelphia Daily News* ran a guest column by a well-known conservative writer named David Horowitz. In an often provocative way, the piece made a 10-point argument against the idea that African Americans should be paid reparations for the harm done by years of slavery and segregation.

The column provoked a few spirited letters, pro and con, and an op-ed piece a few weeks later taking Horowitz on. And nothing more.

Okay, but why raise the issue again?

Why do I tell you this? Because it demonstrates the unfortunate point that sometimes what's considered legitimate political speech is determined not by what is written or said but by who is reading or listening.

A version of that same opinion piece, in the form of a paid advertisement offered to college and university newspapers, is now at the heart of a controversy over political correctness and freedom of expression that has been consuming some of the nation's most prestigious universities.

Now, Eichel describes how much of the nation is unaware of the controversy, that university papers that published the ad are accused of racism, that the office of one that did was stormed by protestors, that all copies of other papers were stolen by protesters.

The point? That a larger issue, free speech, is in jeopardy, and that the author of the ad . . .

. . . is, in his own way, merely expressing an opinion on a public issue, and it's hardly a fringe viewpoint. His conclusion, if not his reasoning, is shared by millions upon millions of Americans.

Nowhere it is written that political discourse has to be polite or popular to be legitimate. A lot of

students undoubtedly found Horowitz's views offensive. But as an editorial in the Brown paper noted the other day, that reaction makes it "the very kind of speech that must remain free."

Precisely.

Larry Eichel
Philadelphia Inquirer[8]

Lessons for a columnist: Stay alert. Don't let important stories slip unnoticed out of public view. Use your columnist's *freedom of selection* to focus on topics that involve wider issues, wider principles.

BE CANDID WITH READERS

As in no other journalism, column writing enables you to build special links with readers. That creates unique responsibility and opportunity.

Your opportunity is to build something akin to a family of followers who read you faithfully with warmth, respect and trust.

Your responsibility, if you want that trust, is to be open and candid with readers, fully revealing on your personal ideology and agenda, if any, that might be driving your selection of topics and how you write about them.

That is, columnists should put their personal cards on the table for all to see and write in a spirit of, "This is where I stand."

Writing for the *Boston Globe*, Robert A. Jordan does that as he accuses President Bush of anti-union maneuvers. His opener:

Democrats and one of their strongest allies, organized labor, are beginning to realize their fears about President George W. Bush.

Less than a month after he assumed office, President Bush issued four executive orders aimed at reducing the political and economic clout of organized labor . . . .

There follows point-by-point discussion of Bush's orders, and this revelation of the columnist's personal involvement (emphasis added):

Unions, as a New York Times article explained, are forbidden by law to donate money, including dues or fees from workers directly to candidates. Such money can be used for political purposes only in get-out-the-vote drives, issues advertising and other such purposes. And (*as yours truly, who is also president of* a union representing white- and blue-collar workers at The Boston Globe, is aware) only when unions set up political action committees and ask their members to donate can such money go directly to a candidate's campaign . . . .

Robert A. Jordan
Boston Globe[9]

Note above that columnist Jordan not only reveals his personal involvement in union activity, he also credits the *New York Times* as a source.

In big-league journalism, writers credit even competitors when credit is due.

David S. Broder, a *Washington Post* columnist so skillful he himself is regarded as an authoritative source, is careful to be open and candid with readers on his sources. This in a column on the federal budget:

As a result, said *Congressional Quarterly, the nonpartisan, private news service*, spending for fiscal 2001, which began on Oct. 1 is likely to be $100 billion more than allowed by the supposedly ironclad budget agreement of 1997 . . .

David S. Broder
Washington Post[10]

Lesson: Even star columnists build authority and credibility into their writing by locating — and quoting by name — authoritative sources. *Readers have a right to know where you got the facts that you are asking them to believe.*

Clarence Page of the *Chicago Tribune* establishes his authoritative credentials in a column that opens this way:

Washington — Tabloid revelations about the Rev. Jesse Jackson's "love child" are devastating to everyone who ever had faith in him, including, undoubtedly, his wife.

Many wonder whether Jackson can recover from the National Enquirer's scoop that he fathered a child, now 20 months old, whose mother . . . was a Washington official in his Rainbow/PUSH Coalition.

Even more tantalizing for the media and Jackson's foes is that his affair was going on while he was praying with then-President Clinton as a "spiritual adviser" during the Monica Lewinsky scandal . . . .

Those are the facts, as Page sees them. Now, he delivers his opinion *and reveals the experience on which his opinion is based*:

Can he recover? Maybe. *But after covering Jackson off and on for about 30 years* I think these wounds look permanent. If this is not the end of the rainbow for the Rainbow/PUSH Coalition leader, you can at least begin to see the beginning of the end from here . . . .

Clarence Page
Chicago Tribune[11]

Note above that columnist Page reports in his fourth graf his 30 years of covering Jackson. As readers move through the hundreds of words that follow, they know they are reading a reporter with solid experience.

Think about it: As a columnist, you're asking readers to trust your opinions and observations. Surely, your readers deserve to know how you arrived at those opinions.

You need not devote hundreds of words to outlining your credentials. Georgie Anne Geyer, a syndicated columnist specializing in foreign policy, files a column datelined Pristina, Kosovo, on guidelines laid down by Bernard Kouchner, former head of the U.N. peacekeeping mission there. Geyer opens her second graf this way:

When I interviewed Kouchner a year ago last fall . . . [12]

It's particularly important to be candid with readers if there is real *or perceived* conflict of interest in your writing. For example, it's a journalistic sin to use your column to further your own financial interests — or those of friends.

Cal Thomas, a widely syndicated columnist, comments on the stock market, revealing his principal source *and his personal ties with the source*:

Whenever I want sound financial advice, I don't go to politicians. I turn to Ric Edelman, *who is my financial adviser*, and a best-selling author and broadcaster. You can check him out on "Oprah" this Friday, or you can visit his Web page (www.ricedelman.com). (*I receive no goods or services for this unsolicited plug and pay full fee for Edelman's services.*)

Cal Thomas[13]

PITY THE POOR READERS

War, famine, poverty, political fighting, disease . . .

Pity the poor readers. We ask them to follow our litany of gloom and doom, to plow through hundreds of words on enormously complex issues.

When *you* ask readers to do that, ask yourself how you can help them. The answer, of course, lies *not* in avoiding the complex, *not* in pandering to readers with pablum-like dialogue but, rather, the answer lies in writing that's open, engaging, *readable*.

It's easy to see when a columnist does that.

For example, David S. Broder (a columnist I admire greatly) sometimes gets so focused on the *subject* that he seems to forget the *reader*. I think that happened on this lead:

Bankruptcy and ergonomics were not topics George W. Bush talked about when he was running for president, so it is not surprising that few if any voters gave much thought to those matters when deciding how to mark their ballots last November. But elections have consequences, even for issues that go undiscussed in the campaign. And it turns out that millions of Americans will find their lives changed because Bush's views on bankruptcy and ergonomics are radically different from those of his predecessor, Bill Clinton, and his opponent, Al Gore . . . .

David S. Broder
Washington Post[14]

Note the difference when Broder uses a reader-friendly writing device we discussed earlier — an opening vignette in a neck-of-vase structure:

Shortly before 7 a.m. Saturday, Feb. 10, President Bush, up early as usual, read an editorial in The New York Times titled "Mr. Hagel's Reform Ruse," ripping a campaign finance reform bill sponsored by Sen. Chuck Hagel, R-Neb. According to the editorial, the Hagel bill "would open more loopholes than it attempts to close and would do nothing to stop the flow of corrupt money into the system."

Bush picked up the phone and awakened his top political aide, Karl Rove. "Call Hagel and tell him to keep going."

That phone call signaled an important shift in the dynamics of the coming debate on overhauling the campaign finance system . . . .

David S. Broder
Washington Post[15]

Which Broder lead do you find more palatable and, thus, more informative? It's worth emphasis: If readers can't — or won't — follow your tortured convoluted writing you've lost your chance of informing them on an issue of compelling importance.

Whenever possible, translate complex issues into simple examples readers can understand easily.

For example, Scott Lehigh of the *Boston Globe* has the formidable task of leading readers through a complex controversy over the quality of public education. Precisely how poorly are students doing? Lehigh:

Here's an example. Asked how much an $18,000 car will be worth after one year if it loses 30 percent of its value each year, one student subtracted 30 from 18,000 — and, compounding the calculational error, arrived at $17,990. Or consider this essay excerpt from a student asked to examine the role of a secondary character in a "work of literature" he had read.

"Tinker Bell also gets Peter out of a lot of trouble. You wouldn't believe it because she is a very tiny little lady that shines and flys around also. Tinker Bell makes Peter and everyone else fly by farry dust."

As grade-school work, that would be disquieting. In the 10th grade, it's tragic . . . .

Scott Lehigh
Boston Globe[16]

Lesson: As a columnist you're paid to lend personal interpretation to complex issues. But sometimes you best serve that purpose by putting aside your writer's ego, stepping out of the column and resorting to the reporter's old trick of *reporting, not pontificating*.

WRITING PERSONAL COMMENTARY / **319**

And do remember your readers are not professional journalists tasked, as you are, with staying atop all news, all the time. Background them early in your column so they'll understand your later message.

William Pfaff, a syndicated columnist, does that on a story that's a week old before he comments on it. His intro on February 16 *opens* with background:

Paris — The commander of the US submarine Greeneville, *which struck and sank a Japanese school ship Feb. 9, killing nine*, has been reassigned pending an investigation. Whatever the investigation's outcome, the press says he is un-

likely to command a ship again.

If so, it would be a refreshing change in a US Navy that, in recent years, seems to have renounced the principle of command responsibility . . . .

William Pfaff[17]

And for goodness sake, lighten up! If you do, you can make even a column on taxes palatable:

Washington is filled with talk these days about cutting your taxes. President Bush has proposed a $1.6 trillion tax cut, which would give a reduction to people at all income levels. So you can relax about your taxes now, right?

Wrong!

While the politicians talk a good game, across town at the Internal

Revenue Service, it's business as usual. The green-eyeshade crowd over there is still churning out forms and regulations so obtuse and demanding that no honest person with more than a very simple income situation can hope to comply without help . . . .

Walter S. Mossberg

Wall Street Journal[18]

WRITING SPORTS COLUMNS

Nowhere else in journalism are there as many columnists as in sports.

Nowhere else are columnists given more freedom.

And, probably, nowhere else do individual columnists attract such large and loyal followings of readers.

About 75 percent of all adult male readers and 47 percent of women report they regularly read newspaper sports sections. Sports editors, in turn, employ columnists liberally, with metropolitan papers sometimes assigning two or three columnists to the same game, along with spot-news reporters.[19]

Actually, the line in sports between news coverage and commentary is thin. The best spot-news reporting in sports is much more analytical and interpretive than in other news reporting.

If you want a career in sportswriting, therefore, you'll need to edge into personalized commentary sooner than your colleagues in, say, political or economic reporting. And, you'll probably have a chance at a column sooner, too.

Broadly, two types of columns are popular in sports:

- *Game columns* are sidebar offerings in addition to the spot-news account or "game lead." Game columns frequently focus not so much on who won and who lost, but why and how.
- *Fixture columns* are published, say, three times weekly and are designed to attract groups of loyal readers, some of whom buy newspapers principally to read their favorite columnist. Fixture columns generally are "anchored" in the same place — the left-hand column of a sports section's front page, for example — so readers can find them easily. Writers don't always peg their columns to specific games. Rather, they roam freely across the sports world, its personalities, its business.

ELEMENTS OF GAME COLUMNS

Spot-news reporters are assigned to write the game lead, the wrapup story on winners and losers.

Game columnists have no such panoramic responsibility and thus are free to concentrate on examining key elements behind who won and who lost — and, particularly, why. Four elements are most important.

#1: GAME STRATEGY

Sports readers, like armchair soldiers, want to know strategies that decide who wins, who loses.

Baseball columnists, for example, may focus on the coaching strategy behind "rotation," the order in which hitters go to the plate, or pitching strategy.

Football columnists may examine defensive and offensive play — whether the passing game works or whether running backs carry the day.

In basketball, columnists score points with readers by examining such things as the merits of man-to-man defense and zone defense.

And, in all of this, columnists must display solid expertise, because those armchair strategists know the game, too.

#2: Turning Points

In sports, as in war and love, there are moments pivotal to the outcome — true turning points when victory slips from the hand or is seized.

The drama of those moments can be intense in sports: a pass interception that breaks a football team's spirit, a homerun that sparks a rally.

Reader-fans savor those moments and will read your commentary on them even if they saw the game on television. (Television, we find, doesn't turn off newspaper reading; in fact, it spurs fans to seek in newspapers a confirmation and explanation of what they saw.)

#3: Star Performances

Writers of spot-news game leads must range across the entire face of a contest, wrapping up all factors influencing the outcome.

Smart columnists find in that an opening they can exploit: Seldom can game leads give reader-fans the full depth of coverage they want on sports heroes.

Sports are about people, and reader-fans closely follow the fortunes of their heroes, according them much more attention than is accorded public officials or business leaders.

So, columnists often focus on star performers to excellent advantage.

#4: Other Influences

Key influences on many games include player hijinks off field, weather, injuries, officiating — and all are great subjects for columnists.

Rain can kill a passing game in football and slow the running game; injuries to a star center can stop a basketball team in mid-court; officiating — good or bad — can influence any contest.

In the spot-news lead, such factors must be mentioned, usually only briefly. But in-depth examination awaits columnists who are free to devote hundreds of words to them.

BUILD LINKS TO READERS

Many sports columnists build extraordinarily close links with readers. Their secret is writing *tone*.

For example, Tennessee's basketball coach loses his job, and the *Chattanooga Times Free Press'* lead sports story *reports to readers*:

Knoxville — University of Tennessee men's basketball coach Jerry Green resigned Tuesday and took a $1.1 million buyout after the administration offered him the choice of quitting or coaching without a contract extension.

Tennessee athletic director Doug Dickey announced at an afternoon news conference that Green — who led the Volunteers to an 89–36 record and four NCAA Tournament appearances in four years after coming from Oregon — had turned in his letter of resignation. After the Vols started this season 16–1, Green came under fire from fans, boosters and the administration as they limped to a 22–11 finish that culminated with a loss to Charlotte last Friday in the first round of the Midwest Regional . . . .

Andy Staples
Chattanooga Times Free Press[20]

On the same page, with equally prominent top-of-page display, columnist Mark Wiedmer *chats with readers*. Note how his conversational tone differs from the staccato, hard-news language of the lead story.

Knoxville — They made Jerry Green an offer he couldn't refuse.

Color Green's Tuesday resignation as the University of Tennessee men's basketball coach in any hue you choose, but no one turns down $1.1 million to take a five-year vacation.

And no school makes that offer to a guy with 89 victories in four years if that school is not *desperate* to make a change.

In fact, UT athletic director Doug Dickey was apparently so desperate that he met with Green last Saturday, less than 24 hours after the Volunteers' season-ending loss to Charlotte in the opening round of the Midwest Regional in Dayton, Ohio. To further sweeten the deal, he even agreed to throw in a full year's salary for each of Green's four assistants, which added another $300,000 to the buyout.

That's right. Your University of Tennessee paid $1.4 million to once again start over in men's basketball . . . .

Mark Wiedmer
Chattanooga Times Free Press[21]

The difference between *reporting to* reader-fans and *chatting with* them is apparent in how this columnist opens his conversation with reader-fans over the day's first cup of coffee:

Good morning, Cubs fans. I know what you're thinking. You're thinking that the idea of an all-New York World Series would motivate your team to bring that kind of cachet to Chicago.

And here's what I'm thinking. You're a few clowns short of a circus.

In New York, there seems to be an urgency to put together and pay for a championship-caliber team. The Yankees always do it and the Mets are aggressive as well. It's an obligation to fans out there. But not here. Not even close . . . .

Steve Rosenbloom
Chicago Tribune[22]

CATCH THE MOOD

At the *Chicago Tribune*, columnist Skip Bayless leaves to a spot-news writer the nuts and bolts of reporting the NCAA basketball tournament.

For Bayless, it's *mood* that counts, and how to better catch that than in focusing on an individual:

Dayton, Ohio — Up the steeply banked arena ramp chugged Illinois coach Bill Self. Tie loosened, face drained of the usual pink glow. Self looked as if he had had a long day at the office. Who wouldn't after coaching and scouting the kind of turnover-plagued, sudden-death games that make the NCAA tournament a blast for everyone but coaches?

For No. 1 seed Illinois, the long climb toward the Final Four began

Friday morning with an 11:15 a.m. game against a team that lost to Arkansas by 68 points, 115–47. Purple-clad Northwestern State had far less business being in the NCAAs than the Northwestern Wildcats would have. But with seeds being spat out as if the bracket monster took a giant bite of watermelon, Self was worried . . . .

Skip Bayless
Chicago Tribune[23]

Columnist Michael Holley of the *Boston Globe* also is after mood — a moment during pre-season workouts conducted by a conditioning coach for the Chicago Cubs:

Mesa, Ariz. — It was so early that the desert sun was still yawning, and Mack Newton already had worked Tom Gordon and the Chicago Cubs into a lather. A lot of the Cubs weren't ready for this guy. No way. Not during spring training, which most ballplayers consider a six-week family reunion.

But you can't be casual on Newton's watch . . . .

Michael Holley
Boston Globe[24]

COLLECT BITS AND PIECES

In sports, as in all news reporting, little bits and pieces of information come floating along that individually may not merit coverage. Collected in a "sum-up" column they may create a pattern.

Thomas Boswell of the *Washington Post* watches the Redskins' new coach for two months and sees the pattern:

When the Redskins hired Coach Marty Schottenheimer, did they realize he'd come to town driving a dump truck? In two months, he's hauled out more scrap than the . . . sanitation department.

Any Redskin who hears a beeping noise behind him better move fast. Marty may be backing up the truck to attach the winch to you, then drop you elsewhere. Especially if you weigh 320 or 340 pounds.

If you're a free agent, be careful what you ask for. If you say, "I may leave town," Schottenheimer tends to respond, "Can I help you pack?" Semi-decent pass receivers, crafty, creaky old vets and moderately promising young pass-rushers are replaceable in his view of the NFL. So long, buddy. Shake a tree and 10 more just like you will fall out. Let somebody else pay you millions . . . .

Thomas Boswell
Washington Post[25]

TAKE LONG LOOKS AHEAD

With spot-news reporters writing the standard look-ahead lead, a columnist on Friday looks ahead to — and beyond — a heavyweight fight:

Las Vegas — There will come the day when the lightning in Evander Holyfield's hands loses amperage, when the elastic in his legs runs out of stretch, when no amount of will or canny boxing wit can compensate for the sucker punches of time.

History says that day is nigh. Perhaps not as nigh as Saturday night against an outclassed 28-year-old John Ruiz. But who can say for sure? Two months from his 38th birthday, Holyfield is well into the fighter's twilight, when in an instant all that you knew about a champion is wrong . . . .

Steve Hummer
Atlanta Journal-Constitution[26]

NAG A BIT

Tuck in your shirt. That's what our moms always told us, but what did they know? Now, there is a great international shirt-raising movement.

The other day at a tennis clinic, a number of women asked—begged, beseeched, goaded, teased—the young dude Jan-Michael Gambill to raise his shirt high enough so they could get a glimpse of his abs. Needless to say, he obliged . . . .

That's George Vecsey of the *New York Times* on a new fad in sports: athletes — men and women alike — ripping off upper garments in moments of victory or pure pandering to sexual impulses. Vecsey, who longs in his columns for purity in sports, concludes by suggesting that everybody should keep their shirts on.[27]

Columnists can serve as the conscience of sports, applauding or booing as appropriate.

TELL 'EM A STORY

No slam-bang sports action today, folks. No fisticuffs in the ring, no crushing tackles on the gridiron. For Ira Berkow of the *New York Times* it's story time:

Morgantown, W.Va.—One year ago, Tyler David Hostetler, age 8, died. Last week, he played in a Little League game. This is the story.

The soft, spring rain had stopped and the evening sun angled through the clouds as Jeff Hostetler walked the family's 6-month-old buff-and-white cocker spaniel, Rookie, down a path from his spacious house. It was about 7 p.m. last June 14 when they headed to Cheat Lake, which sparkled alongside his property. Hostetler moved with Rookie down a hill — this is West Virginia, after all, "almost heaven" as the locals often refer to it — and the hills and

mountains are indelible to the
majesty of the terrain . . . .

Ira Berkow
New York Times[28]

Jeff Hostetler is a former New York Giants quarterback. His son
Tyler was nearly killed in an accident, and recovered to get back into Little League baseball. The story runs *nearly 3,500 words* and is just that —
a story, a story of inspiration and drama.

That is effective column writing.

WRITING FEATURE COLUMNS

For many readers, it's a long, arduous journey we force on them, over our
front page of worldwide woe and through our editorial page of deep-think
reflection.

So, readers value feature columnists who put light-hearted twists on
woe — or avoid it completely and, instead, offer a stress-free stroll in a
different direction.

Broadly, this gives you two attractive opportunities: write close to the
news, or write away from the news.

WRITING CLOSE TO THE NEWS

The advantage of this is that the event you are about to kick around already is fresh in readers' minds and you can get down to work with limited backgrounding.

For example, President Bush puts math education high on his list of
priorities. That puts Dave Barry, *Miami Herald* columnist, into high gear:

President Bush says our schools need to do a better job of teaching mathe-
matics, and I agree with him 150 per-cent. Many high school students
today can't even calculate a square root! Granted, I can't calculate a
square root, either, but I *used* to be able to, for a period of approximately
15 minutes back in 1962. At least I *think* that was a square root. It might
have been a "logarithm."

But whatever it was, if I had to learn how to do it, these kids today
should have to learn it, too. As Pres-ident Bush so eloquently put it in
his address to Congress: "Mathe-matics are one of the fundamen-
taries of educationalizing our

youths." with a 10-foot pole . . . .
I could not have said it better

Note Barry devotes just 14 words to the "set-up" of his column ("President Bush says our schools need to do a better job of teaching mathematics").

The closer you write to the news, the less set-up needed.

Note also the mangled quote attributed to Bush. It's a wry reference to Bush's struggle with the English language, much discussed at the time.

With that, Barry is off on a delightful romp that includes a test question developed by "the American Association of Mathematics Teachers Obsessed With Fruit." Barry says it goes like this:

"If Billy has twice as many apples as Bobby, and Sally has seven more apples than Chester, who has one apple in each hand plus one concealed in his knickers, then how many apples does Ned have, assuming his train leaves Chicago at noon?"

The problem is, these traditional algebra problems are out of date.

Today's young people are dealing with issues such as violence, drugs, sex, eating disorders, stress, low self-esteem, acne, global warming and the demise of Napster. They don't have time to figure out how many apples Ned has. If they need to know, they will simply *ask* Ned, and if he doesn't want to tell them, they will hold him upside down over the toilet until he does.

And then Ned will sue them, plus the school, plus his parents for naming him "Ned" in the first place.

Ultimately, the ACLU will get the Supreme Court to declare the number of apples a student has is protected by his constitutional right to privacy . . . .

Dave Barry[29]

Barry tries (and mostly succeeds) to write funny all the time. Other columnists who write about "serious" issues find relief occasionally in using a featurish approach.

Take Molly Ivins. She normally opens her syndicated column as if mounted on a fast horse, leading a posse intent on lynching idiots in high places. Today, she sneaks up on the bad guys:

I got repetitive stress syndrome from over-knitting. I prefer to think of it as Extreme Knitting. It was during one of my periodic attempts to quit smoking. (Now amid another one, I'm six months out and doing well, thank you.) With impeccable timing, I decided to quit at almost exactly the moment that the Republicans decided to impeach Bill Clinton.

Now, Ivins sharpens the point:

So there I am, a one-week no-smoker, and I know there's no way I am getting through the Judiciary Committee's Theater of the Rank and Absurd on this matter without smoking unless I can find something to do with my hands.

In desperation, I rushed off to the knit shop and demanded yarn and needles . . . . I'd knit while listening to Republicans enumerate the sins of Bill Clinton.

The Late Unpleasantness lasted for quite a while, involved vast amounts of repetitious bloviation and was altogether fairly sickening from all points of view. By the end of it, I had a dozen badly knit scarves and repetitive stress syndrome.

It was not exactly agonizing, but it hurt all the time . . . .

So off I went to the physical therapist. I had massage and shots and ice packs and hot lamps, and I can't even remember what-all else . . . .

Finally, Ivins & Posse catch up with the bad guys:

Fortunately, my living is not dependent on knitting. Suppose it had been?

I bring this up because President Bush held a private meeting with congressional leaders on Feb. 27, and they decided to kill the new ergonomic workplace rules . . . .

Molly Ivins[30]

Ivins devotes the rest of her column to lynching Bush for, she says, selling out to big business and ignoring workers injured on the job.

Lesson: Lead your readers *gently*, *indirectly* to your point, and you'll increase chances of them catching your serious message.

Of course, feature columnists *need not have a deeply serious point*. Bob Greene, then of the *Chicago Tribune*, didn't:

It feels almost unpatriotic — not to say unsophisticated and out of touch — to confess being neither shocked, surprised, distraught, disillusioned or particularly upset by the news of the breakup of Tom and Nicole.

Tom is Cruise; Nicole is Kidman. Judging by the news coverage of their recent separation, you would think the event was startling on the level of, say, George and Barbara Bush splitting up.

But for some of us, the urgent coverage of the marital discord of these two actors was puzzling to the extreme. "Tom and Nicole"? First of all, we've never met them, so the first-name references seem a little presumptuous; second, if their 10-year union symbolized something special and enduring about American public life, something whose end spoke volumes about national expectations and disappointments . . . .

Well, for many of us, the real news was not that Tom and Nicole are no longer Tom and Nicole; the real news is that their onetime oneness evidently was supposed to be a part of our consciousness. Tom and Nicole's separation warrants headlines? Somehow we missed the wedding . . . .

Now, a wry thrust:

But this is not really about Cruise and Kidman — although . . . it may be a good time to weigh in with an opinion about why they broke up. Every publication in America has offered authoritative analysis of why the two parted, so here is ours:

They probably don't like each other as much as they once did . . . .

Bob Greene
Chicago Tribune[31]

Note characteristics of Greene's column:

- It avoids serious issues in the headlines *but* plays counterpoint to an event much talked about.
- Greene cleverly makes himself the "goat" (sort of, Gee Whiz, what's all the fuss about?)
- Greene includes "some of us," pulling readers in with a "me-too" attitude you can envision in conversation across the kitchen table.

WRITING AWAY FROM THE NEWS

Bombings in the Middle East. Chaos on Wall Street. The Chinese are really mad at Americans, and Molly Ivins is riding hard over the energy crisis.

None of that for Loran Smith, a Georgia columnist who offers country-boy memories for readers who were there, and, for readers who weren't there, nostalgia for times they never knew.

For Smith, it's springtime:

Even though I don't like for my feet to get cold, I find it refreshing to go barefoot about this time of the year. Perhaps it reminds me of my youth when the planting was about to begin and you could walk in freshly tilled soil, fallow land that would soon produce gardens and crops.

Life was being renewed, and springtime brought hopes for a good crop which would pay the bills and hopefully provide enough money left over for a few clothes and some shoes.

But as the old mule pulled along the plow and you walked behind your daddy as he turned the earth, you had not a care in the world, and there was no thought of ever needing shoes again . . . .

Loran Smith[32]

And off we go, across fields and into the woods, where boys hunted squirrels for dinner that night . . . barefoot in rural Georgia because "ill-fitting-hand-me-down shoes were not comfortable" . . . .

Brian McGrory of the *Boston Globe* opens *far* from the news beat:

There was a story circulating through the dog parks of Washington, D.C., a few years back . . . A short but commanding woman was exercising her golden retriever in the early morning . . . when a fellow dog owner making typical small talk asked her name and what she did for work.

"My name is Donna," Donna Shalala casually replied, "and I'm secretary of health and human services."

Ah, dog ownership. It doesn't matter if you're the head of the largest government agency in the world, which Shalala was, or the guy who works the overnight shift vacuuming her office. Dogs, and all the pleasures and obligations that accompany them, are the greatest of equalizers . . . .

For just a moment, McGrory gets serious: Get a dog. They'll introduce you to nice people. The exercise you get walking them is good for *you*, as well as the dog.

Then, McGrory (whose dog is named Harry) lets readers look into his personal life:

When I first picked Harry up on a December night, there was no way I could know then what I am certain of now, that he is, the cliches aside, the best friend I will ever have.

My dog has outlasted one wife, moved with me from Boston to Washington and back to Boston, lived in five houses and apartments, has recently shared his L. L. Bean bed with a regal black Labrador named Riggs and sprawls patiently by my side when I take to the keyboard trying to wring words from thoughts. In return, he seeks a few biscuits, an occasional rub, and seems endlessly soothed by the sound of my voice. Mostly, he encourages inclusion: Whatever I'm doing, he'd like to do as well. The daily walks are as much mine as his . . . .

Brian McGrory
Boston Globe[33]

Lesson:

As a newswriter, you look into the lives of others.

As a columnist, open your own private closet for a peek, reveal a bit of yourself, and you'll no longer be a dispassionate stranger hidden behind the anonymity of a byline. Rather, you'll be an acquaintance, *a friend invited in for a cup of coffee.*

OTHER WINNING COLUMNS

Columnists can — and do — follow where the writing muse leads. But two subjects promise special reader interest: lifestyle and health.

Lifestyle, of course, is a hugely broad subject, encompassing fun, travel, fashion, career . . . and columnists turn regularly to those human endeavors.

For Marjorie Williams of the *Washington Post*, the lifestyle subject of the day is raising children:

A warning: This column contains very bad news. If your house is less than spotless — if dust bunnies hold hospitality suites for new recruits under your bed . . . if eight or 10 desiccated pieces of Halloween candy still dot your children's bureaus . . . if that faint cobweb up near the ceiling in your dining room has started to feel like a member of the family — then you may want to skip this news entirely . . . .

That's the *bait*. And note how inclusive columnist Williams is, describing household conditions that undoubtedly have many readers saying, "So, my house isn't the only one that's dirty." Now the *hook* — the message:

A researcher at the University of Michigan reports that the children of people who keep clean houses do better in later life than the children of people who let the dishes stack up in the sink. According to Rachel Dunifon, of the university's School of Social Work, home cleanliness can predict a child's educational attainment and income more than 25 years later . . . .

Onward marches Williams, describing the research and researcher ("yes, she grew up in a very clean house, and reports that her mother feels pleasantly vindicated by her research").

Now, with every homemaker-reader undoubtedly firmly behind her, Williams despairs of ever keeping a clean house and says she's going to write a research proposal on the subject "just as soon as I've dumped these dishes in the sink."[34]

Health is a hugely important topic. In writing about it, you have three compellingly important responsibilities:

- Be accurate. People make life-and-death decisions on what they read in newspapers. Never let your journalistic enthusiasm (or ill-founded optimism of researchers) lead you beyond the intrinsic merits of the news. (The first published report of a cancer "cure" I ever saw was in *1957*.) *Always* quote authoritative — and balancing — sources.
- Write entertainingly. You cannot lead readers into an important health story unless your writing is open, engaging, readable.
- Translate jargon.

Writing in the *Wall Street Journal*, Tara Parker-Pope, a health columnist, has a challenge: She has to inform readers that many medications can interfere with libido, but the problem is worse with the popular class of antidepressants known as selective serotonin reuptake inhibitors, or SSRIs.

See the challenge?

Here's how the columnist meets it:

A new television commercial tells the dirty little secret of many popular antidepressants: They can ruin your sex life.

Columnist Parker-Pope quotes sources in government, drug companies and universities and breaks the complex issue down to understandable language: taking these antidepressants can cause "sexual dysfunction, ranging from loss of desire to problems with arousal and an inability to reach orgasm."[35]

No wink-and-nudge writing here, no pandering to lewd side-jokes — just straight talk on an important health issue.

WRITING ARTS CRITICISM AND REVIEWS

Want to tuck yourself away unnoticed in a quiet corner of the newsroom, comfortably far from the thundering herd of spot-news reporters?

If so, don't go into arts criticism.

The arts — music, drama, dance, books, films — are front-line offerings in newspapers and magazines, and critics and reviewers are under all the pressures and strains of competitive journalism.

In fact, the best arts coverage is a combination of hard-driving *news* reporting and deeply analytical and expert commentary.

Broadly, arts commentary divides in two parts:

- Insider coverage written at a high level of expertise for readers knowledgeable in the field. *Dance Magazine* and *Opera World*, virtual bibles for their respective artforms, are examples of insider publications.
- Coverage for general-circulation newspapers and magazines, in which your commentary is the "interface" or translation between the complexities and beauties of an artform and readers who may not be experts.

WHAT YOU OWE READERS

As in any specialized reporting, you carry heavy responsibilities in arts commentary. Keep the following in mind:

FOCUS ON READERS

Like sportswriters or technical writers of any kind, arts commentators tend to be attracted to journalism out of love of the subject they cover. Many write first in defense of the artform and, second, to express their personal opinions on a subject about which they feel great passion.

That's the wrong order of priorities.

In arts commentary, as in all journalism, reader needs and desires — not the artform, not the artist — must come first.

STRONG PREPARATION

Merely liking movies or loving music isn't enough preparation for arts commentary.

First, many readers of arts commentary are far too expert to be fooled by a writer's superficial grasp of a subject.

Second, if you are inadequately prepared — if you don't know your subject thoroughly — you can jeopardize unfairly an artist's career, a film's marketplace prospects or a symphony orchestra's fund-raising capabilities.

REPORTING SUBSTANCE

Nowhere in journalism can you escape them — the good old Five Ws and How.

Impressionistic writing, passionate opinion, flights of poetic fancy— all belong in arts commentary. But so does letting readers know the who, what, where, why, when and how.

You need not give away clues about whodunit, but at least sketch a play's plot line. Let readers know enough about a movie so they can decide whether to attend. And, let them know where to get tickets, and at what cost, if that's an issue.

CLARITY OF WRITING

. . . The four new pieces he presented tended to be evolving, programmatic narratives where ensemble textures and a keenly controlled sense of dynamics took precedence over collective venting and individual statements . . .

Understand? If you're a music expert, you might. If not, you probably have been shut out of this review, published in a major metropolitan newspapers with hundreds of thousands of readers of all ages, interests and demographic characteristics.

The author (whose identity I am concealing to protect the guilty) saw and heard something that resonated deeply in his own closet of musical knowledge and memory. But, I submit, that writing doesn't share the emotion and passion with readers.

Clarity of writing — clear communication — is a major goal in arts commentary, as in all journalism.

HONEST, INFORMED WRITING

Your review should pay due deference to what the artist — the dancer, singer, painter — is trying to accomplish. And do report the director's intent in a film or play, and of course it's only fair to report audience reaction.

But, above all, arts commentary should include your honest, *informed* opinion — honest in that you must write what you think, informed in that you must base your opinion on solid understanding and appreciation of artist and artform alike.

Avoid the "cheap-shot syndrome," the stretch for a wickedly funny line even at the expense of informing readers properly or respecting art and artist.

Invariably, the cheap-shot lines go something like this: "The Our Town Symphony played Mozart last night. Mozart lost."

First, that fails the first test of good writing; it doesn't communicate or inform. Second, cheap-shot writing debases art, journalism — and the writer.

HOW THE PROS DO IT

Joe Morgenstern of the *Wall Street Journal* leaves no doubt what he thinks of a new film:

"15 Minutes" is worth that much of your time, but only if you're a masochist. A thrill-less thriller to chill any movie lover's soul, it's a botched attempt at social satire and a blot on the escutcheon of Robert De Niro, who should have run before taking the money. If Detroit had produced an equivalent lemon, we might have been seeing the world's first one-wheeled, square-tired car with no cooling system, steering wheel or brakes . . . .

Now, however — and this is key, I think — the reviewer casts the movie against a *larger issue in filmmaking*:

In a week when two truly worthy films are going into national release — "The Widow of Saint-Pierre" and "When Brendan Met Trudy" — I've put "15 Minutes" at the top of the page simply because it's such a flagrant example of a distribution pattern that is turning adult moviegoers into stay-at-homes. Slapdash star vehicles like this one, fueled by huge marketing budgets, reach thousands of multiplex screens around the country, while new releases of merit are often confined ... to a scattering of theaters in big cities . . . .

Joe Morgenstern
Wall Street Journal[36]

At the *Los Angeles Times*, critic Kenneth Turan didn't like the film much better:

Like many ambitious, provocative films, "15 Minutes" is a bit of a mess. Both audacious and unwieldy, exciting and excessive, this dark thriller is too long, too violent and not always convincing. But at the same time, there's no denying that it's onto something, that its savage indictment of the nexus involving media, crime and a voracious public is a cinematic statement difficult to ignore . . . .

Kenneth Turan
Los Angeles Times[37]

Nevertheless, the studio that released the film found plenty of rave reviews for an *advertisement*: "A Slam Bang Thriller," Larry King, *USA Today*; "'15 Minutes' is an 'A' all the way," Gene Shalit, "The Today Show"; "Riveting," Jim Ferguson, Fox-TV.[38]

Lessons:

- Pitch your review's theme and language to your *likely audience*. Movies are loved by film buffs and non-buffs alike. Note writers of the two reviews above opened their writing to non-buffs by using clear, non-technical language.
- Seldom is there unanimity among any reviewers over any artform. If you like De Niro's film, that's OK; if you don't, that's OK, too. Just be certain you make logical, informed observations about it.
- Moviegoers can't depend on studio ads for dispassionate, objective guidance on which films to attend. *That's* why we have independent reviewers.

Below, a reviewer takes a narrow approach to his audience, writing for insiders, pop music fans *in the know*:

The best vintage R&B always put feeling over craft, confession over cliché. That's why the current renaissance of classic soul — whether in the hands of traditionalist D'Angelo or the quirkier Macy Gray —

has found a grateful and growing
audience. Add Musiq Soulchild to
the list of artists to thank . . . .

Steve Appleford
Los Angeles Times[39]

Lesson: Not all art is for all readers, and trying to pull everybody into such a subject is a waste of energy.

KEEP ARTISTS HONEST . . .

Make it your reviewer's mantra: *Good* reviewers are *great* reporters.

Mary Campbell of the Associated Press looks at opera as an investigative reporter:

New York — Turns out Luciano Pavarotti, the King of the High C's, gave up his crown some time ago without telling anyone.

The 60-year-old tenor wasn't even trying for that lofty note last Saturday night at the Metropolitan Opera when he sang the role of Tonio in Donizetti's "Daughter of the Regiment," the part that made him a superstar 24 years ago.

Without informing his adoring public, he had transposed the fiendishly difficult aria, "Pour mes amis," a half-tone lower to make it easier to sing. He duly hit all the high notes, which were actually B naturals.

It didn't work during the second performance, on Wednesday. His voice cracked on a B, and he gave way to an understudy at intermission . . . .

Mary Campbell
The Associated Press[40]

The *Chicago Tribune's* television critic, Steve Johnson, watches David Letterman "in his emotionally charged first broadcast back from heart surgery." Letterman introduces the medical people who "saved my life." But, one "doctor" actually is a stand-in actor. And that leads the critic into an assault on fakery in television that leaves viewers who responded to the program's genuine emotional wallop as "feeling sucker punched."[41]

Sportswriters and arts commentators alike might deny it, but they share commonalities: In arts commentary, as in sports writing, "boosterism" — unthinking, unwavering support of the home team (artist) — is out. Honest, hard-hitting reporting is in.

SERVICE OVER ART (YOURS)

Sometimes you must put aside *your* artform — colorful, passionate writing — and simply settle down to giving readers nuts-and-bolts information.

For example, in his column, "All That Jazz," Don Heckman of the *Los Angeles Times* avoids what must be considerable temptation to wax poetic about jazz. Instead, this:

The books about jazz, like the CDs, just keep coming. Information in and of itself, as the Ken Burns jazz documentary frequently affirmed, is not nearly as illuminating as the actual music, of course. But there are many entries in the continuing flow of material that are valuable either as overviews of larger areas of jazz or as penetrating insights into individual lives. Here's a sampling of some recent publications . . . .

Now follows painstaking looks at new books on jazz, awards won by jazz musicians, schedules for forthcoming performances — simply a workmanlike summary of what's happening in jazz around town.[42]

A *Times* movie critic, Kevin Thomas, reviews "The Widow of Saint-Pierre" in detail for *film buffs*. For a wider audience of non-expert *moviegoers*, Thomas provides information crucial in all reviews:

• MPAA rating: R, for scenes of sexuality and brief violence. *Times* guidelines: Both the sex and the violence are brief and discreet, but the film is too intense and mature in themes for children.

"The Widow of Saint-Pierre"
Juliette Binoche, Pauline
   Madame La;
Daniel Auteuil, The Captain;
Emir Kusturica, Neel Auguste;
Phillppe Magnan, Judge Vernot;
Michel Duchaussoy,
   The Governor.
A Lions Gate Film release. Director Patrice Leconte. Producers Gilles Legrand, Frederic Brillon. Screenplay by Claude Faraldo.

Cinematographer Eduardo Serra. Editor Joelle Hache. Music Pascal Esteve. Costumes Christian Gasc. Art director Ivan Maussion. In French with English subtitles. Running time: 1 hour, 52 minutes.

Exclusively at the Royal, 11523 Santa Monica Blvd., West Los Angeles, (310) 477–5581; the Playhouse 7, 673 E. Colorado Blvd., Pasadena, (626)844–6500; and the South Coast Village, Sunflower across from Maggiano's South Coast Plaza, Costa Mesa, (714) 540–0594.

Kevin Thomas
Los Angeles Times[43]

That's how to take art to buffs and non-buffs alike!

SUMMARY

- No journalist has complete freedom, but being a columnist writing personal commentary comes close to it.
- In contrast with objective newswriting, column writing requires you to express your personal views and to assume high visibility in your community.
- Columnists must sharpen their reporting skills, the basis of all strong journalism, and build expertise in their subjects.
- Strong columns offer authoritative information from credible sources, along with balanced, informed opinion.
- Good *jobs* can be obtained by columnists who are strong reporters, even if they don't write brilliantly, but building strong *careers* requires outstanding writing skill, as well as reporting strength.
- To win near-fanatical readers, write a sports column; to amuse, write humor; to cause change, write a hard-news column.
- Nationally prominent columnists hit hard but fairly and write to explain the day's news complexities.
- Columnists must be candid with readers, building their trust by revealing any personal ideology that drives their writing.
- Readers have a right to know the sources and information on which columnists' opinions are based.
- Nowhere else in journalism are there as many columnists as in sports, and nowhere else are columnists given more freedom.
- Game columns examine the why and how of a contest, and fixture columns are published three or four times weekly and range more widely.
- Game columns frequently focus on strategy, turning points, star performances and other influences, such as coaching, weather, officiating.
- Many sports columnists chat with readers in conversational tones, leaving other reporters to cover spot-news developments.
- Feature columns written with light-hearted twists or focusing on the human element can give readers welcomed relief from worldwide woes reported on our front pages.
- Lifestyle and health are favorite subjects with feature columnists — and readers.

- Arts criticism is among front-line offerings by newspapers, and reviewers are under all the pressures of competitive journalism.
- Strong preparation is required for arts commentators who write for audiences that include experts.
- Reviews must include honest informed opinion — honest in representing the critics' opinion and informed in that opinion is based on solid understanding and appreciation of the artform.

RECOMMENDED READING

I discuss column writing and arts criticism at more length in "Writing Opinion for Impact" (Ames, Iowa: Iowa State University Press, 1999).

The Masthead, published by the National Conference of Editorial Writers, covers the full range of opinion writing. Watch also the *American Editor*, the *Quill* and *Editor & Publisher* for discussion of writing opinion.

The *New York Times* and *Los Angeles Times* are musts for aspiring columnists. Both papers carry columnists particularly strong in hard-news analysis and arts criticism. They have strong sports columns, too, as do the *Atlanta Journal-Constitution*, *Boston Globe*, *Washington Post*, *Dallas Morning New*s and *Chicago Tribune*.

EXERCISES

1. Study three consecutive columns by William Safire of the *New York Times* (or another columnist designated by your instructor) and, in about 300 words, comment on the following: Does the columnist display specially strong news instincts? Is the column written close to the news? Does the columnist quote — or appear to have — authoritative sources? Does the columnist offer balanced, informed opinion? How would you grade the writing ability of this columnist?

2. With your instructor's approval, select a hard-news story current on your campus, and write an opinion column about it. Be certain

to interview authoritative sources and to present "added-value reporting" in your column. Present balanced and fair accounts of opposing viewpoints, but take a strong informed position of your own. Write the wordage required.

3. Write a humor column tied to a news event currently on front pages. Avoid intensely personal humor whose meaning may be lost on a general audience of readers. Write the wordage required.

4. With you instructor's approval, write a sports column. This can be a game column or a fixture column that ranges widely in topic. Do appropriate sources and bring "added value" to your writing. Present conflicting viewpoints, then take a strong personal stand on your topic.

5. With your instructor's approval, review an arts performance on your campus. Write for a general audience of newspaper readers (not "insiders" expert in the artform.) Do the reporting required to give your column an authoritative tone. Demonstrate the requisite respect for the artist's intention and efforts, but take a strong informed position in expressing your opinion. Write the wordage required.

NOTES

1. "O'Neill Makes a Not-So-Hot Impression," March 16, 2001, p. A–14.
2. Syndicated column for March 21, 2001.
3. Syndicated column for Oct. 18, 2000.
4. "Does Worker-Grading System Fuel Bias?", March 21, 2001, p. A–21.
5. "Powell Better Remember to Pack a Defined Policy," Feb. 23, 2001, p. B–9.
6. "Cycle of Death," March 5, 2001, p. A–23.
7. "Forsaken for a Rich Fugitive," Feb. 1, 2001, p. A–21.
8. "The Body Politic," March 21, 2001, p. A–21.
9. "Assault on Organized Labor," Feb. 27, 2001, p. D–4.
10. Syndicated column for Oct. 18, 2000.
11. "Could This Latest Episode be The End of The Rainbow?", Jan. 21, 2001, Section 1, p. 19.
12. Syndicated column for Feb. 16, 2001.

13. Syndicated column for March 21, 2001.

14. "Business in The Driver's Seat," March 14, 2001, p. A–25.

15. Syndicated column for March 11, 2001.

16. "Unions Get an F in Honesty over MCAS," Feb. 16, 2001, p. A–19.

17. Syndicated column for Feb. 16, 2001.

18. "Personal Technology," March 15, 2001, p. B–1.

19. Simmons Market Research Bureau, quoted in Newspaper Association of America's "Facts About Newspapers, 1998," p. 8.

20. "Money Talks, Green Walks," March 21, 2001, p. D–1.

21. "A Field of Green Sends Green out to Pasture," March 21, 2001, p. D–1.

22. "MacPhail Not About to Adopt New York Model," Oct. 18, 2000, Section 4, p. 3.

23. "In The Wake of The News," March 17, 2001, section 3, p. 1.

24. "Cubs Hope They Can Bear up," Feb. 26, 2001, p. D–1.

25. "Departures Bring Home a Message," March 14, 2001, p. D–1.

26. "Father Time Remains Boxing's Ultimate Foe," Aug. 11, 2000, p. C–2.

27. "Sports of The Times," Sept. 3, 2000, p. 31.

28. "Brush with Death Bonds a Family," June 14, 2000, p. D–1.

29. Syndicated column for April 22, 2001.

30. Syndicated column for March 9, 2001.

31. "And Now the News, in a Flibbertigibbet Nation," March 4, 2001, section 1, p. 2.

32. "When Spring Tiptoes into Play, It's Shoe-Shedding Time," *Athens (Ga.) Daily News and Banner-Herald*, April 15, 2001, p. A–9.

33. "Pet Project: Saving Lives," Feb. 27, 2001, p. B–1.

34. "Products of Clean Living," March 14, 2001, p. A–25.

35. "Health Journal," March 16, 2001, p. B–1.

36. "Review/Film," March 9, 2001, p. W–1.

37. "Movie Review," March 9, 2001, p. F–1.

38. This ad appeared in many newspapers on March 9, 2001. It can be seen in the *Los Angeles Times* of that date, p. F–5.

39. "Pop Music Review," March 9, 2001, p. F–10.

40. Dispatch for Sunday papers, Nov. 12, 1995.

41. "Comedic License?", Oct. 18, 2000, section 2, p. 3.

42. Don Heckman, "All That Jazz," *Los Angeles Times*, March 9, 2001, p. F–24.

43. "Movie Review," March 9, 2001, p. F–12.

PART SEVEN
Ethics, the Law and You

Ethics, the Law and You

Well, we've come far, you and I — over the basics of reporting and through the fundamentals of strong writing.

But our journey is not yet ended. Two crucial factors, though implicit throughout this book, need explicit emphasis:

First, a principled journalist (and who needs the other kind?) must report and write from *the moral high ground*. To your skills as reporter and writer, then, you must add a keen sense of journalistic right and wrong, embodied in a thoughtful personal code of ethics.

Second, while aggressively serving the public's right and need to know, you must be careful to *work within the law*. Legal challenges against journalists and newspapers are frequent and can be damaging to career and pocketbook, alike.

In Chapter Twelve: Codes of Ethics, Rule of Law, we'll take a two-part look at all this.

We'll start with *doing the right thing*, reporting and writing within an ethical framework you should create personally after methodically studying existing codes drawn by newspapers and journalism organizations.

Then, we'll turn to the law, some of its pitfalls — and steps you can take to avoid them. No journalist, no newsroom can operate ignorant of the law or insensitive to its penalties.

12

Codes of Ethics, Rule(s) of Law

WHY LINK PRESS LAW with ethics in the same chapter? Because they are linked in the newsroom.

After more than 45 years in journalism, I am convinced that many — not all, but many — of our legal problems arise out of our own ethical shortcomings.

Put simply, inaccurate or sloppy journalism by arrogant or uncaring journalists yields a very high percentage of the lawsuits against the press.

And, the public attitude that law courts are the place to deal with the press grows out of a wider disenchantment with real — or perceived — ethical transgressions by the media.

The disenchantment is measurable. In one survey, 51 percent of respondents said the press has too much freedom; 20 percent disagreed that newspapers should be allowed to publish freely without government approval of a story; 23 percent disagreed that newspapers should be allowed to criticize public officials.[1]

Juries drawn from *that* public sit in judgment of us when individuals sue newspapers and reporters, which they often do out of anger over real — or perceived — lack of fairness and balance in our reporting about them.

Our first and best defense against legal problems is to *do the right thing ethically.*

But, what is the "right thing"?

AREN'T THERE ETHICS RULES?

No, there are no *rules* — not in the sense that ethics are codified systematically industrywide or embodied in mandatory regulations journalists must follow.

However, there are guidelines. Professional journalism societies and editors' conferences discuss nothing quite so much as ethics and how to do the right thing. And all journalism societies have *recommended* codes of ethics.

Some newspapers have their own codes of ethics, but many really are codes of *conduct* put forward as a condition of employment to protect marketplace image.

Whether written by journalism societies or individual newspapers, codes tend to be sweeping in content and aimed at establishing only wide parameters of conduct — serve the public, avoid conflict of interest, monitor the powerful. Such codes may give you only limited help as you attempt to pragmatically sort out the rights and wrongs of a story you're juggling under the stress of competitive pressure and deadlines.

Existing codes *are* helpful, however, as you try to sketch at least the broad outlines of your personal code of ethics, your personal definition of what you will do as a journalist and what you won't.

WHAT EXISTING CODES SAY

Two commonalities run through ethics codes written by major journalistic societies:[2]

- Fair, impartial and accurate service to the public is what journalism is all about.
- Journalists carry heavy responsibilities — not special rights — in serving the public's right and need to know.

Let's look at the fine print.

AMERICAN SOCIETY OF NEWSPAPER EDITORS
STATEMENT OF PRINCIPLES

This premier national organization of editors sets the tone for its Statement of Principles (emphasis added):

Preamble

The First Amendment, protecting freedom of expression from abridgment by any law, guarantees to the people through their press a constitutional right, and thereby *places on newspaper people a particular responsibility.*

Thus journalism *demands of its practitioners* not only industry and knowledge but also the pursuit of a *standard of integrity* proportionate to the journalist's singular obligation.

To this end the American Society of Newspaper Editors sets forth this Statement of Principles as a standard encouraging the highest ethical and professional performance.

Clearly, ASNE regards journalism as not a job, not a career—but a *calling.* The codes adds:

RESPONSIBILITY

Journalism's primary purpose is to "serve the general welfare" with information the people need to judge the issues of our time. Journalists who abuse their professional power for selfish or unworthy motives are "faithless to that public trust."

PRESS FREEDOM

Press freedom belongs to the people, and must be defended against encroachment "from any quarter, public or private." Journalists must ensure the public's business is conducted in public.

INDEPENDENCE

Journalists must avoid conflict of interest — or the *appearance* of conflict — and neither accept anything nor pursue any activity that compromises their integrity.

TRUTH AND ACCURACY

News must be accurate, free from bias and in context, with all sides presented fairly. Editorials and analysis must meet the same standards of accuracy.

IMPARTIALITY

Being impartial "does not require the press to be unquestioning or to refrain from editorial expression." However, there must be clear distinction between news and opinion.

FAIR PLAY

Respect the rights of people involved in the news, observe "common standards of decency" and stand accountable to the public for fairness and accuracy.

SOCIETY OF PROFESSIONAL JOURNALISTS CODE OF ETHICS

Your duty, SPJ says, "is to serve the truth."

Your obligation is to "perform with intelligence, objectivity, accuracy and fairness."

On ethics, the SPJ code is detailed:

- Nothing of value — gifts, favors, free travel or special treatment — can be accepted. Never compromise your integrity or your employer's.
- Secondary employment, political involvement and "service in community organizations" should be avoided if such activity compromises your integrity.
- Publish nothing from "private sources . . . without substantiation of their claims to news value."

- Seek news that serves public interest and "make constant efforts" to assure public conduct of public business.
- Protect your confidential sources.
- Plagiarism "is dishonest and unacceptable."

ASSOCIATED PRESS SPORTS EDITORS ETHICS GUIDELINES

The sports editors' guidelines strike first — and hardest — at a tradition in sports journalism of accepting favors from teams.

- A newspaper, the guidelines say, must pay its staffer's way for travel, accommodations, food and drink.
- Reporters *and* editors should avoid outside activities or work that might create conflict of interest (scoring baseball games, writing for team media guides).

The guidelines mirror those of other journalism societies in calling for sportswriters to spurn gifts — including free tickets.

NATIONAL CONFERENCE OF EDITORIAL WRITERS BASIC STATEMENT OF PRINCIPLES

Your chief duty is to "provide the information and guidance toward sound judgments that are essential to the healthy functioning of a democracy." Toward that end, you should:

- Present facts honestly and fully; it's dishonest to base an editorial on half-truths.
- Draw "fair conclusions from the stated facts."
- Never use your influence for personal favors.
- Give voice to "diverse opinions" and have the courage of your own "well-founded convictions."

STANDARDS AND ETHICS OF THE WASHINGTON POST

These standards broaden the question of ethics to include the *newspaper's* responsibilities.[3] They are:

- To listen to the voiceless.
- To avoid any and all acts of arrogance.
- To face the public politely and candidly.
- The *Post* pledges itself to an "aggressive, responsible and fair pursuit of the truth without fear of any special interest, and with favor to none."

From its staffers, the *Post* requires:

- Pay your own way; take no gifts from news sources.
- No outside work without permission.
- Avoid obligation to news sources and special interests.
- Avoid active involvement in any partisan causes *and* disclose any involvement by *family members* that might compromise the paper's integrity.

OUR ROOTS: SOCIETAL VALUES

Resonating throughout journalism's discussion of ethics are *societal values* accepted by most of us as characteristics of civilized society.

Humankind has developed values in the debate since time of the Greeks over which principles or standards to use in judging human conduct. These are important to our discussion:

Truth-telling. Without honesty, no moral framework exists, and, of course, truth-telling is at the very core of principled journalism.

Justice. Society promises impartial, fair treatment for all, along with reward or punishment as deserved. Being just is essential to journalism, as is monitoring whether society applies justice evenhandedly to others.

Humaneness. Help people, don't harm them, and assist the weak and vulnerable. That's crucial to civilized conduct, and is expressed in journalism by determination to avoid intentionally harming people in the news and to use our power to assist the needy.

Freedom. Independence and autonomy are essential to liberty and to principled journalism.

Stewardship. Guard and respect the rights of others; protect and pass to others who follow the benefits you enjoy. Protection of the First Amendment is first on our agenda.

OUR JOURNALISTIC PRINCIPLES

Reflecting our wider societal values, journalism has developed job-related principles you can consider for guidelines.

Serve the public. Change things for the better. Assist the needy, comfort the afflicted, attack social injustice. Public service is woven into journalism's very fiber.

Monitor the powerful. Be the watchdog. Monitor power — government, business, organized religion, special interest groups. *Hold the powerful accountable to the public.*

Be balanced and fair. "Objectivity" may be impossible to achieve because each of us is the sum total of past experiences, education, personal beliefs. But, regardless of your personal prejudices and beliefs, you can — you must — be balanced and fair.

Be compassionate. Cover the news as it must be covered, but deal compassionately and respectfully with people in the news.

Be independent. Avoid any inappropriate outside influence on your journalism, be independent in your thinking, and take personal responsibility for it. This includes avoiding "herd journalism" — unthinkingly stampeding after a story merely because other journalists are in the chase, or letting a media opinion setter (*The New York Times*, for example, or *Washington Post*) influence unduly your definition of what is news.

Be courageous. Penalty can be attached to autonomous moral reasoning: You can lose your job for answering to your conscience and defying editors' orders; you can be shunned by colleagues and friends by taking a principled stand. In matters of conscience you must consider the price — and whether you're willing to pay it.

Consider your loyalties. You have duty to yourself and your conscience, to truth and doing good. But you also have loyalty to your employer, who pays you to help get the newspaper or magazine on the streets, the newscast on the air. Consider loyalties in your decisionmaking process.

DECISION-MAKING: A METHOD

There is no single truth in ethics or, certainly, no formula that automatically yields decisions on right and wrong.

And, as you've seen, existing codes provide only general guidance.

What to do? How can you work you way — fairly and with balance and justice — through a complicated question of ethics? How can you be certain your reporting and writing are on the moral high ground?

Two suggestions:

First, avoid snap judgments, the automatic decisions based on "instinct" that, in turn, is based on nothing broader than your personal background and beliefs.

Second, employ your own broader system for weighing all societal values and journalistic principles that apply to an ethical dilemma. Do this regularly and with discipline, and you'll find your "instinct" giving way to much more trustworthy and methodical consideration of relevant influences.

A route for structured moral reasoning is adapted from the "Potter Box," developed by Dr. Ralph Potter at Harvard University:[4]

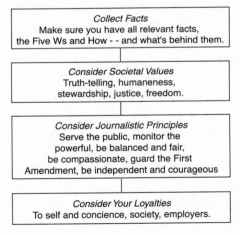

How to be a good journalist

Envisage the decision-making process this way:

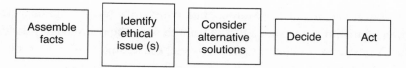

Note in the above these factors:

- An ethical issue in fact may be several ethical issues. *Precisely* what issue or issues do you face? Conflict between serving the public and being compassionate for someone caught in the spotlight? Conflict between loyalty to the public and your employer? Or your conscience? Isolate for examination the societal values and journalistic principles involved.
- Is there more than one solution? Can you, for example, decide that a politician's embarrassing private life must be reported but that his innocent family can be spared the spotlight? Can you monitor the powerful but avoid unwarranted intrusion into a government official's private life?
- Decide and act. We're in journalism, pressed by deadlines. *Methodically* walk through your decision-making process, then decide and act.

WHERE YOU CAN EXPECT TROUBLE

Expect ethical challenges to arise, broadly, on two levels:

First, certain conceptual underpinnings of press ethics sometimes take the media, as an institution, into conflict with other powerful institutions in society.

Second, you'll need to deal personally and pragmatically with serious ethical concerns involved in daily reporting and writing.

CONTROVERSIAL CONCEPTS

Libertarianism holds that the people are capable of making rational, intelligent decisions *if* informed sufficiently well.

Early in our nation's history, the press assumed the role of surrogate of the people, responsible for publishing information crucial to informed participation in our democracy.

The press, as an institution, thus constantly pushes against other powerful institutions in society that want to deny the people that information. A desire to conduct the people's business behind closed door, out of sight of the people, is manifested frequently at every level of government, from local school board to White House. Many other powerful institutions — business and organized religion, for example — sometimes are even more secretive.

As a reporter, you'll be the tip of the free-press spear, forcing your way into closed meetings that should be open to scrutiny and demanding release of documents and information the public has a right and need to know.

Utilitarianism holds that moral conduct must aim at general well-being — creating greatest happiness for the greatest number of people.

This gets controversial when we employ that concept in, for example, a story that serves the larger public's right and need to know *but* injures innocents.

If a politician's personal life becomes of public interest, we cover it, as we covered President Bill Clinton's sexual escapades. Innocents on the sidelines — a wife, a daughter — can be injured.

We explain that the public has a right and need to know and, without perhaps ever using the term "utilitarianism," we thus justify our intrusive journalism. Inevitably, in a career in journalism, you'll handle a story such as that — and you'll have to explain to friends and neighbors, as well as critics of the media, that you do so to serve the public's greater need.

Social responsibility is the theory that because the press has special freedom and power, it has special responsibility to society beyond merely being law-abiding and providing profits to shareholders.

Some social commentators, including economist Milton Friedman, argue otherwise, saying no corporation is responsible for more than increasing its profits and playing within the rules of the game.[5]

Media commentators developed a contrary view: that the press enjoys privileged position in our society and such freedom carries special concomitant obligations.[6]

Our special status includes such things as favorable postal rates and taxes (some states don't tax newspapers sales) and, especially, the power to critique, on behalf of the people, other institutions in society.

Here's one practical impact of all that: You and your newspaper are expected to serve, even at considerable cost, as a medium of social uplift and education for the poor and downtrodden. You are expected, for example, to serve even those readers not attractive to advertisers (from whom the bulk of our revenue flows). Conversely, society does not expect Ford Motor Co. or General Motors to sell cars at below cost for people who cannot afford the sticker price. That's the difference between our business and the car business. Rejoice in it.

People's right to know is a concept widely accepted, although not explicitly granted by the U.S. Constitution.

The First Amendment gives the press the right to freely print the news. Journalism's early fight for free flow of information carried that right forward to the belief that the people have a *right to know* news and that the press has a *duty to print it.*

This, in turn, supports the idea — widely accepted in press and public, alike — that the media are the Fourth Estate, a fourth branch of the system that (with legislative, judicial and executive branches) governs the country.

And it's that Fourth Estate concept — the people's right to know — that makes it your duty to force open school board meetings, to monitor how judges conduct their courtrooms, to examine the mayor's spending habits.

The adversarial relationship is one of the basic — and most misunderstood — conceptual underpinnings of our free press.

For journalists, adversarialism may mean probing, questioning coverage, no holds barred, of news and the people and institutions who make it.

For some of the public, adversarialism means herds of stiff-legged newshounds circling their prey and waiting, under the guise of serving the people, to dart in and rip out somebody's jugular vein.

And, watching camera crews chase celebrities or White House correspondents shout questions at the president of the United States, it's easy to see how such public perception is created.

Your dilemma: Much of your career will be spent trying to get news from people who don't want to give it to you. Further, even public officials who *should* give you the news often are surrounded by skilled public relations practitioners, spinners and news managers whose mission is to keep you from the real story or, at least, ensure you get a sanitized version.

Your solution: Constant pressure, with escalating application of "muscle," if needed, to get the news the public has a need and right to have. If that sounds adversarial, it should. But don't make mad-dog adversarialism your only tactic. Gentle, professional insistence sometimes works, too.

DAILY ETHICS ON THE NEWS BEAT

You'll struggle to convert ethics theory into practical application early in your journalism career, maybe in your first week, if not your first day on the job.

Here's where the struggle starts:

STORY SELECTION

You're expected to find news, to generate story ideas, and hundreds — thousands — of possibilities are out there.

Beware: Are you selecting stories with true news value and relevance to your readers, or are your personal mindset, beliefs and, yes, prejudices taking you in other directions?

In hard news, this isn't much of a problem. Simply go with the self-selecting breaking news.

In features or timeless stories, however, your personal power of selection is stronger, and you must be certain you're not gravitating toward stories simply because you personally find them agreeable.

Also, your story selections must meet reader desires, of course, but don't neglect your responsibility to select stories that you, as a trained journalist, know are important, even if your readers don't.

SOURCE SELECTION

Ever notice how you automatically gravitate toward people like you, people who think as you do, who believe as you do?

That, of course, is the danger as you select sources for your story — subconsciously seeking sources who agree with you. After all, people who agree with your views just make more sense, right?

You must seek sources on all sides of controversies and, importantly, ensure your balancing sources have authoritative credentials. If the mayor, a Republican, is in the news, you've not sought properly authoritative balancing comment if your only Democratic source is a street sweeper.

FACT SELECTION AND ARRANGEMENT

If you're a good reporter, you'll collect 20, maybe 30 or more facts for every one you plug into your story.

With principled fairness and balance, you must select those that properly represent all conflicting views. Again, a problem is that facts simply look better if they support your personal view.

With equal care, you must weave those facts into a balanced, authoritative account. If your mayor is a Republican, and your lead and subsequent 29 grafs represent his views, you've not properly arranged your facts if you hold the Democrats' response to a few words in the 31st graf.

Be careful particularly in selecting quotes and partial quotes. For example:

The mayor says, "Our local economy is headed down for six months but will recover in the second half of the year."

You're unethical in writing a lead that reports partial truth by predicting doom and disaster because "the mayor says our local economy is headed down."

LANGUAGE SELECTION

Note differences in tone and meaning:

The mayor said he failed.

The mayor acknowledged he failed.

The mayor admitted he failed.

That's right, "said" is neutral; "acknowledged" implies he did so under pressure; "admitted" implies criminality.

Note the difference between, "He *walked* to the podium," and, "He *strutted*" . . . , or, The mayor "smiled" or "smirked" or "grinned."

Some language can be extremely prejudicial. Make sure yours is fair and balanced, not prejudicial or judgmental.

TIMING AND CONTEXT

Your 56-year-old mayor was arrested for drunk driving when he was 17.

That fact has limited impact if revealed deep in a personality profile, published on page 29, three years before he's up for reelection.

That same fact has major impact if reported breathlessly as a page-one exclusive the day before voters go to the polls.

That's how timing and context change meaning and impact of news stories.

Breaking news sets its own context and timing. It breaks, we cover it — now. But proceed carefully when timing and context are *your* choice.

REPORTING TECHNIQUE

Inaccurate, sloppy reporting is deplorable. That's clear.

What's not so clear is how to develop reporting techniques that 1) get the news, your first responsibility, and 2) are ethical.

For example, is it ever appropriate to lie or masquerade as a police officer to get a story of compelling interest to readers?

No? Not even if you could break a story on child prostitution? Or systematic abuse of the elderly in a care facility? Or dope dealing in local schools?

How about using hidden cameras or recorders? Would you steal a government document for a scoop? Of course not? Well, would you accept a document filched by a source and given to you?

In the abstract, such questions are nearly beyond answer. But in journalism, abstraction quickly gives away to reality, so work out — now — your personal code of ethical reporting technique.

Your essential dilemma: Are any news stories so important that you're justified in deceiving, masquerading — lying — to get them?

(My advice: *Never* masquerade or lie. Don't use secret cameras or recorders. Consult senior editors if offered important purloined documents. The *Pentagon Papers* story, dealing with the Vietnam War, and other important stories were broken because sources inside government revealed documents labeled "secret" to reporters — and they were documents the public had a right and need to see.)

AH, YES! THE TRUTH!

The mayor looks straight at you — and lies.

Where It All Began

CONGRESS SHALL MAKE NO LAW RESPECTING AN ESTAB-LISHMENT OF RELIGION, OR PROHIBITING THE FREE EXER-CISE THEREOF; OR ABRIDGING THE FREEDOM OF SPEECH, OR OF THE PRESS; OR THE RIGHT OF THE PEOPLE PEACE-ABLY TO ASSEMBLE, AND TO PETITION THE GOVERNMENT FOR A REDRESS OF GRIEVANCES.

First Amendment, *U.S. Constitution*

You know he's lying; he knows you know. And guess what: The mayor expects that your rigidly "objective" reporting will get that lie into print untouched.

There was a day when it might have done so. Many are the reporters, admonished to keep themselves out of the news, who wrote shadings of the truth, untruths and outright lies launched by scally-wags.

A case study is Sen. Joseph McCarthy of Wisconsin who created a global stir in the 1950s by charging, with no substantiation, that communists were infiltrating high places in American government. Pledged to being "objective," reporters of that era had great difficulty putting McCarthy's charges into factual context.

Born of that experience was a new turn in American journalism toward *same-day* balancing comment from opposing sources, not waiting for a reply the next day, and defining "objectivity" more broadly to include *careful, balanced* background analysis and interpretation.

Reporters seldom find "truth." After all, who knows what it is? However, you *can* find balancing comment and facts.

THE RULE(S) OF LAW

Warning: Big change ahead.

Your path toward journalistic professionalism now turns from *voluntary* codes of ethics to *mandatory* caution in the law.

Mandatory, that is, if you are to avoid expensive, career-threatening legal problems, especially in libel.

Yes, the press is the only business institution with freedoms guaranteed in the U.S. Constitution. And, yes, courts down through the generations have built other safeguards for our independent, free press.

Nevertheless, we operate in a threatening legal environment, and no reporter or newsroom can operate ignorant of the law and the dangers in it for journalists.

First, understand the law is hugely complicated (witness the books — *libraries*! — dedicated to explaining it). We cannot, here in Chapter Twelve, fully treat the law of the press.

Second, understand that lawyers are best suited to discuss the law. And I am not a lawyer, nor are most editors. So when in serious doubt, *consult a lawyer*.

Nevertheless, there is merit in discussing law from a journalist's viewpoint.

YOUR BIGGEST CONCERN: LIBEL

Though the U.S. Constitution's guarantee of a free press is marvelously simple and direct in language, press law has become complex and multifaceted since the First Amendment went into effect in 1791.

For you, as a reporter, *defamation law* is the crucial facet. Why?

- Because you *personally*, as well as your newspaper, can get sued by someone angry over what you write.
- Because newspapers lost 63.7 percent of defamation suits, before appeals, in the 1990s, a reflection in part of public distaste for the media.[7]
- Because judgments in the millions of dollars are made against newspapers (in the 1990s, 11 were for more than $10 million each) and because just the cost of defending against libel suits, win or lose, can run into millions of dollars.[8]
- Because journalism — yours and your newspaper's — will suffer a "chilling effect" of fear over being sued, unless you learn to work within the law and thus gain the confidence you'll need to aggressively pursue the people's need and right to know.

THE BASICS

Defamation is false communication that harms the reputation of persons — or businesses — and thus lowers them in the eyes of their community or deters others from associating with them.

Only judge and jury decide 1) what reputation is and 2) whether or how it is damaged.

But, you are at risk if your reporting and writing hold a person or business to public shame, disgrace, ridicule, hatred.

Defamation comes in two forms:

- *Slander* rises from injury to reputation through the *spoken word.*
- *Libel*, our principal concern, rises through writing, pictures, cartoons, advertisements or another tangible medium that injures reputation.

Be particularly careful with writing that alleges criminal behavior, incompetency, inefficiency, fraudulent or other dishonorable conduct and harms professional reputation or causes financial loss.

A single word — "murderer," "whore," "communist" — can be held to be libel, as can one sentence or single paragraph.

A libel *must be published*. But not necessarily under a six-column headline on page one. Many libel cases rise out of seemingly unimportant stories — a couple grafs only — buried deep in a newspaper. In fact, a libel need not be published in a newspaper or magazine. A memo to your editor, a letter to a friend, a draft story on a bulletin board — all can be judged libelous if circumstances suggest someone other than the writer and target saw the offending material.

Persons claiming libel must prove they were *identified*. But that doesn't mean only by name, age and address. If identity can be inferred from a story, you may have identified a person.

For example, don't write that a 63-year-old man living in an apartment near the bank was responsible for the stick-up, and think you're safe because you didn't name him. Everybody in the neighborhood might know the man and make the identification.

When you *do* identify the holdup man, do so fully.

No: John Smith, 63, who lives near the bank, was arrested. (There may be *two* John Smiths nearby.)

Yes: Police charged John Smith, 63, of 1987 Elm St. with the holdup.

The plaintiff (the person or company filing suit) *must prove you were at fault* in publishing the defamation, through negligence or recklessness or, of course, that you intended to defame.

Plaintiff also must prove harm through financial loss, injury to reputation or emotional distress.

Defamation can arise out of context and overall impression, not only out of literal language. For example, you need not write "whore" or "prostitute" to defame if a jury could conclude from your story that a woman is of bad moral character or a person of ill repute.

Always read your story once more, asking yourself, "Would a reasonable person reading this story draw an unfair, defamatory conclusion about the subject?"

YOUR LEGAL DEFENSE

Provable truth is your only (there's just one) *unconditional defense* in a libel suit. That means you — not the cop you talked to on the beat, not your source at headquarters — must be able to convince a jury that all your facts are probably true.

Note: That includes what's between quote marks. *You* can be sued successfully for something you quote a *source* as saying, if you cannot prove its truthfulness.

Qualified privilege is a second line of defense. This rises from reporting fairly, accurately and without malice official proceedings, such as court hearings and legislative meetings, and from official records. Malice is defined as publishing a story you know is false or publishing with "reckless disregard" of whether it is true or false.

Qualified privilege can cover reporting false or damaging information. For example, a U.S. senator has absolute privilege in stating on the floor of the U.S. Senate that a colleague is a "crook." You have qualified privilege in reporting — fairly, accurately, without malice — what was said.

The defense of *fair comment and criticism* gives you strong protection in writing opinion on people or issues of public interest and importance, even if you're unfair. But you must be certain the facts on which you base your opinion are provably true.

The Associated Press Stylebook and Libel Manual puts it this way:

Everyone has a right to comment on matters of public interest and concern, provided they do so fairly and with honest purpose. Such comments or criticism are not libelous, however severe in their terms, unless they are written maliciously. Thus it has been held that books, prints, pictures and statuary publicly exhibited, and the architecture of public buildings, and actors and exhibitors are all the legitimate subjects of newspapers' criticism, and such criticism fairly and honestly made is not libelous, however strong the terms of censure may be.

"Fair comment" is particularly strong protection if your opinion is based on provably accurate facts and directed at public acts, appearances and performances.

YOUR JOURNALISTIC DEFENSE

You cannot prevent someone from suing you. Even plaintiffs with obviously ill-founded or spurious cases have the legal right to proceed against you.

However, you *can* report and write in ways that head off complaints or, if you still get sued, give your lawyers a solid defense.

BE FAIR, ACCURATE, BALANCED

Many libel suits arise out of what plaintiffs perceive to be unfair, inaccurate journalism. Do the *right thing* journalistically, and you reduce odds of being sued.

A story that fails the good-journalism test likely will fail legal test.

HANDLE ACCUSATIONS CAREFULLY.

If your story alleges criminal activity, misconduct in office or dereliction of duty, be careful. If the story could cause financial loss, be doubly careful.

Libel is damage to reputation, remember, and judges and juries are harsh with journalists who inaccurately charge persons or companies with improper behavior.

364 / WRITING TO INFORM AND ENGAGE

WRITING TO INFORM AND ENGAGE

BEWARE OF "PRIVILEGE"

Not all public records are privileged and thus safe to quote in your story. State laws vary on what is public and official and thus privileged. A piece of paper from a police officer or city official may *not* be public, official or privileged.

And do remember: Your reporting must be fair, accurate and balanced if you claim "privilege" as a defense, even if the record is official and public.

BEWARE "NEUTRAL REPORTAGE"

Some courts see privilege operative when you report damaging statements or charges made by responsible sources *if* your story truly is newsworthy and concerns public officials or public figures *and* if your reporting is impartial, balanced and provides opposing views.

For example, "neutral reportage" might be operative if you report charge and counter-charge by shareholders critical of a company president.

However, some courts view "neutral reportage" as merely license for journalists to report false and damaging charges, and deny a defense based on this principle.

REJECT THE "FAIR GAME" TRADITION.

Many journalists once believed (and the idea lingers today in some newsrooms) that certain people — particularly public officials and public figures — are "fair game" for rough treatment without regard for the law of defamation.

Wrong.

Everyone has rights under the law of defamation and, increasingly, many people, including public officials, are using the law as a club.

It *is* true that public officials are held to a high standard of proof. So are public figures, those people who seek the limelight or are thrust into it. Public officials and figures must prove "actual malice" — that you knowingly wrote a falsehood *or* wrote with "reckless regard" for the truth.

Two problems:

- Even life-long politicians and government officials presumably used to press coverage, are suing in defense of their professional and private reputations.
- The courts have left ill-defined who is a public figure. Even a well-known lawyer and prominent socialite have been deemed "private" individuals.

Best rule: Be fair, accurate and balanced in writing about everyone.

OTHER DANGER AREAS

FALSE LIGHT

Even if your writing is not defamatory, you can get into big trouble if it portrays an individual in "false light" that would be offensive to a person of ordinary sensibility.

For example, writing that implies a person is a racist could be deemed to create false light even if racism is not expressed explicitly. Omitting facts and thus creating false light also can trigger a lawsuit.

Your defense is truth. If what you write is provably true, it cannot hold the individual in false light.

PRIVACY

A person has the right to privacy, to be left alone. That principle is embedded deeply in American life and law.

As a journalist, you'll frequently invade personal privacy in pursuit of news in which the public has legitimate interest. And that's the key: Courts have ruled you can write safely even about people *unwillingly* involved in news *if* the public has legitimate interest in them.

For example, the public has legitimate interest in a person held hostage yesterday in a bank robbery because there is *current newsworthiness* in the event.

However, there may not be current newsworthiness in your reporting that the town's leading doctor was arrested on a DUI as a teenager 30 years ago.

OTHER LEGAL CONCERNS

REPORTER'S NOTES

Lawyers are divided on whether you should store permanently your notes.

Some say notes, on paper or disk, can be useful in defending against a lawsuit, particularly if they demonstrate painstaking fact-finding and interviewing went into your reporting.

Other lawyers disagree, saying not even reporters can make much sense out of their scribbles a few days later and, anyway, a plaintiff's lawyer can find ways of using your notes against you.

On this lawyers do agree: Be consistent in what you do. If you store some notes, store them all; if you throw some away, throw all away.

Check a senior editor on whether you newspaper has a policy on keeping notes.

SUBPOENAS

A subpoena is a court order to perform — to appear in court, to turn over notes, to reveal other information.

Many newspapers resist subpoenas on grounds they infringe on freedom of the press. If you are served with a subpoena, go immediately to a senior editor.

SHIELD LAWS

Journalists argue we should have legal recognition of the same confidential relationship with sources that doctors have with patients, clergy with their flock, lawyers with their clients.

Some states recognize that spirit with laws that shield reporters from being forced to divulge the identity of sources, to turn over notes, or to testify in court or before administrative and legislative bodies.

However, don't count too heavily on shield laws. The U.S. Supreme Court has ruled that reporters can be compelled to testify in criminal

Help!

Help is closer than you might think if a legal question arises. Check these:

The Associated Press Stylebook and Libel Manual contains an excellent rundown on defamation, privacy and other legal issues, and it's written in language non-lawyers can understand. This is *must* reading for any aspiring journalist.

State press associations have libel experts on retainer, available to you if your newspaper is a member (as most are). Consult senior editors on using this resource.

The Libel Defense Resource Center is a media-financed organization in New York City that offers assistance. Telephone (212) 889–2306.

The Student Press Law Center provides quick telephone or email advice on legal problems. Contact at 1815 N. Fort Myer Drive, Suite 900, Arlington, Va., 22209–1817; telephone (703) 807–1904; e-mail: splc@splc.org. Web site: http://www.splc.org.

And, of course, don't overlook media law experts in your journalism or law school.

cases if their testimony is essential to an accused's defense — even in states with shield laws.

Your state press association or, of course, senior editors can acquaint you with shield laws, if any, in your state.

OPEN RECORDS LAWS

Open records or "sunshine" laws at both the federal and state level require that certain meetings and records be open to the public. Making sure they stay open is a job for journalists.

If you learn of public business being conducted secretly in closed-door sessions or if you are prevented from covering public business, contact a senior editor immediately.

State press associations are excellent sources of background on state open-records laws.

COPYRIGHT

Federal copyright statutes protect the rights of writers and photographers to the product of their creativity, particularly the right to be paid for use.

Information in those materials — ideas, theories, news—cannot be copyrighted. But the *manner of expression* — words, sentences, the writing — can be copyrighted.

The doctrine of "fair use" may permit you to use limited portions of someone else's writing, as in quoting from a book in a review, for example. The test of what usage is fair lies in whether your usage has hurt the commercial value of the work. Many copyright issues arise over use of music lyrics, dramatic works, photos and recordings.

TRADEMARKS

Some trademarks — Coca-Cola, Xerox, Pepsi — are the most valuable assets companies own. If such trade names slip into the public domain through misuse (as did "aspirin" and "nylon") enormous commercial value is lost.

So, expect a stiff letter from a company attorney if you misuse a trademark. Use generic terms such as "soft drink" and "copying machine" unless you indeed mean Coca-Cola, Pepsi or Xerox.

SOURCE CONFIDENTIALITY

Don't lightly break a promise to sources that you'll protect their identity. A court could rule your promise was a contract and that you're liable for damages if you break it.

That happened in one case in which reporters promised anonymity to a source but were overruled by editors who published the source's identity.[9]

Best rule: Use anonymous sources very sparingly, only when you cannot get an essential story some other way, *and check a senior editor in advance* to be sure your newspaper will back up your promise.

TRESPASSING AND OTHER SINS

News stories important to the public are broken by reporters who trespass, conceal their identities and disguise their intent. However, aside from being unethical, such tactics can be illegal. Fraud charges were levied against television reporters who went undercover in an investigation of a supermarket chain. Plunging through a front door after police on a drug raid can be trespass.

Good rule: Always identify yourself as a reporter and use aboveboard techniques to get the news.

LAW IN CYBERSPACE

Bottom line: The law of defamation in print applies in cyberspace, as well. Libel is libel, whether on paper or the Internet or other electronic services.

One huge difference, however: Unleashing libel on the Internet can widen tremendously the geographic area of publication and expose you to greater danger. For example, Internet publication could end up in Britain, where libel laws are much more severe than in the United States.

Remember that if a third party sees your communication, libel law can apply. Watch those e-mails!

WHEN TROUBLE ERUPTS

Despite your best efforts to be fair, accurate and balanced in your reporting, it's likely you'll be threatened with a lawsuit sometime in your career.

A few pointers for that day:

First, never talk to a complaining lawyer. Only lawyers talk to lawyers. What you do or say *after* you get a complaint can be important to your defense, and unprincipled lawyers have been know to try to elicit damaging post-publication comments from reporters.

Second, listen politely and carefully to any complaint, taking full notes on what is said and letting the aggrieved party blow off steam. Often, getting a chance to shout a bit about a perceived wrong is enough for people who otherwise might file a lawsuit.

Third, *make no comment on the merits of your story or the complaint.* Libel law is complex, and what might look to you to be libelous might not be. But admission of error can be damaging.

Fourth, don't try to work your way out of trouble alone. Don't, for example, promise to write another story "that will set things right." Any corrective or apology must be written by a senior editor or the newspaper's attorney. Give them full and frank details on what happened so they can construct a proper defense.

It needs emphasis: Senior editors are paid, in part, to keep you out of trouble. And, of course, defending you is integral to defending the newspaper.

Many newspapers carry libel insurance, that covers reporters and editors. But there have been cases of newspapers settling lawsuits out of court and leaving reporters to their own defense.

SUMMARY

- Principled journalists must report and write from the moral high ground and work within the law while serving the people's right and need to know.
- Many legal problems stem from inaccurate and sloppy journalism by arrogant or uncaring journalists.
- Public disenchantment with the press is measurable — 51 percent of respondents in one survey said the press has too much freedom.
- Juries drawn from a critical public sit in judgment of us when individuals sue newspapers and reporters.
- In ethics, there are no rules in the sense of systematic industry-wide codification of ethics but all journalistic societies have recommended codes of ethics.
- Commonalities in ethics codes are statements that fair, impartial and accurate service to the public is what journalism is all about and that journalists carry heavy responsibilities, not special rights, in serving the public.
- The American Society of Newspaper Editors' code regards journalism not as a job or career but a calling.

- The Society of Professional Journalists' code says your duty "is to serve the truth" and your obligation is to "perform with intelligence, objectivity, accuracy and fairness."
- The *Washington Post*'s code says the newspaper's responsibilities are to listen to the voiceless, avoid arrogance and face the public politely and candidly.
- Societal values behind newspaper codes include truth-telling, justice, humaneness, freedom, stewardship.
- From those values, journalists have developed job-related principles such as serve the public, monitor the powerful, be balanced and fair, be compassionate, independent and courageous.
- In making decisions in ethics, collect all facts, consider societal values and journalistic principles and your loyalties to self and conscience, society and your employer.
- Controversial concepts embodied in journalistic ethics include libertarianism, the belief that the people will make rational decisions if informed sufficiently well, and utilitarianism, the belief that moral conduct must aim at general well-being.
- Beware that your personal beliefs and prejudices don't unduly influence or distort your selection of stories, sources, facts and language.
- Although adherence to a code of ethics is voluntary, respect for the law is mandatory.
- Beware libel, which is written defamation or false communication that harms the reputation of persons or businesses and lowers them in the eyes of their community.
- A libel must be published and persons claiming libel must prove they were identified and that you were at fault in publishing defamation through negligence or recklessness.
- Provable truth is your only unconditional defense in a libel suit.
- Fair comment gives you strong protection in writing opinion on people or issues of public interest and importance, but you must be certain your facts are provably true.
- The best journalistic defense against libel is to be fair, accurate and balanced in your reporting and writing.

RECOMMENDED READING

I discuss ethics more fully in Conrad Fink, *Media Ethics* (Needham Heights, Mass.: Allyn & Bacon, 1995). Leading journalistic codes of ethics are published in that book.

See also my discussion of ethics in reporting and writing in Conrad Fink, *Introduction to Professional Newswriting* (New York: Longman, 1998) and, for a discussion of ethics in opinion writing, Conrad Fink, *Writing Opinion for Impact* (Ames, Iowa: Iowa State University Press, 1999).

On libel, see *The Associated Press Stylebook and Libel Manual*, and Kent R. Middleton, Bill F. Chamberlin, Matthew D. Bunker, *The Law of Public Communication, Fourth Edition* (New York: Longman, 1997).

EXERCISES

1. Read again the Preamble to the American Society of Newspaper Editors Statement of Principles, reproduced in this chapter. In about 350 words, interpret its meaning for a career journalist. How do you perceive the "particular responsibility" the preamble places on newspaper people? How do you interpret "standard of integrity proportionate to the journalist's singular obligation"? Make this essay a statement of *your* sense of journalistic integrity.

2. Do you agree journalism has a *social responsibility* exceeding that of other industries? Or, is Milton Friedman correct in saying no corporation is responsible for more than increasing its profits and playing within the rules of the game? In about 300 words, discuss whether special responsibilities fall to journalism and those who practice it.

3. In about 300 words, discuss your thinking now that you see journalists and newspapers can be held liable for millions of dollars in damages in libel suits. Do you feel a "chilling effect"? Is your reportorial ardor dampened by the realization that journalists work in a legally dangerous climate? How will you reconcile your need to be cautious in your reporting, yet

aggressive in pursuit of the news the public has a right and need to have?

4. Should journalists have legal defense of their confidential relationships with news sources? Why? What are arguments for and against giving journalists the defense of confidentiality accorded lawyers, doctors and clergy? Can the First Amendment and service to the public be truly operative if we don't have confidential sources? Would you argue a journalist should be able to preserve confidentiality even by refusing to, say, testify in a murder trial? Wouldn't such a legal right conflict with the right of the accused to a fair trial? Discuss this in about 350 words.

NOTES

1. "State of the First Amendment 2000," First Amendment Center, 1207 18th Ave. South, Nashville, Tenn. 37212, p. 16–17.

2. Major codes are published in Conrad Fink, "Media Ethics" (Needham Heights, Mass.: Allyn and Bacon, 1995).

3. Ibid., p. 130–135.

4. This decisionmaking process was developed in Dr. Potter's 1965 Ph.D. dissertation and is discussed in more detail in "Media Ethics," op. cit., p. 8–27.

5. Friedman's statement and its context are discussed in "Media Ethics," op. cit., p. 111–119.

6. The role of the Hutchins Commission and Prof. Theodore Peterson in defining social responsibility is discussed in "Media Ethics," op. cit., p. 15.

7. These figures are from the Libel Defense Resource Center's 20th annual report and are summarized in Lucia Moses, "Punitive Damage Awards on the Rise in Media Libel Cases," Editor & Publisher, Feb. 14, 2000, p. 18.

8. Ibid.

9. For a summary, see Lawrence Savell, "Legally Speaking," Editor & Publisher, Oct. 23, 1993, p. 3.

Name Index

Subject Index